Memoirs of a Cold War Son

SINGULAR LIVES

*The Iowa Series in*

*North American Autobiography*

*Albert E. Stone, Series Editor*

# Gaines Post, Jr.

Foreword by Albert E. Stone

*for Richard and Patti Boerner,
with fond memories of
Cornell rowing, and
the joy of reunion in
Sept. '17 —
Gaines Post*

## *Memoirs of a Cold War Son*

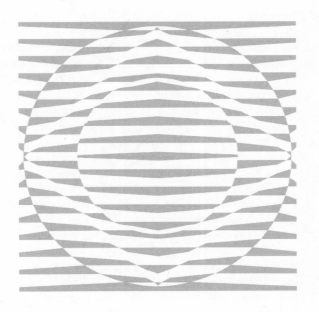

University of Iowa Press ψ Iowa City

University of Iowa Press,
Iowa City 52242
Copyright © 2000 by the
University of Iowa Press
All rights reserved
Printed in the United States of America
Design by Richard Hendel
http://www.uiowa.edu/~uipress
No part of this book may be repro-
duced or used in any form or by any
means, electronic or mechanical,
including photocopying and recording,
without permission in writing from the
publisher. All reasonable steps have
been taken to contact copyright holders
of material used in this book. The
publisher would be pleased to make
suitable arrangements with any whom
it has not been possible to reach.

The publication of this book was
generously supported by the University
of Iowa Foundation.

Printed on acid-free paper

Library of Congress
Cataloging-in-Publication Data
Post, Gaines, 1937–
Memoirs of a Cold War son /
by Gaines Post, Jr.; foreword by
Albert E. Stone.
p.    cm.—(Singular lives)
ISBN 0-87745-701-8
1. Post, Gaines, 1937–  2. Cold War.
3. United States—Politics and
government—1945–1989.
4. Europe—Politics and
government—1945–  I. Title.
II. Series.
CT275.P6885  A3   2000
973.92—dc21            99-057732

00  01  02  03  04  C  5  4  3  2  1

*To*

*My children, Katherine & Daniel*

*My nephews, John Gavin Post &*

*David Gaines Post*

*My godsons, Maury Sterling &*

*Sebastian Dawson-Bowling*

# Contents

## *Foreword*  ALBERT E. STONE

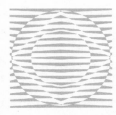
Gaines Post, Jr.'s *Memoirs of a Cold War Son* is the twentieth volume in Singular Lives: The Iowa Series in North American Autobiography. All autobiographies are unique, yet they share common literary features and conventions. This work is no exception. Post's evolving self is shown as an actor in, or a witness to, significant public events and processes of the Cold War. The accepted term for such a literary convention is *memoir*, but pigeonholing this book as such can also be misleading.

Post's story asserts throughout allegiance to the forces of time, place, event, and institution as determinants of his autobiographical identity. History dictates the terms on which the immature teenager living in Paris in 1951 with his once-motherless family turns into the adult Army officer in Germany caught in the Berlin airlift crisis of 1961. Moreover, the creator of both selves—the insecure son and the first lieutenant—is the much older and wiser college professor-historian writing in nineties California. Post is, therefore, doubly caught and at the same time doubly liberated. Cold War history has molded him in essential ways that are honestly and sensitively chronicled here. But the maturing author makes sure that Gaines Post is always at the center of the story. Whether as actor or as witness, it's *his* story, no matter how representative of his Silent Generation he becomes. In this sense the book becomes a confession as well as a memoir, a revelation of innerness. Readers should, therefore, be careful not to confuse this autobiographer with biographers working the same territory such as Stephen Ambrose or David McCullough. Nor should they assume a stance of undiscriminating acceptance of this very personal Cold War history. Even as memoir, the truths autobiography affords meld both external event with internal emotion and expression.

Nonetheless, historical event and personal experience move inexorably forward toward the remembering author. Temporal momentum is sometimes discontinuous, often overlapping, but also allows private life to run on a separate track from public. Post is sensitive to such shifting relationships. Though privileging war and presidential elections, for instance, he interweaves private concerns, like the psychologically vulnerable mother who is the chief emotional reality in his formative experience. In both narrative streams, Post establishes connections and patterns. One instance of significant overlap involves the word "bully." To the timid and vulnerable boy, the Madison neighborhood bully is an unnamed but omnipresent threat. On the wider screen of history, "bully" denotes sucessively Hitler, Senator Joe McCarthy, and finally Krushchev. These public figures define, in mysterious ways, his mother's lingering bouts of crippling depression. Other sequences of public-private experience arrange themselves as paired opposites to be reconciled by the growing youth: northern boyhood in academic Madison vs his family's southern roots; a reserved historian father and a lively but fragile mother; Europe vs America; World War II (the "good war" even in the wiser writer's opinion) and the Cold War ("the war that wasn't"); adolescent agnosticism vs patriotic military service. Of this pattern of contraries, Post observes,

> Madison, Paris, Haskell. If these places were people they would not stay together for long at the same party. . . . the Left Bank, West Texas, the University of Wisconsin, the Second World War, my parents: this chorus guided me through the fifties believing in fair play, diplomacy, and the long term, all of which were contrary to the nation's official version of the Cold War.

This pattern produces a revealing credo and apologia for himself and his era when Post next observes: "my generation has been called 'silent,' as if we simply ducked and held our tongues. . . . In fact, we had a more dynamic collective personality than we have ever been given credit for. Our ambivalence offered us both protection and maneuvering room, in an unprecedented state of war. . . . We began to dissent without leaving home or renouncing institutions."

Such meditations of a one-time "Cold War agnostic" do not affirm a final self. Indeed, Post is always seeking "a best self" within and around intransigent circumstances. This motivates him throughout: from West High to Cornell (where rowing and ROTC meant as much as grades and Phi Beta Kappa); from Fort Sill (where his officer class contained but a single black) to Giessen, Germany, tending nuclear warheads and escorting German and Austrian generals about the field of maneuvers. His ideal is to become an "educated European-American." The process culminates in Lieutenant Post winning a Rhodes Scholarship to Oxford. With quiet pride and quieted agnosticism he declares, "I had been elected to the male elite of my generation at the height of American imperium." He feels completely confidant that, after the Berlin crisis is past, Oxford will make him one of "the men who fit Cecil Rhodes' ideal of civil servants and officers who would rule well."

The author, to be sure, has reservations about this smug summit self. For one thing, he voices doubts about the tunnel vision often betrayed by both youthful actor and author. From a mid-nineties perspective he pauses to reflect on the young officer's outlook and assumptions about the future:

> Recalling 1961 here will not resolve the debates among historians over Krushchev's intentions, Kennedy's strength of will, or the likelihood of war over Berlin. I simply want to say, this is how it appeared to a junior officer in a battalion of V corps. This is how I remember it. . . .
>
> I remember thousands of fragments. Sometimes these turn up haphazardly, answering impromptu signals that have no apparent design. Sometimes they accept conscious invitations to come help me teach, write, or review my life.

In the epilogue, other reservations about his story and the decision to limit it chiefly to the 1950s are expressed. While exploiting the richnesses of memoir and confession—the latter reflecting a younger self's tunnel vision—he acknowledges other gaps and contradictions, noting other ways of periodizing the era. Though the Berlin crisis was and is his personal and therefore narrative climax, the writer realizes that historians often see the Cuban Missile Crisis and even the Bay of Pigs fiasco as larger turning points. Less openly admitted, perhaps, is the "whiteness" of this memoir. No reference is made to the Brown decision of 1954 or, until the last retrospective epilogue, to Martin Luther King, Jr. Civil liberties here greatly outweigh civil rights. What bulks larger in the final summary of Post's afterlife is Vietnam and the resulting political conflicts of the sixties. Indeed, the Cold War agnostic who dominates the earlier chapters of this story is reborn, after having been suppressed by the junior officer in Germany. The older Post hopes that both Camus and patriotic militarism can survive in the riots and protests of the later tempestuous era. Learning from his students, the professor voices his objections to Vietnam in a letter which, in revealing candor, he admits he never mailed.

Still, estrangement and disillusion are all but swallowed up by a happy marriage that puts to rest the shyness about women and sex that dogged his youthful development. Academic career hopes of a former Rhodes Scholar are another matter. Though many of his generation's elite became college presidents, Post discovered a more suitable path. "I suspected that I wasn't cut out for administration after all. How can anyone manage faculty politics and raise money when he believes he is still fighting the Second World War?" This is the story's surprising last line. But to this admiring reader at least, a truer Post has already declared himself. Just before this admission of continuing entrapment in the wartime past he still calls "good," a deeper reason for stepping away from a presidency is his abiding preference for being alone. He knew all along, he writes, that beginning as a boy on the streets of Paris in 1951, the central self was and remains committed to solitude and independence. The acts of autobiography as both memoir and confession have, I think, made this dual recognition possible and plausible.

# *Acknowledgments*

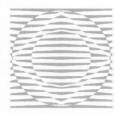For jogging or supplementing my memory, and occasionally disagreeing with it, my brother, John F. Post, has been indispensable. Cousins have lent a hand as well — Wynona (Post) Bryan, Marvina (Post) Hauger, Crickett (Cannon) He-bert, Henry Post, Dorothy Jane (Post) Sanderson, John S. Rike III, Anne Katherine (Rike) Winstead. I also thank the late Roland Blum, William Avery Crawford, Philip Curtin, Doris Dedner, Brig. Gen. (ret) James Dickey, John Guse, Edwina Gilbert Holder, Edward Ingraham, William Kay, Gavin Langmuir, Andrew Mailer, the late Douglas McKee, Robert Nathan, Sally O'Neill, William Pfaff, Sam Reynolds, Peter Riesenberg, William and Nancy Sachse, Carolyn Saunders, Neil Smith, William Craig Stubblebine, Dorothy Worthy. David Lutz, an undergraduate at Claremont McKenna College when I started planning this book, did excellent preliminary research on the 1950s.

I am obliged to these institutions for access to documents and published material: in Paris, the American Library, American School of Paris, Benjamin Franklin Documentation Center (U.S. Consulate), Bibliothèque de documentation internationale contemporaine

(University of Paris, Nanterre), and Centre de documentation juive contemporaine; in Germany, the USAREUR Military History Office (notably Bruce Saunders) and the USAREUR Library and Resource Center (both in Heidelberg), U.S. Army Library of Grafenwöhr Post, CARE Museum (Giessen), and Justus von Liebig University (Giessen); the Bodleian Library and Rhodes House (Oxford University); the Honnold-Mudd Library of the Claremont Colleges.

Friends and colleagues emboldened me to write from the heart and reach out to a wide audience. I am indebted to Mike Bryan (a no less demanding reader for being my second cousin), Robert Faggen, John Keene, Joe Spieler, William Sterling, Richard Sylvester, Rob Urstein, and Hugh Van Dusen. Robert Fossum went through the penultimate draft with great care and perception.

Claremont McKenna College granted me the sabbatical leave during which I began this book, and the staff of the college's faculty support center helped me over many logistical hurdles. At the University of Iowa Press, I gratefully acknowledge the assistance of Al Stone, editor of the Singular Lives Series, as well as Holly Carver and Edie Roberts.

My wife, Jean Bowers Post, has encouraged me every step of the way, my best critic as always. My brother, lifelong comrade, understands better than anyone my wanting to tell this story. I dedicate the book to six members of a younger generation who will want to look back from time to time.

# Introduction

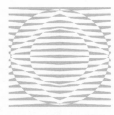 I have been fighting the Second World War all my life. That is not what I expected to discover when I began this book. As a professional historian, I had thought I would compose a general account of the Cold War in the 1950s, spiced with occasional anecdotes to illustrate how memory affects my reading of history. But something happened as I began to write during a sabbatical leave in Paris, 1995–1996. Memory became more important to me than history, and this book became a memoir.

I lived in Europe at both ends of what became a distinct historical period. I was a ninth grader in Paris, 1951–1952, at the start of America's massive military build-up in Western Europe when NATO's young headquarters were in the City of Light. I was an army lieutenant in Germany, 1960–1961, during what turned out to be the last major European crisis of the Cold War. As I was reconstructing those times while sitting at my desk or walking around Paris, the Second World War kept appearing, summoned by memories and emotions that my professional training had taught me to mistrust as unscholarly.

Although my father had been too old to serve, the war brought gloom to our house in Madison, Wisconsin. Dad had been to Europe several times before marrying. His study contained books in Latin, French, German, and Italian. There was a picture of the cathedral of Chartres, a Dürer engraving of Saint Jerome reading in his cell, a papal bull made from parchment, a small phonograph on which Dad played opera recordings by Enrico Caruso, Marcel Journet, Claudia Muzio, and Frieda Hempel. I blamed his unhappiness on Germany's destruction of European things he treasured. But he was losing more than Europe.

My mother had hung over the mantel a large watercolor of the Thames in London, yet she stared at the floor much of the time. "Your mother is sick, boys," was about all Dad would tell my brother, John, and me, although I overheard him saying "nervous breakdown" on the telephone to close friends. He did not tell John and me that she was losing her mind. In those days mental illness was taboo, especially around children, and "crazy" was a cruel epithet for people whose state of mind, it was widely believed, was their own fault. I knew nothing about the alcoholism — not uncommon among hardscrabble ranchers in West Texas — that had killed her father when she was fifteen, about her unfulfilled undergraduate dream at Southern Methodist University of becoming an actress, about her feelings of intellectual inferiority as a faculty wife in a northern university, about her regret that she had no European experiences to share with Dad and his colleagues.

In September 1939 the outbreak of war had extinguished Mom's first opportunity to see Europe. Dad had won a Guggenheim Fellowship for research, and they would have left John and me with her mother in Haskell, Texas, for the year; John had just turned three, and I was two years old. Instead they took us in tow to Cambridge, Massachusetts, where Dad did his research in the Widener Library. Back in Madison during the war, I did not understand that Mom was retreating before the combined forces of two rambunctious boys, family bookkeeping, wartime rationing and scrap collecting, neighborhood peacekeeping, a temperamental husband, and volunteer work, such as reading the papers of GIs who took extension courses from the University of Wisconsin. I knew only that she was badly wounded and that I could not make her well. I blamed Hitler and the neighborhood bully for this. Hitler, I had heard, killed the sick.

As a boy, I did not distinguish between these two wars that my family fought simultaneously. My brother and I practiced tactics for defending our home against invaders, who were German more often than Japanese. In the gutter, we burned leaves or old paint buckets to lay down smoke screens. We made a mortar out of an old bike pump and cherry bombs. We put our front line at the low wall near the sidewalk, booby traps at every door, obstacles on the stairway up to the second floor, trip wire outside our parents' bedroom at the head of the stairs, last ditch around the double bunk in our bedroom down the hall. Movies, comic books, and neighborhood war games gave us the know-how for these rehearsals, and we were sure we could kill a bunch of the enemy before they killed us.

But I was never confident I could protect my mother. Helping her around the house and "behaving," as Dad ordered, neither cheered her up nor stopped my recurrent nightmare of thousands of bombs falling from invisible planes onto invisible targets. After Mom started seeing a psychiatrist, I heard the words "shock treatment," which had the same cadence as "storm trooper" and scared me to death. Dad promised John and me that she would get well after the war was over, and I prayed for the miracle weapon that I supposed would end it quickly, a single bullet specially made to kill every enemy soldier. After v-j Day, Mom did not improve. As fathers and brothers started returning from Europe and the Pacific, she was preparing to leave for a mental hospital. My war was not over.

The Second World War remained my allegory for life. It had Nazi thugs and innocent victims, fatalistic good-byes and improbable homecomings. It bred collaboration and resistance, loneliness and solidarity, cowardice and courage. The war left me with fear of loss, guilt that I could not defend victims, and longing to be a hero in a "good war" against evil. It predisposed me to resist thuggery broadly defined. I still take the war personally, too personally.

Why has my generation's military service in the Cold War not elicited memoirs, movies, or memorials? I suppose the most obvious reason is that veterans of this war who did not stay on for Vietnam have no traumatic reasons for dreading their memories and needing comfort — no nightmares, no bloodshed, no buddies in body bags. In fact, few such veterans even think of themselves as veterans, having faded in and out of service like subatomic particles leaving only faint traces. But the faintness of my generation's traces extends beyond military service, and it has much to do with peculiar timing.

The Second World War shaped us. Born during the Great Depression, we were raised on the war, too young to join our war heroes but old enough to absorb their struggle as the central political and moral reference point for our lives. We are the only generation to have had childhood nightmares about Hitler, the only one whose adolescence coincided with McCarthyism, the only one in its twenties when President Kennedy called upon Americans to ask what they could do for their country and then fell to an assassin before we had done much. We are the only generation under eighty-five not to have a GI Bill when it left military service, most of us having been too young for Korea and too old for Vietnam, and the only one over forty not to have one of its ranks occupy the White House. We may be this country's last truly Eurocentric generation. History has schooled us and passed us over. We are called "silent." It is time we told our stories. This is mine.

# Memoirs of a Cold War Son

CHAPTER 1    *Rue St-Julien-le-Pauvre*

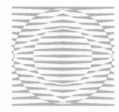My father, brother, and I sailed for France shortly after my fourteenth birthday in September 1951. Before then I knew Europe only from fragments around the house, the *National Geographic* map of Europe that papered the wall next to my bed, stereoscopic pictures in West Texas parlors, the Second World War. Since the end of the war, the bits of Europe in Dad's study seemed to brighten along with his hopes of returning to manuscripts that had survived. A professor of medieval history at the University of Wisconsin, he had sabbatical leave to do research in the French archives.

I did not want to quit Madison for a year in Paris, not even though my mother now lived there. She had been in mental hospitals in Wisconsin for a few years after the war. Shock treatments had not ended her severe depression, and her doctors recommended a lobotomy. "There's no other cure," Dad was told. He refused. Instead Mom was released from the hospital and left Wisconsin. This was around the time when *The Snake Pit* appeared in movie theaters, the nation's first fumbling attempt to confront mental illness. I said nothing when friends echoed the sensationalist publicity, nothing about the resemblance I saw between Mom and posters of Olivia de Haviland. I did not want to see the film; either Dad or the theater forbade me in any case. Mom stayed for a while with her mother in Texas, then went to Europe early in 1949, seeking her separate peace in its ruins.

Europe seemed far away, a place I still imagined from wartime photographs and newsreels of blitzkrieg, burning cities, refugees, concentration camps, death. Meanwhile, the beginnings of the Cold War, the "loss of China," and the outbreak of the Korean War had brought new enemies and nightmares. Communism threatened Europe, Asia, and the American way of life. Communism was "red fascism" and "totalitarian," an ideology likened to Nazism. Joseph Stalin, *Time* magazine's "Man of the Year" in 1942, was now Hitler's evil successor. The conviction of Julius and Ethel Rosenberg early in 1951 for espionage, along with President Truman's firing of Gen. MacArthur a month later, proved to many that Communist agents and sympathizers could be found anywhere in the United States. We heard this constant refrain from our own senator, Joseph McCarthy, and in radio dramas like *The FBI in Peace and War*, which taught me that the bad guys worked for the Soviet secret police (NKVD in those days).

Dad loathed McCarthy, whom Granddad Post, a former West Texas cowpuncher, described as a "whomper-jawed hypocrite." In neighborhood and school fights over McCarthy, of which there were many, I followed Dad's lead. Political venom seeped into normally harmless "so's your old man" standoffs, which escalated into feuds with overtones of disloyalty if you did not support Joe. Still, I feared Communism. News, radio, and movies told me that Europe was again some sort of battleground, only this time without actual battles. The Iron Curtain sounded like a black metal drop in a vast auditorium, and I wondered how it might hurt Mom.

I didn't know what to expect, and Dad offered little reassurance. He was preoccupied with teaching and the household, unschooled in child psychology. I had been taught to wait for my elders to explain things when they were ready. That, I thought, accounted for Dad's impatience whenever I asked when Mom would come back. In fact, he was emotionally far more vulnerable than I would ever have imagined, and he would change the subject to spare both of us the hurt. He had left some of her clothes hanging in the bedroom closet, and

I had not given up hope. But I had adjusted to her absence and was surprised when Dad told John and me that she wanted to see us.

The world was larger then and distances greater. We took the Milwaukee Road to Chicago, the New York Central from there to New York City. My brother and I had stamped steamer trunks and suitcases with odd-looking labels, our first hint of the language barrier we would soon have to cross. Cie Gle [Compagnie Générale] Transatlantique struck me as a jingle, not the name of a mighty steamship company. After a few days in New York, which was foreign enough for me, we embarked on the *Liberté*.

When we lost sight of land, I felt completely unmoored. I associated large bodies of water with mental hospitals on the shores of Lakes Mendota and Winnebago, where Dad took John and me on some of his trips to see Mom after the war. He would ask us to wait near the car while he spent a couple of hours inside with her. If they did not appear at the front door during the first hour, I knew she would not come outside to sit with us on a bench under large elm trees. When she did, I had little idea of what to say. On the *Liberté*, there was little I could hold on to. Not the rolling of the ship, the throbbing of the propellers, the seasick smell of seawater, the cramped tourist-class cabin, the gray roof of sky bolted to the dark ocean at a featureless horizon. Movies didn't help. A grainy black-and-white French detective film foretold a dismal year. In it, Jean Gabin and other unsmiling characters spoke a language I did not understand on rainy backstreets of Paris at night, and a slim young woman attempted suicide by jumping into the Seine from a bridge. I recognized the look on her face before she jumped.

I found a glimmer of hope in the menu for dinner one evening. The dishes were listed in French on the left — *saumon froid à la Parisienne, gigot d'agneau rôti, salade de chicorée aux oeufs, entremets, poire* — in English on the right. On the cover was a sketch of Notre Dame viewed from rue St-Julien-le-Pauvre on the Left Bank, with assorted doorways to the left of the street and the small Romanesque church of that name to the right. Dad told us one of those doors led into the apartment that Mom had found for us. I imagined her walking out the door, crossing the cobblestone street, and opening the gate to the park next to the small church. I decided to hold on to that menu.

We landed at Le Havre on 1 October. Blue-clad stevedores wearing berets clambered aboard. Europe, a narrow band of skyline when

I had first seen it a few hours earlier, turned into bombed break-waters, piers, warehouses, and railroad yards. I pictured dive-bombers and dogfights. I wondered why the French hadn't repaired things; in the long interval since V-E Day, our Madison street, West Lawn Avenue, had been resurfaced, and I had progressed from grade school to junior high.

In my passport, stamps totaling 3,500 francs adorned the visa the French consulate general in Chicago had issued in August. A lot of money, I thought, until I started carrying francs aboard the *Liberté*. The Department of State, two pages after its seal and Dean Acheson's signature, had added a restriction against travel to Bulgaria and Czechoslovakia, as well as to Japan and Okinawa; no problem for us, this official mingling of wars. When the French authorities at Le Havre stamped *entrée* in my passport, their eyes conveyed authorization, not welcome.

On the boat train to Paris, the novelties grew. Compartments separated people into tiny communities behind glass windows and sliding doors. Going into the corridor was an adventure. Freight cars on sidings resembled old toys: rusty little containers with small wheels, curved roofs like bread loaves, two round bumpers at each end; droll playthings, not in the same league with the real thing we knew at home on the Milwaukee Road, Chicago & North Western, and Illinois Central. We saw hedge-lined fields, no silos, few tractors, roads bordered with symmetrical trees, and villages of stone. At grade crossings, men and women cranked the gates by hand. Everyone seemed to be old and dressed in dark blue.

Mom met our train at Gare St-Lazare, an enormous barn with bulky iron girders. I was thrilled to see her on the platform. Her smile overwhelmed my anxiety that her eyes might blame us for her leaving, that she might change her mind as soon as she saw us. As she hugged me, I remembered her fragrance, traces of which I had sought in her bedroom closet at home when I missed her badly. We gathered our luggage, waved to several acquaintances we had made on the boat, and found a porter who led us outside to the taxi queue. While we waited, I looked at Mom out of the corner of my eye as I watched oddly shaped black cars hiss by on the cobblestone just as in the Jean Gabin movie. She wore a brown suit and hat. She was as slender as I remembered, even prettier than the photo she had sent to Dad back in the spring as if to introduce us to the woman we would find in Paris. Soon it was our turn for a taxi. "Rue St-Julien-le-Pauvre," Mom said to the driver, "c'est près de Notre Dame." I was astonished: she spoke French!

The centuries-old building at #10, one of a row built over vaulted medieval cellars, is about fifteen feet wide and seven stories high (six *étages* if you count in French). We lived on the ground floor, which since the 1960s has been occupied by restaurants under at least three different owners. When I was in Paris in May 1989, the name "Les Colonies" had been freshly painted over the door, the front window had been narrowed, and the elegantly dressed proprietress was putting finishing touches on decorations. She responded cordially to my request to look inside, saying the whole interior had been redone. I recognized some of the woodwork, showed her where our kitchen had been, and pointed out the skylight our cat had used as his private entrance.

That was my home from October 1951 to June 1952, a time that proved far from dismal and gave me life-long moorings. In reconstructing that period, I have come to appreciate how much history is linked to memory and the senses. Much of our historical consciousness involves remembering personal encounters with events, people, artifacts, and moral dilemmas. Often at random, without textbook regard for continuity and causation, we remember the smell, the weather, and the mood during these encounters.

In the late Joseph Brodsky's poem "A Halt in the Wilderness," an old Orthodox church in Leningrad has been replaced by a new concert hall, but dogs still return to the spot they once knew well:

> Perhaps the earth still holds that ancient smell;
> asphalt can't cover up what a dog sniffs.
> What can this building be to such as dogs!
> For them the church still stands; they see it plain.
> And what to people is a patent fact
> leaves them entirely cold. This quality
> is sometimes called "a dog's fidelity."

Brodsky's dogs help me recall my encounters with Europe and the Cold War with what fidelity I can summon. First impressions linger long after the things that impressed me have changed. True, these impressions are confused with what I learned later, yet they still retain their ancient smell. Needing to remember Mom while she was away gave me an unusually active and faithful memory before this story began.

Madison remained far away from Paris. Telephoning the States took at least two operators and one hour just to get through and was prohibitively expensive to boot. I met Communists and Russians and learned these were not synonymous, found free games on café pinball machines, faced riot police. I saw church windows 600 years older than my country. I liked our neighborhood, snails, and the French. Homesickness faded as Paris became a homecoming.

The French Communist Party (PCF) plastered our neighborhood with anti-American posters. The party controlled the largest confederation of labor unions and had substantial support from intellectuals, but it also had internal frictions, both before and after its ouster from the coalition that governed the Fourth Republic until May 1947. After that, any member who challenged the party line from Moscow risked expulsion for being a Trotskyite. The number of Communist seats in the National Assembly — though not the party's percentage of the vote — fell sharply in the national elections of June 1951. Ambassador David Bruce and his staff at the American embassy viewed this and other setbacks as evidence of the declining strength of French Communism. In a comprehensive report on party strength in May 1952, they concluded that the PCF no longer constituted a serious threat to the French state, though it continued to draw credit for its wartime resistance and to be capable of some damage through occasional strikes as well as "peace" propaganda against colonialism, NATO, and America.

In 1995 I began corresponding with William Avery Crawford, the author of this report, later to become ambassador to Romania. Now a retired Foreign Service officer, Crawford has quite a tale to tell about his brush with McCarthyism while we were both in Paris. As a young officer in 1944, he had responded to a State Department call for volunteers for Russian language training. After courses at Harvard, he had completed tours of duty at our Moscow embassy and at the department's Soviet desk, studied for a year at Columbia University's Russian Institute, and in 1950 had been assigned to the Paris embassy.

President Truman's Executive Order 9835 of March 1947 had established "loyalty boards" in government agencies, and Senator McCarthy's allegation in February 1950 that the State Department was aswarm with Communists had increased pressure on the diplomatic service to rid itself of anyone disloyal to the United States. To Crawford's astonishment and roughly coinciding with the submission of his report, he received a letter from the department's Loyalty Security Board asking him to explain a secondhand report that he had written a letter in 1945 indicating he was "extremely enthusiastic about Russia." He recapitulated his enthusiasms to the board, with the caveat that neither Communist ideology nor the Soviet system of government was among them. He was pursued no further, but his case illustrates the atmosphere of distrust in Washington and the flimsiness of many of the allegations.

In the French National Assembly, the Communists voted against military budgets, tax increases to pay these bills, and proposals supporting NATO, German rearmament, European recovery, or anything else that Moscow and the PCF put under the umbrella of American imperialism, the alleged successor to Nazi hegemony. That umbrella covered everything from generals to drinks. In 1944 French Communists had acclaimed Gen. Eisenhower for his role in the liberation of their country. In January 1951 chanting "Eisenhower get out!," they staged hostile demonstrations outside his temporary headquarters at the Astoria Hotel — on the Champs-Élysées near the Arc de Triomphe — when he returned to take command of Supreme Headquarters Allied Powers Europe (SHAPE). When Gen. Matthew Ridgway arrived in Paris in May 1952 to succeed Eisenhower, a full-fledged riot erupted as marchers tried to reach Place de la République. Police shot and killed one demonstrator and arrested around 700 of the 5,000 participants, including Jacques Duclos, head of the PCF's delegation in the National Assembly, who taunted authorities for acting as "valets" for their American masters.

Three years earlier, Paris streets had run with Coca-Cola, which the Communists denounced as a foul symbol of American imperialism. They were not alone. French wine producers feared competition from this syrupy alternative beverage, and *Le Monde* saw Coca-Cola as a symbol of the American "civilization" that threatened French "culture." Thanks to prolonged litigation and the faith of well-placed French politicians in the ability of their countrymen to follow their national palate, my brother and I could find Coca-Cola in local cafés.

French officials reacted to the Communists in assorted ways.

They suspended civil servants who participated in the strike called by the Communists to protest Eisenhower's arrival early in 1951. They expelled the pro-Communist physicist Irène Joliot-Curie from the French Atomic Energy Commission, having already dismissed her like-minded husband, Frédéric, as head of the commission. Responding to Soviet propaganda that Communism had saved the world from Hitler, the French government pointed out that the Soviet Union had done nothing to help Poland and the West in 1939–1940.

In early 1952 the French foreign minister, Robert Schuman, declared that, while France would like to find an honorable end to its war in Indochina, France would certainly not "open doors to Communism." In the spring the Center-Right government of Antoine Pinay adopted tougher methods than usual. Paris police closed the doors of a theater that staged a Communist anti-American play, and police in major cities throughout France invaded PCF headquarters in search of firearms and other evidence of subversion. Nearly 10,000 police and security guards confronted half that number of demonstrators against Ridgway. In June, as my family prepared to return to Madison, the French interior minister, Charles Brune, announced to the Anglo-American Press Club that his government would not outlaw the Communist Party because it would be even more dangerous hidden. He assured everyone that police would soon start spraying demonstrators with indelible blue dye for future identification. The *New York Times* mused that the French might consider red for the extreme Right and plaid for demonstrators from the Center. Outside New York, however, painting Communists blue was not the American way, and Washington was not convinced that France took the Communist menace seriously enough.

I remember the atmosphere of demonstrations and strikes, the symbol of Picasso's dove of peace, and the most ubiquitous evidence of French Communism: posters denouncing atomic weapons, German rearmament, NATO, and American imperialism. Most of them told us to leave: "Les Américains en Amérique!" and "Americans go home!" Beneath these, enterprising employees of Trans World Airlines had added, "via TWA." Around the corner on rue Galande, which ages ago had been the first leg of the Roman road from Lutetia (Paris) to Lugdunum (Lyon), an especially lurid anti-American poster on a wall opposite our *boucherie* displayed a large black spider feeding on victims caught in its web against a blood red background. As we walked by that sign one evening on our way to a restaurant near Place Maubert, our butcher pointed to the poster, waved his meat cleaver at us, and jokingly shouted, "Go home!" His laughter filled the narrow corridor of the ancient street. My parents laughed back and waved.

Laughing at Communism was permissible in Paris, partly because some French Communists laughed at themselves. The grave digger who lived above us at #10 let us know early on that he was a Communist and proud of it. He wore a soft cap and owned two beautiful retrievers, one black, the other yellow. Before long the dogs wagged their tails whenever John and I approached, and the owner, who shared Dad's interest in stamps, wanted to know what conditions were really like in the United States. The two men sometimes stood on the cobblestones chatting away after a day's digging, one wearing muddy boots, the other carrying notes on Roman law. The Frenchman, Dad reported, was a decent fellow with a sharp mind and lively sense of humor.

Our landlord, a Russian painter named Nikolai Vasil'evich Makeev, had left his country in the early 1920s along with hundreds of other intellectuals whose revolutionary euphoria had turned into disenchantment with the repressive policies of the Bolshevik regime. Like many of them, Makeev settled in Paris, part of a large and disparate Russian community in exile. He rented his apartment to us while he spent the year in the south of France with his young Belgian mistress and baby. He left oil paintings behind. Propped against walls and easels in the dingy storeroom at the back, they seemed like silent relatives of his. It was spooky in there.

Makeev asked us to feel at home, retain Leonid, and take good care of Kotik. Leonid cleaned the apartment every week. He was a shy, short, and swarthy man who spoke French with a thick Russian accent, pronouncing our name "Posht." He wore dark baggy trousers tied around his waist with a rope, and he walked with a shuffle. He was warmhearted, dependable, and unfailingly courteous, especially to my mother, who had the least trouble of any of us in carrying on a conversation with him. Kotik, an affectionate black-and-white cat who lived up to his Russian name ("little tomcat"), divided his time between the apartment and, through the skylight in the water closet, a feline society that favored rue St-Julien-le-Pauvre.

He passed back and forth through the skylight, jumping down onto the shoulder of anyone who happened to be using the toilet; sometimes we forgot to warn guests. Kotik danced with his dinner now and then, and Mom called his ballet characteristically Russian. After devouring half of a cow's lung, to which she treated him every couple of weeks, Kotik would play with the remnant, tossing it in the air and pirouetting across the multipurpose middle room from Mom's dressing table to the portable counter covering the bathtub opposite the kitchen stove.

In 1977 I described Kotik and the apartment to Nina Berberova, who had taught at Princeton University in the 1960s and whom my wife and I had just met during a research leave I spent there. We had been introduced to her by Richard Sylvester, a close friend, Slavicist, and expert on the poetry of her first husband, Vladislav Felitsianovich Khodasevich. Nina came to dinner. During my account over coffee, the candles on our dining-room table guttering as we leaned back in our chairs after dinner, Nina began to nod, as if she had heard it all before, and soon said she knew the apartment.

"Are you sure?" I asked, "it's at #10."

"My dear," Nina replied, "I have been in that apartment. I knew Makeev. I was married to him." She leaned forward into the candlelight, accentuated each verb, and paused at the end of each sentence, savoring the dramatic effect of her story. She told us she had married Makeev in the 1930s. He had been a Socialist Revolutionary during the First World War and one of the youngest delegates to the Constituent Assembly in 1917, where he was a close friend of Aleksandr Kerensky, head of the provisional government before the Bolsheviks seized power. Nina lived with Makeev until 1946, emigrated to the United States in 1950, and later sent money to him every year at a nursing home in Provence until his death in 1975. In her memoir, *The Italics Are Mine*, she identifies him only with the initial "N." When my wife and I returned to Paris in May 1989, Nina's books were all the rage there, and her picture in bookstore windows seemed to say, "See, I do know this place." She died in 1993. Three years later Dick Sylvester and I found Khodasevich's grave in a cemetery in Boulogne-Billancourt; we observed what Dick said is a Russian custom, taking hard-boiled eggs to the graves of loved ones around Easter.

Since that evening in Princeton, I cannot return to #10 without thinking of Nina. Her revelations, and now the memory of them, have combined with my introduction to Russians on rue St-Julien-le-Pauvre. How much of the long history of Russian idealism and expatriation did I intuit in 1951–1952? Probably less than this confusion of memories can reliably tell, but in 1952 it was certainly enough to send me home doubting that the only good Russian was a dead or a White one.

Rue St-Julien-le-Pauvre, the park, and the church across the street: these defined my corner of Paris, a secure base for exploration, a reassuring destination every time I return. Shortly before Germany invaded France in the spring of 1940, the writer Julian Green, born of American parents living in Paris, had visited this same corner where he had memories of finding inner peace when he first stumbled upon the little church at the age of sixteen during the First World War. For still deeper personal reasons, this church, street, and park form the soul of my Paris. After a long struggle, my family was restored in that place at the very moment when my childhood feelings became adolescent emotions. There I shall always feel centered, not free of doubts but pretty sure of who I am. There I am closest to my parents, now dead, not blind to their faults but consoled. This ancient neighborhood may seem indifferent to the comings and goings of generations, but it knows I lived there just as I know it marked me for life.

We walked out the narrow door of #10 into life itself. At #8, the new Gallery 8 featured abstract art and advertised exhibitions of works by Dubuffet and Giacometti. Around the corner, on rue de la Bûcherie, George Whitman had just opened Librairie Mistral, the bookstore he later renamed Shakespeare and Company to preserve the name of Sylvia Beach's post–World War I establishment on rue de l'Odéon. He stocked works that were censored back home. It did not take me long to memorize the numbers of the best pages in *Lady Chatterley's Lover*, and in September 1995 I thanked Whitman for letting me browse as a boy. He had lost many of his front teeth since then.

Our little park and garden, called Square René Viviani, afforded the city's best view of Notre Dame and entertained throngs of children on weekends and holidays. Its guard swigged red wine from a bottle in his onion-roofed shelter right across the cobblestones from our front window. In the church of St-Julien-le-Pauvre, named after a medieval bishop who gave his money to the poor, the University of Paris had held its assemblies in the Middle Ages. A Melchite chapel since the nineteenth century, the church exposed John and me to icons and Orthodoxy for the first time. Next door to the church, in the Caveau des Oubliettes, once a dungeon, we heard folk songs about the virtues of drinking a little without rolling under the table. Down to the right, past The Tea Caddy and a baroque doorway, hunched up against the angle between two taller buildings across rue Galande, a produce shop displayed its colorful still life next to artists who painted the view across rue St-Jacques of the tower and gargoyles of St-Séverin.

Although not Catholic, we soon considered Notre Dame "our lady," too, because of the comfort we drew from her familiar profile and quotidian bells. John and I attended midnight mass there on Christmas Eve, the third Christmas since the end of rationing in France. We returned to the bountiful *reveillon* Mom had prepared at #10, with rich pâtés, runny cheeses, and a chocolate *bûche de Noël*. Singly or together, members of the family would step into Notre Dame just to get their bearings. I still do that. In March 1996 I sat on the center aisle at a Saturday evening mass given by the Archbishop of Paris, Cardinal Jean-Marie Lustiger. When Lustiger came down the aisle after the service, nodding left and right, our eyes met for a split second. He looked to the other side, then paused, looked back at me as if he had noticed something needy or kindred, and extended his hand to shake mine. I have never felt so overwhelmed by such a simple gesture nor so ready to describe someone as holy. A few days later I learned that Lustiger is a converted Jew, that his mother died at Auschwitz.

To the south and east of our apartment, rue Monge led from Place Maubert to the ruins of a Roman arena, and rue St-Jacques to the Sorbonne and Panthéon. We walked down rue de la Huchette to Place St-Michel. We followed boulevard St-Michel to the Roman baths and medieval house of Cluny, Luxembourg Gardens, and Montparnasse; boulevard St-Germain to the Odéon theater and former monastery chapel of St-Germain-des-Près. To the north and east, bridges linked us with the Gothic masterpieces, revolutionary prison, and large flower market on the Île de la Cité. Except for the boisterous central market (Les Halles), the Right Bank seemed formal and formidable, with royal gardens, concert halls, opera, museums, department stores, fancy shops, and the archives where Dad worked. We took buses and the Métro when distance or time required, railroads for day trips to

Fontainebleau, Versailles, and Chartres. Posted inside every public conveyance were signs reserving seats for *les mutilées*, a lacerating reminder of wars.

Whatever the outing, my parents took care to look for detail, nuance, the idiosyncratic. For Dad, the point was to imagine the story behind an object; for Mom, to understand human nature. Dad gave lectures on history, architecture, food, and wine, exercising our minds, senses, and patience. He took us to the Louvre, where the Mona Lisa could not hold a candle to the Nike of Samothrace or nude statues. We met Dad one day for lunch at a café near the Archives Nationales and then walked north together to the Conservatoire National des Arts et Métiers, where Foucault's pendulum and Lavoisier's laboratory equipment made a deeper impression on John than on me. We attended *Cyrano de Bergerac* at the Comédie-Française and *La Traviata* at the Opéra, whose opulent foyer and staircase I have associated with Verdi ever since. We saw acrobats, clowns, and animals at the Cirque d'Hiver, its one ring more thrilling than our three-ring memories of Barnum & Bailey had led me to expect, although Dad agreed there was nothing comparable to watching the circus train unload and huge tents go up outside Madison at dawn one summer day before Pearl Harbor.

We used Dad's Zeiss binoculars to follow his lessons on rib vaulting and stained glass at Notre Dame, Sainte-Chapelle, Chartres. He had bought the binoculars in Germany in the late 1920s. When the war broke out, he loaned them to the U.S. Navy in response to a nationwide call, assuming they would become a casualty. To his surprise, the navy returned them after the war, reconditioned and accompanied by a certificate that Dad mounted above his desk near the engraving of Saint Jerome. Once, when our attention flagged, he recaptured it by recalling how one of his undergraduate students had named the "flying buttocks" as an innovation of Gothic architecture. With Dad sometimes daring us, we ordered the French version of hamburger steak at the Restaurant des Beaux Arts on rue Bonaparte, snails and tripe at Pharamond's near Les Halles, *choucroute garnie* at Brasserie Lipp on boulevard St-Germain. He loved the St-Germain quarter. In Robert Doisneau's 1952 photograph of the abbey church, taken from the boulevard side of the Deux Magots, a tall man in a dark suit is walking away from the camera, his head and limbs at familiar angles. I think it is Dad.

Mom traced personalities in the *ferronnerie* (wrought ironwork) above window ledges and around balconies. She covered her head with a dark scarf before entering churches. She introduced John and me to a Parisian teenager named Jacques, who lived on rue du Dragon just south of boulevard St-Germain. She taught us how to shop, purchase Métro tickets, get haircuts, ask directions, argue politely. She knew the French better than Dad did, just as she knew how to calm a horse by touching its mane or make Leonid feel respected. In her everyday dealings with Parisians, she usually found something everyone could laugh at. One day, her container of crème fraîche started to drip on the floor of the *laiterie*, and several women began to show concern. "Oh, il fait pipi" (oh, it's peeing), Mom said, to the delight of all.

Paris was a dirty gray in those days, merely flecked with the colors of shops, posters, gardens, and window boxes. The smell of urine was everywhere, especially strong around the sidewalk pissoirs used by men and boys. Dad told us these nineteenth-century urinals were also called *vespasiennes*, after the first-century emperor who had public urinals built in Rome. (Unlike the French, he charged a fee for using them; on his deathbed, according to Suetonius, Vespasian said, "I think I am becoming a god.") The pungency of autumn leaves seemed peculiar without the seasonal rituals of Badger football and the World Series. A wave of homesickness hit me in early October on the family's first walk in the Luxembourg Gardens, as it does to this day whenever I stand at the Medici fountain there, a reflex locked within memory.

My brother and I noticed that our parents neither bragged nor apologized about being American, that they could discuss the qualities of something French without comparing it to the American equivalent (cheese being the major exception). They were genuinely cosmopolitan, having adapted the West Texas virtues of integrity and hospitality to both their social life and worldview. They saw no necessary contradiction between patriotism and love of other countries and none between strong convictions and an open mind. They read the European edition of the *New York Herald Tribune* as well as French newspapers. In the *Tribune*, they followed Art Buchwald's columns on Paris while I turned to the comics (Dick Tracy, Smilin' Jack, Donald Duck, Joe Palooka) and sports, perplexed to see that

Ted Williams was recalled to active duty in the spring of 1952 for service in Korea.

My parents gave and took with the French, disarming affronts and returning a twinkle in the eye. I heard Mom use the phrase *çe n'est pas juste* (that's not fair) with devastating effect when the French knew it was warranted. I saw Dad join the laughter after ordering four churches (*églises*) instead of nuns (*religieuses*) at the local patisserie for our dessert one evening. Thanks to such examples, I survived the embarrassment of asking the barber to cut my horses (*chevaux*) instead of my hair (*cheveux*).

John and I learned how to buy croissants, milk, wine, salade niçoise. We dueled with baguettes and drank café au lait from deep soup bowls. We ate mild radishes with unsalted butter and wild strawberries in buttery pastry shells. We tried foods that we would have rebelled against at home, although I never did learn to like calves' brains, which Dad taught the chef at one of our neighborhood restaurants how to cook *au style du Texas*. We drank wine at dinner, Dad wishing he could afford to buy cases of 1947 because, he correctly predicted, that would turn out to be one of the great vintages of the postwar years. We admired the way Mom conversed with shopkeepers and closely examined certain paintings. While looking at the twelfth-century windows at Chartres, we heard Dad say, "Boys, no one will ever be able to re-create that blue." We saw both professional regret and wartime sadness in his face when he told us that a charred bundle of parchment was all that remained of a manuscript he had hoped to read in the cathedral library; a stray bomb had hit one of the cathedral's storage sites.

Left on our own, John and I found small carnivals with dodgem rides, shooting galleries, lottery wheels. We took the Métro to the edges of the city if necessary, once nearly getting into a fight with a gang of French boys who resented our aggressive style of driving the tiny electrical cars. We went to movies that opened on the Champs-Élysées, such as *The African Queen* with Humphrey Bogart and Katharine Hepburn, *The Lavender Hill Mob* and *The Man in the White Suit* with Alec Guinness, a demonic French film about Bluebeard, and *Fanfan la Tulipe*, a farce of adventure and sex at the time of Louis XV. Ads for the Folies-Bergère caught our eyes. We sat at cafés with Jacques, whose quick mind and kind patience gave us just what we needed in a French companion; watching him was an education in facial language and speaking from the front of the mouth.

John and I played the soccer game at the Café Le Petit Pont around the block and got used to calling it "football." To our delight we were often joined by Gavin Langmuir, a Canadian war veteran wounded at Normandy who quickly became our idol. Working on his Harvard Ph.D. in medieval history, Gavin had bumped into Dad at the Préfecture de Police when both were applying for *cartes de séjours.* His high regard for our father impressed John and me as much as his war record. Whenever Gavin came to dinner at #10, everyone understood that he must arrive early for a few games of soccer. Now retired from Stanford and living in Palo Alto, Gavin recalls a convivial atmosphere at #10, "almost like their second honeymoon." Mom was "lovely company, mentally sharp with a livelier sense of humor" than Dad, who himself was "anything but pompous." Gavin does not remember any tensions in our apartment. I do.

My imagination was hard at work that year as I got to know my mother again. I had little to go on except memories, hopes, and fears. Mom clucked at John and me to bundle up against the cold, as she had done in Madison during the war; the apartment at #10 was poorly heated, and it snowed several times that winter. She called me "kid" and "hon" again, hugged me when I came home from school, tilted her head as she listened to me recount my day. She hummed her favorite tunes from Chopin and Boccherini and called to Kotik in a bilingual melody. She pantomimed Kotik's ballet and impersonated shopkeepers. She slapped her hip with one hand after good jokes, just the way I had seen her do on her brother's ranch in Haskell County. Pans chattered in the kitchen, sauces and herbs were topics of conversation at dinner, and she welcomed our praise of her French cuisine, which often surpassed that of restaurant chefs. She was a warm and generous hostess, sometimes pairing Gavin with Alice, a graduate student of voice at Indiana University whom we had met on the *Liberté,* who sang arias after dinner at #10. Mom smoked Gauloise Bleue cigarettes and looked French at sidewalk cafés. The French obviously admired her wit and her legs. She happily described how she would redecorate our house in Madison. Mom's well, I would rejoice to myself, there's nothing to worry about. She'll come back to Madison with us. She loves us.

Or is she, will she, does she? I dreaded reminders of her wartime breakdown. Once in a while, eyes staring at the table, she would sup on bread crumbled into a glass of clabber, go right to bed without saying a word, and sleep past breakfast. She would take long walks alone, leaving no note. One time I saw her coming out of Notre Dame, head down and scarf unremoved as she turned north toward the Right Bank instead of south toward home. I did not follow her, confused as I was by apprehension that I would make matters worse if she saw me and by remorseful doubt that I could help her even though I was no longer the child who had been unable to stop the war. On rainy nights her wanderings made me think of the woman who tried to kill herself in the movie on the *Liberté*, and the bridge in the movie began to look like the Petit Pont. One weekend a French film company talked its way past the concierge in our absence to invade our apartment and use its picturesque front window as a backdrop. "That's not like the French," Mom sobbed over and over, as inconsolable as she had been during the war when she stopped hugging me and I began to realize I was losing her.

Dad told John and me to go easy on Mom. Help her with chores, don't yell at each other, don't mope, don't show anger, don't ask her where she has been. He asked us to brace ourselves for the possibility that she might not return to Madison with us. I suppose Mom warned him she might not be well enough when the time came. He had never blamed John and me for her breakdown and leaving, but his implication that our behavior would have some bearing on whether she would return marked a minefield. It reminded me of the suspense at home late in the war, when I was afraid I might set off the impending disaster. In Paris Mom gave John and me no explicit warning herself. She probably counted on her own remedies to work in the long run — Europe, bread and clabber, long walks alone. Looking now for clues that she thought she had mended enough to stick with us, I would single out the picture she bought in Paris and hung at #10 before we arrived. It is a print of a woman sitting in a chair bent over her sewing, her tumble of hair hiding her face. I am guessing that the tranquility of the picture expresses what she hoped she had finally achieved after her ordeal. Or does the faceless solitude suggest that she was prepared to live on her own after trying one last time with us?

I do not remember resenting Mom for leaving. Dad certainly didn't want me to. In Madison he had never suggested that she deserted us, didn't love us, or wouldn't come back. She must have understood his loyalty, or their reunion in Paris would surely have collapsed there. On her forty-first birthday they cheerfully abandoned John and me to dine at Lapérouse on the quai des Grands-Augustins; Michelin gave it three stars at the time. I could tell Mom and Dad enjoyed themselves in bed. She did not hide her supreme contentment at breakfast or when we returned from school to find Dad at home earlier than usual. I remember thinking, "My God, she *wants* John and me to know she likes sex!" Dad ruffled papers and blushed.

Dad usually put in full days at the Archives Nationales or Bibliothèque Nationale researching thirteenth-century ideas of public law derived from Roman law. He walked both ways, "the better to know Paris," he would say, not knowing that on rue des Archives he passed by one of the city's oldest houses, the fifteenth-century residence of Jacques Coeur, chancellor to King Charles VII, which was discovered during renovations in the 1970s. At dinner, especially if Gavin were there, I heard strange terms like *utilitas publica* (public welfare), *ratio status* (reason of state), *pugna pro patria* (fighting for one's country).

Dad's chronic indigestion flared up in Paris. A nearby pharmacist prescribed ingesting some sort of charcoal, an odd remedy typical of his profession in France. Effective against symptoms, the charcoal did not reduce Dad's anxieties over career and family. He had been unable to write much while caring for us boys, and this discouraged him as he compared his publications with what he had hoped to achieve by the age of fifty, which he reached in March 1952. He seemed happy with his progress in the archives, and this may explain why he lost his temper less often than had been the case in Madison during and after the war. But he lived in the same minefield he had marked for John and me, and his own memories, hopes, and fears must have guided him. Did he hold himself responsible in any way for Mom's breakdown? I don't know. Did he watch his step in Paris, restraining his natural tendency to anger at minor irritations or any interference with his work? Yes, although not enough to convince me that he was as sensitive as I to Mom's presumed fragility.

Although Paris demanded our tacit fraternal alliance, John and I had our differences. In Madison he had floundered at West Junior High and had become something of a loner. I had higher grades, more friends, and greater athletic skill. He took up photography and model railroads as hobbies, tutored by an older boy named Stan

Mailer who lived across the street. Stan built HO-gauge rolling stock from scratch and collected photos of steam engines. The two of them let me know I was not welcome in their projects. When I persisted, John ridiculed my lack of talent; retaliation, he told me years later, for my mocking his awkwardness at baseball and basketball.

In Paris John caught fire academically and started a diary. I found the diary and sneaked looks at it, fascinated by introspection I had never seen before. One day I came to an entry ending, "Damn you Gaines if you read this!" I never read his diary again. I backed away, annoyed at his secrecy and rebuffed by his brooding inquiry into a world of ideas that both of us seemed to know were beyond my reach. He sometimes went out of his way to illustrate this point at my expense, and I sometimes went out of mine to criticize him for thinking more about himself than about Mom. Each of us began to spend more time alone.

I liked walking Paris streets alone, particularly when worried about Mom. Her own search for solitude provided both example and grounds for me to try to sort things out on my own. Besides, I had already learned how to take care of myself in her absence. In our Madison home I had often found comfort in private corners, where I could daydream, play, and hide. I was conscious of hiding but not sure from what. Unable to find such places in our small Paris apartment, I sought or made them on foot.

Loneliness sometimes led me to parks so I could watch mothers at play with their children. In happier moods, I browsed the stalls along the riverside quays. I had never seen anything like these treasure chests full of maps, etchings, cartoons, posters, jewelry, telescopes, compasses, Gregorian music scores, stamps, medals, original editions of Jules Verne, leather-bound volumes of works by seventeenth-century French jurists and playwrights. I looked for flintlock pistols and pictures of sailing ships; I had become hooked on the Hornblower series by C. S. Forester while in a small English library on boulevard St-Germain.

I found bargain prices for notebooks, Bic ballpoint pens, graph paper. I saw posters in Métro stations and kiosks advertising Maurice Herzog's book *Annapurna*, his heroic story about the first ascent, in June 1950, of a mountain over 8,000 meters. This was an enormous boost to French pride when they needed it. Herzog had dictated the book while recuperating in the American Hospital in Neuilly; "I am having a rather difficult time," he said in the foreword, surely one of the all-time understatements in the history of mountaineering. Initially as an antidote to homesickness and anxiety, later as an avocation, I scouted for free games on pinball machines at cafés on rue St-Jacques and Place St-Michel; my favorites were Le Petit Pont, Le Notre Dame, and Le Départ Saint Michel, all still there today, two with space-age games that leave me cold. I sometimes looked as far afield as Montparnasse and St-Germain, unaware that others went there looking for Simone de Beauvoir and Jean-Paul Sartre or pretending to be Ernest Hemingway.

My perimeter on the Left Bank approximated the line of King Philippe Auguste's late-twelfth-century city wall. Sorties took me to St-Germain (whose "fields" had been outside the wall), Place de l'Odéon, St-Sulpice, Montparnasse, Luxembourg Gardens, Panthéon, Sorbonne, rue Mouffetard. I rarely introduced myself to American tourists, few by today's standards though too many for most Parisians. I marveled at how easily white Parisians fraternized with black Americàns and Africans; the Africans' colorful dress stopped jarring me after a couple of months. Gaining confidence, I explored alleys, "passages," and courtyards. I stumbled upon the building where Benjamin Franklin, John Adams, and John Jay signed the treaty with England in 1783 recognizing America's independence. I found Renaissance turrets on the corners of houses, remnants of Philippe Auguste's wall, open gates, lenient concierges, secluded fountains, impish sculptures.

These were *my* discoveries, and I was proud as I tossed them onto shelves that my mind was nailing together to hold experiences. Dad greeted my early reports with pleasant surprise. Mom seemed to know I could learn on my own, a vote of confidence that she must also have given herself during her recent independence.

I noticed pretty girls but was too bashful to introduce myself. Puberty was especially awkward for an American boy who happened to go through it in Paris while rediscovering his mother there. I envied couples kissing, walking arm-in-arm, talking at café tables. I kept doubts and yearnings to myself, thinking these would perplex Dad and give John all the more opportunity to exercise his new sense of superiority. Mom gave clear enough signals that she would listen sympathetically. Jacques's parents had arranged their apartment so he could entertain girlfriends in privacy, and Mom said she hoped to do the same for John and me back in Madison. But I was too startled to pursue the subject, too embarrassed to dance more than a few seconds with her one evening when music on the radio made her jump from her chair and pull me toward her. She offered to pay for John and me to take dance lessons. We declined, I because I could not bear to relive the misery I had felt at an eighth-grade dance where each boy's partner was determined by the girl's shoe that he picked out of a common pile.

By intuition as well as obedience to Dad, who didn't like dancing either, I counted my growing pains among those subjects that might hurt Mom. So I tried not to inflict my moods on her, whether angry at John or bewildered by sex. I did not understand how hard she was trying to catch up to my age and her maternal instincts.

Uncertain how to respond to Mom's affection or what feelings were permissible for me to have toward her, I developed a crush on her English friend, Dorothy. Dorothy was assistant to the headmaster of a private school for girls, La Châtelainie, in St. Blaise, Switzerland, at the northern end of Lake Neuchâtel. Mom had worked there the year before. According to her passport, Mom arrived in Switzerland in October 1950. An insurance form for residence in that country identified her as "divorcée," and I can only wonder whether she presumed she soon would be or merely gave that status to avoid even more awkward questions. She described the school to John and me but said nothing about her first year abroad, except for vague allusions to the south of France and the dialects of Provence. Her passport shows that she cashed the last of her traveller's checks in Paris in August 1949. The next fourteen months remain a mystery.

In St. Blaise Mom would walk up the hill to the school's scattered dwellings from the room she rented in a doctor's house on the main road to Neuchâtel. She and Dorothy quickly became friends. Dorothy, about thirty, had lost her fiancé during the war. She came to see us at #10 whenever in Paris on school business, sometimes arriving in the headmaster's chauffeur-driven Daimler. Glamorous in her faux-fur jacket and wide-shouldered dresses, Dorothy looked like Lauren Bacall and became one of my earliest ideals of the woman I hoped to marry.

I grew aware that pinball was not the only game in town, that the Left Bank moved to suggestive modern tempos. I saw posters, artists, poets, existentialists, theatergoers. I heard jazz welling up from cabarets. But I had inherited my father's ignorance of popular culture, and I did not comprehend what an extraordinary time and place this was for postwar fashions.

Existentialism was still the popular religion on the Left Bank, although its gods now quarreled among themselves over the problem of political engagement in the Cold War. Albert Camus had already distanced himself from Sartre and de Beauvoir by acknowledging the crimes of the Soviet regime in Eastern Europe and rejecting revolutionary violence cloaked in promises of human justice. In the spring of 1952 the irreparable break came when *Les Temps Modernes*, the journal Sartre had founded in 1945, published a harsh review of Camus's new book, *The Rebel*, and Sartre and de Beauvoir attacked Camus for abandoning the Left and withdrawing from politics.

New journals sprang up, usually mixing literature and politics, such as the English-language *Merlin*, edited by Jane Lougee from New England and Alexander Trocchi from Glasgow. Its first issue went on sale at George Whitman's Librairie Mistral in May 1952. Other international exiles plying the Left Bank included Samuel Beckett, Christopher Logue, James Baldwin, Richard Wright, Eugene Ionesco. Jean Genet's *The Maids* (1947), Beckett's *Waiting for Godot* (written in 1948, though not performed until 1953), and Ionesco's *The Bald Soprano* (1950) would soon be standards in the theater of the absurd. The latter play opened at the Théâtre des Noctambules and would move to the Théâtre de la Huchette in October 1952, where it can still be seen. Another popular small theater, Théâtre de la Poche, staged Ionesco's *The Lesson* in 1951. On the Right Bank Jean Anouilh's *Waltz of the Toreadors* opened in January 1952, and Benjamin Britten's opera *Billy Budd* had its Paris premier a few months later.

Cafés and cabarets vied for the intellectual trade, most of them in the St-Germain quarter. By 1951 the Café de Flore (just off Place St-Germain) had lost Sartre, who tired of being a tourist attraction, but the Flore and its neighbor, the Deux Magots, continued to lure both real and would-be intellectuals. Although patrons discussed existentialist "authenticity," more authentic conversations could be found elsewhere, such as at the Café de Tournon on rue de Tournon between boulevard St-Germain and the Luxembourg Gardens. Today the same can be said for Le Temps des Cerises, a small bistro in the 4th arrondissement, compared to larger establishments that advertise specific times for philosophical discussions.

Nowhere in the world was American jazz more popular than in Paris, and some cabarets featured it: Aux trois Mailletz (rue Galande, a stone's throw from our apartment), Le Caveau de la Huchette (rue de la Huchette), Le Club Saint-Germain (rue St-Benoit), Le Club du Vieux-Colombier (rue du Vieux-Colombier, formerly and today again a theater; Sartre's *No Exit* opened there in 1944). Other cabarets highlighted singers, readings, and skits: l'Arlequin (boulevard St-Germain); Les Assassins, Le Bar Vert, and L'Échelle de Jacob (all on rue Jacob); L'Écluse (quai des Grands-Augustins); La Rose Rouge (rue de Rennes); Le Tabou (rue Dauphine; past its postwar prime, when one could have watched "strip-tease *existentialiste*"). Many of the performers became legendary: Michèle Arnaud, Count Basie, Sidney Bechet, Bill Coleman, Miles Davis, Duke Ellington, Juliette Greco, Billie Holliday, Yves Montand, Charlie Parker, Jacques Prévert. Now I wish I had been looking for legends as well as free games.

Paris has scrubbed its buildings and gilded its statues since then. Métro trains run on quiet rubber wheels. Buses have lost their snub noses and rear platforms. Street-cleaning crews have multiplied in environmentally correct green uniforms. Concierges have been replaced by electronic panels of coded buttons. The waiter has died who yelled "deux shish kebab, deux!" toward the kitchen at Les Balkans on rue de la Harpe. The streets between rue St-Jacques and Place St-Michel have surrendered to cheap tourist eateries. The newest restaurant at #10 serves tapas and paellas. The shop at the end of our street, which had been selling produce at least since Eugène Atget photographed it in the late nineteenth century, now offers sandwiches instead. The graceful nineteenth-century Wallace fountain in Square Viviani has yielded to a ponderous allegory of the compassion of Saint Julien. Pissoirs and pinball have vanished. Restaurant menus now come in photocopy or computer printout, not purple mimeograph. French toilet paper has grown too soft to build character.

But there are still reminders of an older Paris. The extravagance around Place Vendôme and the poverty of beggars in the Métro. Children sailing boats in the Luxembourg Gardens. Old women dressed in black with thick stockings bunched down around their ankles. The Seine lapping against banks and bridges. The cries of street vendors.

The shattering of clay pipes in sidewalk shooting galleries like those where my deadeye brother always won a prize. Baguettes protruding from bags and baskets. The smell of dark coffee and ripe cheese. The way Notre Dame embraces everyone.

Day by day, living in Paris peeled away layers of what had been alien — about France, history, growing up. No single experience peeled more than being caught up in a demonstration against a memorial mass for the late Marshal Pétain. The service and ensuing riot symbolized a national trauma for France. The event also rekindled a moral certainty I had acquired during the Second World War: fascists are bullies and bad; anyone who resists them is good. Politics, memory, and creed converged outside Notre Dame on one of those days that begins like any other but becomes like no other, leaving you with a Delphic riddle that predicts your life yet requires a lifetime to unravel.

Seven years earlier, half of my life but a blink for the French, the Resistance had helped liberate their country. Although dominated by Communists, the wartime resistance movement had represented a wide range of citizens who hoped to reconstruct France along idealistic lines transcending narrow party interests. They envisioned a revolutionary new republic well to the left of center, combining liberalism with socialism in a middle way between Marxism and capitalism.

What had happened to the ideals of the Resistance by 1951? Since 1944, Communists and Gaullists alike had claimed to define and hold the moral high ground in France. But now the Communist Party obeyed Moscow, and many Gaullists had become reconciled to party politics only a few years after Charles de Gaulle founded the Rassemblement du peuple français in reaction against an unstable party system. In other parties as well, former members of the Resistance — Guy Mollet (Socialists), Georges Bidault (Mouvement républicain populaire), Pierre Mendès France (Radicals) — played by political rules they had once renounced for the common good. On the Right, conservatives and Pétainistes regained enough confidence to play politics and enter cabinets. On the Left, intellectuals who had coalesced for liberation now argued over Cold War politics.

France had reverted to prewar habits of class conflict, ideological name-calling, and political instability. And the war was still not over. The old wounds inflicted by collaboration and resistance could re-open at any time. They did in October 1951, within view of #10, rue St-Julien-le-Pauvre.

Marshal Henri Philippe Pétain had died in July as a prisoner of the state on the island of Yeu, near Nantes, at the age of ninety-five. The Communist newspaper, *Le Soir*, printed a picture of Pétain shaking hands with Hitler. The Society of Friends of Pétain, among whom were army officers, clergy, and members of the French Academy, called for prayers for the deceased. The *New York Times* called Pétainism "political tinder."

On Saturday, 27 October, the tinder exploded outside Notre Dame during the memorial mass for Pétain celebrated by Archbishop Feltin. Among those attending the mass were veterans of the First World War and former officials of the Vichy regime. Several thousand veterans of the Resistance, joined by university students, massed on the parvis outside to protest honoring the man who had betrayed the Third Republic in June 1940 and then ruled Vichy France as an arch-collaborator with the Nazis. They had gathered at Place Dauphine behind the banners of different associations, Communist and non-Communist, walked along the quai des Orfèvres, placed flowers beneath the plaques on the south wall of the Hôtel Dieu honoring two policemen whom the Germans had executed near that spot during the liberation. In front of Notre Dame the marchers sang "La Marseillaise" and "The Song of the Partisans." According to Archbishop Feltin, the mass was not meant to honor the man but to pray that God pardon any sins he may have committed. Members of a Catholic resistance group prayed that God enlighten the archbishop. The demonstrators had no doubt about sin and no intention of pardoning it.

My brother and I, true innocents, crossed the park outside our apartment to see what all the noise was about. What we saw was ugly, and the mood was grim, like black-and-white photos of crowds in the 1930s and faces in the war. Demonstrators chanted "Pétain — assassin!," "Collabos en prison!," and "Le fascisme ne passera pas!" The police pushed them across the Pont au Double to the Left Bank and then into rue Lagrange on the east side of the park. Hemmed in by the park fence on one side and buildings on the other, their front ranks battered by police wielding billy clubs and capes containing lead weights, the mass of demonstrators fell back along rue Lagrange. Having let our curiosity take us to the rear of the crowd, my brother and I now struggled against this tide, I suppose because we were new at this and taller than most of the students. The melee soon surrounded and separated us. Three police, clubs at the ready, bore down on me, and I looked for an escape route. I found one, over the fence into the garden, then south along the fence until police who had moved into the park forced me back over the fence into the street. I angled down rue du Fouarre to rue Galande and made my way around to rue St-Julien-le-Pauvre, straightening my jacket and walking slowly so any police on that side of the park would think me a guiltless bystander, which I began to think I was not. About fifteen minutes later, John staggered in the door, head bleeding, glasses shattered and lost. A gendarme, perhaps thinking him a student leader, had hit him across the face with a weighted cape, ignoring whatever pleas he could muster up in broken French.

Mom fetched bandages. Dad explained the historical context. He started with Pétain's emergence from the First World War as a national hero for holding Verdun against the Germans in 1916 and moved on to the fall of France in June 1940, the resistance against Nazi occupation and Vichy collaboration, the liberation in 1944, and the vengeful justice allotted to collaborators, Pétain's death sentence for high treason having been commuted by de Gaulle to life imprisonment.

Bandages could not restore John's lost innocence that day nor a history lesson mine. After the riot, alarms rang in my head whenever I came across any reference to war, collaboration, or resistance. I became more aware of maimed veterans of the Great War as they navigated Paris streets using crutches or go-carts, their faces gaunt and eyes focused on something I could not see. I tried to imagine who built barricades out of cobblestones and who fired the weapons that left pockmarks around doors and windows of buildings on the Left Bank and Île de la Cité during the struggle to liberate Paris in August 1944. I wondered what had prompted students, and indeed members of the police, to give up their lives at places where plaques and bouquets still commemorate their valor. I went out of my way to say hello whenever I saw the Miss Marple—like Englishwoman whom neighborhood gossip identified as a heroine of the Maquis. After the anti-Pétain riot, viscerally as well as intellectually, I sided with the anti-Pétainistes, Communist or not. I could more easily imagine risking my own adult life for a cause.

Paris revived my veneration for anyone who had fought against fascism in the last war, my war. During the war, John and I had vowed to resist the Nazis if they attacked our neighborhood. We could have predicted who among the other kids would join us, who would collaborate with the enemy, who would stay at home. I derived my wartime values and judgments from more than ancestors and contemporary heroes. They came also from awareness of Mom's vulnerability and fear of losing her. The neighborhood bully in Madison, who led a gang of older boys from nearby blocks, would have joined the Gestapo had he lived in Germany. He tormented John and me and taunted our parents because they told him to pick on someone his own size. Dad was unfazed, but Mom, who usually shamed miscreants with volleys of common decency, gave up trying. I watched her retreat, suspected Dad could not make things right, felt powerless myself. I still hate the bully for doing this to me, to the childhood I imagined and the man I wanted to become.

Since the war I have been haunted by images of resistance. Nowhere have they been more vivid than in France. My wife and I spent a week in Burgundy and the Morvan early in the summer of 1996. At an intersection of one-lane farm roads near Mailly-le-Chateau on the Yonne River, we stopped to read the names of ten members of the local Maquis whom the Germans killed there in July 1944. Two elderly women stopped their car and asked if we were lost. No, I replied, just looking at the monument.

"Yes," the driver said, "they died in the Resistance."

"It's sad," I said, feeling inadequate.

"Oui, c'est triste," she repeated, and her companion nodded.

I could think of nothing more to say, although I wanted to spend hours with them hearing the story of this crossroad. I thanked them for stopping, wished them good-day, and drove on, visualizing the fatal capture where one of the roads entered woodland at the edge of the field.

Two days later, in the Morvan, we came across a monument to members of the Maquis Bernard who had died during an ambush of a German column as it crossed a stone bridge over a stream west of Montsauche. Picturing the firefight, I remembered how John and I had ambushed a Nazi train on a bridge of the Illinois Central Railroad on the way home from Dudgeon School.

In Paris in June 1996 I visited the small museum next to Gare

Montparnasse dedicated to Gen. Leclerc (commander of the French 2nd Armored Division that liberated Paris) and Jean Moulin, one of the major leaders of the French Resistance. Moulin was a good and courageous man. Betrayed by fellow *résistants*, he was captured in 1943 by Klaus Barbie and the Lyon Gestapo. Moulin refused to crack. When ordered to sign a confession after most of the life had been beaten out of him, he drew a caricature of his interrogator, his final act of defiance.

I wept as I lingered in front of the last display case, and this puzzled a young French couple who were finishing up their quick tour of the museum. They could not have known that artifacts and sites of the Resistance always take me back to Paris in 1951–1952, when my memories of the war were becoming transformed into a lifelong riddle. Who is the bully, who is vulnerable, what have I to lose, what should I do, can victims recover? Looking back, I see that the riddle and its unraveling are embedded in deep emotions. Anger at the sheer arrogance of Nazi Germany, let alone its inhumanity. Sorrow at the loss of life and human dignity. Regret that I was not old enough to fight in the "good war." Fear that bullies will harm me and those I love. Sympathy for the underdog. Hope that I will have the courage to resist the bullies, and shame that I may not. Determination never to let Nazism "happen here." Frustration at how little I knew about Mom's illness. Despair that the individual is essentially alone, unprotected. At the Moulin exhibit, I wept for him, for Mom, and for the boy still at war inside the man.

Until the anti-Pétain riot, I ignored my country's belittling of the Communists' role in the French Resistance. Afterward, I saw good reason to honor them. They had helped liberate Paris. They would have helped me silence the Nazi on West Lawn Avenue. Until Dad's categorical statement about the blue glass at Chartres, it never occurred to me that American know-how could not duplicate an original. Rue St-Julien-le-Pauvre was a subversive place for an American to grow five inches taller and become a baritone early in the Cold War.

CHAPTER 2 *Americans Abroad*

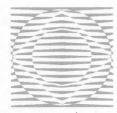29 January 1945. "The Russians are giving them
kraut eating outlaw heathens just what they are
entitled to, and I hope they exterminate the entire German race before they quit, for the Germans are the sole cause of all this trouble in the
world and I want them wiped off the face of the
earth. Just what do you think of that turtle jawed pug nose Churchill
since he is trying to rule all of Europe, and what do you think of the
way he has treated the Greek people, after they fought the Germans
so hard. You know what I have always told you about the English
people, well I think less of them now than ever, it has always been
rule or ruin with the English. I am in favor of giving Russia anything
they want in Europe, I had much rather live under a Russian government than live under a German government, and if Russia wants
all of Europe, I say let them have it."

That's what Granddad Post wrote in a letter to my father as the
war in Europe was drawing to a close. Granddad had never attended
college or traveled farther from Texas than Kansas and then by horse
with herds of cattle in the 1880s. His single-spaced marginless letters
typed by forefingers roamed immense prairies from flu remedies to

world affairs. This would not be regarded as "America's century" had Washington taken his advice.

The Cold War sent unprecedented thousands of Americans to Europe in peacetime for reasons of state. They worked in military affairs, diplomacy, economic recovery, world government, business, finance, law, technology, the arts, education, and other fields. Although they did not see themselves as imperialists, at least not in the Communist meaning of the term, they knew their country had emerged from the war as the world's greatest power, and they symbolized their government's decision to maintain that hegemony at least as long as Communism threatened the postwar order.

These men and women were "magnificent provincials," as GIs in Naples in 1944 were described by a Red Cross volunteer from Boston named Louella in John Horne Burns's novel *The Gallery*. The Americans who went to Europe to fight Communism were healthy, idealistic, confident, effective. Their attitudes toward the Old World ranged widely: from reverence for European customs to disdain; from grief over its near suicide to callousness; from optimism over Western Europe's ability to check Communism to pessimism; from altruism in their efforts to mend a broken continent to self-interest.

In 1951–1952, the first year of America's major military commitment to the Atlantic Alliance, I met some of these cold warriors and went to school with their children. I saw commanders at SHAPE, marines in the Vatican, Harlem Globetrotters at the Palais des Sports. My parents hoped Europe would civilize me. My country wanted to civilize Europe. Europe would give me a past. Americans would give Europe a future. Both my country and I came of age in Cold War Europe.

Educating Europeans in American values had become a long-term tenet of American policy before my European education began. As Americans discovered postwar Europe, they found a devastated frontier. The Western civilization they had studied in school and college had crumbled. A backward area with lousy plumbing now stood between American civilization and a vast wilderness ruled by Communism, and many of the inhabitants of this frontier were susceptible to the idealistic momentum generated by left-wing leaders of wartime resistance movements.

Major statements of American policy justified American aid to Europe in moral as well as economic and strategic terms. Since the world was polarizing around antithetical systems of belief, the United States had a duty "to support free peoples" against "totalitarianism" (Truman Doctrine, 1947). The goal was to revive the world economy so that political and social conditions would emerge "in which free institutions can exist" (Marshall Plan, 1947). The conflict with the Soviet Union was a "test of national quality," and America had "responsibilities of moral and political leadership" (George F. Kennan's 1947 "X" article). America must affirm "our essential values" abroad, demonstrate "the integrity and vitality of our system" in the worldwide "struggle for men's minds," avoid "vacillation or appeasement," and maintain "confidence among other peoples in our strength and resolution" (National Security Council [NSC] paper 68, 1950).

The Soviet Union's detonation of its first atomic bomb in August 1949, the outbreak of the Korean War in June 1950, the intervention of Communist China in the Korean War, Soviet collusion in Korea, European dismay at American weakness in Korea, European fears that Moscow might exploit the situation by advancing westward, the thorny question of incorporating the German Federal Republic in European defense forces, the domestic attacks from Senator McCarthy and the right wing of the Republican Party against a "soft" and "Red" State Department: by the end of 1950, the combined weight of these issues forced President Truman not merely to accept NSC 68 as a statement of policy but to accelerate the achievement of its goals. He agreed to send more American troops to Europe and appoint an American supreme commander for NATO. He recalled Gen. Marshall to government service as secretary of defense, established the Office of Defense Mobilization, declared a national emergency, and planned to treble spending on defense. No longer content to help Europe stand on its own feet economically, the United States would commit substantial military resources to Western Europe and stay there indefinitely. Propaganda would increase correspondingly under the "Campaign of Truth," authorized by Congress as a "Marshall Plan in the field of ideas."

Many American cold warriors arrived in Europe certain that recent history confirmed their country's moral and material superiority. Wishing to re-create the Western European frontier in their own progressive image, they behaved as if Europeans were the provincials. Living in the Latin Quarter, my sense of history stretched and my adolescent world of possibilities opened up by Paris, my family reunited in Europe but of no apparent usefulness to the national interest, I tended to sympathize with the Europeans.

Every weekday morning my brother and I walked across rue St-Julien-le-Pauvre and the park, then down rue Lagrange to Place Maubert, to take the Métro to the American Community School (ACS) near the Bois de Boulogne. We bought *carnets* (booklets) of second-class tickets, often longing for the greater comfort of going first class in the red half of one car on each train. On crowded cars and station platforms, our advantage in height was of little avail against the overwhelming smell of wine and garlic. Hypnotic rows of wires and lights lined the sides of the tunnels, and small signs advertising Dubonnet and La Vache qui Rit were placed where anyone looking out of the cars would see them. The Métro stations measured how much time remained to doze while the train lurched toward the southwestern edge of the city, past entrancing names like Odéon, Mabillon, Sèvres-Babylone, Duroc, Ségur, La Motte Picquet, Mirabeau, to the end of the line, our stop, Porte d'Auteuil. We took the bus or walked west from the Porte d'Auteuil station, skirting the Roland Garros tennis complex (not very complex then), to our school at #45, boulevard d'Auteuil.

The American Community School was established in 1946 in the American Students and Artists Center on boulevard Raspail and moved to Boulogne in 1949. The building that housed ACS from 1949 to 1960 still stands, a townhouse of four stories converted into upscale apartments, still fronted with a gravel yard enclosed by an iron picket fence. On the ground floor was the business office; on the second, the cafeteria, with bland institutional French cooking and an activities room where the glee club practiced. The upper floors contained classrooms, offices, study hall, and library. Grades four through twelve met here when we arrived, kindergarten through grade three at the American Church on the quai d'Orsay. The first wave of the postwar baby boom increased pressure on kindergarten and first grade as the Atlantic Alliance moved more offices to Paris, and by early 1952 ACS transferred all the primary grades to a property elsewhere in the same suburb of Boulogne. In junior and senior high the grades averaged about eighteen students each. My grade, the ninth, was the largest, with twenty-two. The numbers fluctuated as parents moved in and out of Paris on schedules determined by priorities unrelated to the academic calendar.

I was stunned by an institution that was more like a prep school in the East than a public school in the Midwest. ACS was the first private school I had ever attended, and it also had the smallest classrooms and fewest students. The large majority were sons and daughters of American business executives (IBM, TWA, Paramount Pictures, and the like) and civil servants (including diplomat Graham Martin, who was later U.S. ambassador to South Vietnam and evacuated by helicopter from the embassy roof when Saigon fell in April 1975). Most of these kids lived in the posh 16th arrondissement or suburbs; the ACS bus did not go as far east as the 6th arrondissement, let alone the 5th. More boys wore coats and ties and more girls suits than you would have seen in all the public high schools of Wisconsin put together. Some of them had French names, evidence of Franco-American collaboration before the war. Larry Parks, son of Gordon Parks, the *Life* magazine photographer, was the only black student, and there was probably a higher percentage of Jews than in Madison's schools. Most of the juniors and seniors planned to attend private colleges in the Ivy League or Seven Sisters. Many of them seemed sophisticated enough to be in college already, and I admired how casually they undertook every challenge, from tests to school dances. They even persuaded the administration to set aside a smoking room for them, a seismic impossibility at West High School in Madison.

One of the most memorable characters came to school in a chauffeured Rolls Royce, wore fancy suits, and draped his fur-collared overcoat over his shoulders without putting his arms into the sleeves. Neat trick, I thought, but he wouldn't have survived a Wisconsin winter. A popular and politically ambitious senior stole my best notebook and then acted like the victim when I confronted him with the evidence. He became a successful businessman. There was a gangly junior from Tennessee, a star of the ACS basketball team, who knew his French accent was atrocious but loved to tease Madame Dubus, our French teacher, by launching easy words of one syllable on long hound-dog trajectories — as in "*quoi* . . . ?" A Paris-born senior named Nicholas Daniloff would become the Moscow bureau chief of *U.S. News & World Report* in the early 1980s; arrested by the KGB for espionage in September 1986, he was used as a pawn in U.S.-Soviet relations leading up to summit talks between President Reagan and Chairman Gorbachev on the reduction of nuclear arms.

In my class, a hyperactive organizer in his second year at ACS had gathered a small gang about him, and he let me know that I could attach to its periphery if I acknowledged him as leader. I decided not to, preferring the company of two other independent classmates who invited me to their homes, one of them in the refined village of Maisons-Laffitte west of Paris near the forest of St-Germain. I felt uneasy around any gang that treated me like a follower, sensing I was more likely to lose part of myself inside it than outside, the part that was trying to work things out alone.

Most of our teachers were from the States, a few from France and the British Commonwealth. Now we would call them old-fashioned. They did not try to be charismatic or trendy. They emphasized basic skills and subjects for college prep. There were no calculators, no computers, no cassettes, no VCRs. The term "multimedia" would have drawn blank stares, and World Wide Web would have sounded like a horror film. The academic atmosphere was serious without being bookish, competitive without being cutthroat.

Miss Robertson, a tall Australian, wore jackets with thick shoulder pads and taught English. A tough disciplinarian, to the dismay of the goof-offs, she drilled us on grammar from the pluperfect to prepositional phrases. We read more Shakespeare in a year than Madison high schools assigned in four. We had to memorize long passages, and I still thank her whenever Henry V cries, "Once more unto the breach, dear friends." On the Métro one afternoon in February, I happened to be riding in the same car as Miss Robertson. She was reading a French newspaper headlined "LE ROI EST MORT." George VI had died that morning, and Miss Robertson was weeping. I liked her.

Madame Dubus used creative lipsticking to accentuate rosebud lips. If anyone misbehaved in class, she would look up over her glasses, pucker, and snap, "Qui cause là? Tu es méchant!" Madame Dubus had a large bosom. When she took off her glasses and let them rappel over that mighty ledge on the chain she wore around her neck, the boys in class lost all interest in the language and concentrated on her problem of locating her glasses in the void the next time she needed them. This was high drama, as she herself knew, and both parties tacitly agreed that the boys would not laugh until something else came along to let the pent-up humor escape without offending her. One day I summoned up the courage to ask her what my given name meant in French, having nearly recovered from the shock of seeing it spelled in neon in the window of a certain kind of shop. She paused, blushed, replied "girdles," paused, and then smiled flirtatiously. We all knew she wore one. I doubt that we understood how much Madame Dubus taught us with that smile.

Activities that would be unremarkable in an ordinary American high school became singular at ACS. The glee club sang before French audiences. Reporters and photographers from *Life* held the school captive for a few days, and helped stage the Halloween costume ball, while preparing a story about American teenagers abroad. Officials in the European Recovery Program arranged for our Thanksgiving assembly program to be recorded by ABC for radio broadcast in the United States. Dances took place at the American Church and in the basement of TWA's Paris offices. The basketball team defeated Lycée St-Germain in the semifinals of the Paris League, then routed Lycée Berthelot for the championship of Paris and the Île de France.

Class and school trips included the United Nations General Assembly at the Palais de Chaillot, where we went a few weeks after Andrei Vishinsky's tirade against Western proposals for disarmament and free elections in Germany. The proposals, he shouted, had made him laugh so much the previous night that he couldn't sleep. We also visited the French National Assembly, SHAPE, the Place des Vosges and Musée Carnavalet in the Marais district, Orly Airport, the Musée de l'Homme, the Palais de la Découverte. Guest speakers told us about the United Nations and UNESCO, the European Youth Movement, China, the forthcoming American elections. The place to be seen after school was the snack bar in the American embassy at the northwestern corner of Place de la Concorde, where you could order hamburgers, milk shakes, and cinnamon toast. The children of American businessmen could purchase American foodstuffs at the American National Interest Commissary in the 18th arrondissement; Clark and Butterfinger candy bars were popular at ACS. Friends of army brats asked them to procure goodies from the military post exchange.

ACS reflected the institutional scaffolding of American policy in Europe and the centrality of Paris at this time in the Cold War. Parents worked at the American embassy and for Voice of America, both of which had expanded since 1949. They sat on committees and staffs of the United Nations: the sixth General Assembly opened in Paris in November 1951 and concluded in February, the last session before moving to the United Nations' new permanent headquarters in New York City; UNESCO stayed in Paris. They helped administer Marshall aid under the European Recovery Program as officials in the Economic Cooperation Administration (ECA), a federal agency established in 1948 and superseded at the end of 1951 by the Mutual Security Agency (MSA).

A few ACS parents represented the United States in the burgeoning military and civilian administration of NATO, which had been founded in April 1949. But most military families sent their children to Paris American High School in the 16th arrondissement; it would soon move to new quarters a few miles west of Boulogne in St-Cloud, closer to SHAPE. ACS, since 1960 called the American School of Paris, moved to those premises in 1967 after NATO and U.S. forces left France at President de Gaulle's behest. From 1960 to 1967 the American School occupied the former hunting lodge of the eighteenth-century château in nearby Louveciennes, where Madame du Barry had entertained Louis XV.

SHAPE started up early in 1951. The bulk of American land and air forces in Europe belonged to the Central Command, headquartered southeast of Paris at the palace of Fontainebleau, a favorite retreat for Francis I and Napoleon. NATO's Financial and Economic Board, also based in Paris, coordinated aid policy with the Organization of European Economic Cooperation, a European body in which the United States was an associate member. Paris was home to the secretariat of the Temporary Council Committee, established by the North Atlantic Council in September 1951 to reconcile defense requirements and economic capabilities. The NATO Defense College opened in November, teaching courses in military, political, and economic affairs to international classes of officers and civil servants in the artillery wing of the Ècole Militaire, whose eighteenth-century architect had also designed the Place de la Concorde and the Petit Trianon at Versailles. Early in 1952, having overcome British resistance to the idea, the North Atlantic Council decided to locate its permanent headquarters in Paris, where the new office of secretary general would direct an international secretariat in the Palais de Chaillot.

Acronyms tripped off students' tongues like a catechism. I must have heard ECA and NATO fifty times a day in the fall, the same for MSA in the New Year as families adapted to bureaucratic metamorphoses in Washington. Repetition and tone conveyed a system of belief, in language understood only by the chosen few and in truisms for measuring good and evil. It was a humanitarian and arrogant faith combining two traditions in American political culture: America is the promised land; American intervention will make the world safe for our exceptional way of life. "Losing China" and "saving Europe" had biblical overtones; postwar world history would tell the story of American sin and redemption. Everyone in government service seemed to belong to this faith, even altruists who embraced the French.

The authority of the faith was summoned with the greatest dogmatism when finding fault on a large scale, as some of my classmates were inclined to do. Thus, the United States should have joined Germany to fight the Soviet Union in 1945, a refrain that insulted my memories of war. Or the French are incompetent; "Air France is air chance," as the saying went. Or the French are ungrateful, and giving them economic aid is a thankless waste of money. Or Truman is weak, and Ike will be strong; Eisenhower had already defeated Truman in March 1948 in a straw vote at ACS, and four years later he was an even heavier favorite there.

Entering ACS a week after fall term began and suffering from an acute case of homesickness, I knew I was in trouble. The reception from some schoolmates made me regret that I lived in the Latin Quarter and that my father was just a professor at the University of Wisconsin instead of someone important at ECA. Both facts made my brother and me unique at ACS, and in the early going I did not need singularity.

I confessed these worries to Mom one day at a café near the Porte d'Auteuil Métro station, where, much to our relief, she met John and me after school during our first week of classes. When I finished, she arched her right eyebrow. I hadn't seen this storm warning since before her wartime breakdown, and as I instinctively braced myself it did not occur to me to celebrate this meteorological evidence of her recovery. She gave us a stern lecture on the value of teaching and scholarship, the significance of Dad's Fulbright Fellowship, and the proper way to judge people, places, and the national interest.

"Your dad is a great and good man," she concluded, looking me in the eye as she delivered a commandment: "Don't you ever forget that."

I heard echoes of this thunderclap for the rest of the school year. They told me there was something heroic in teaching medieval history and in raising two boys alone, that Dad might be as important as a diplomat, a general, or a business executive.

Mom's lecture helped a lot, but so did touch football, and by the end of October John and I no longer felt complete aliens at ACS. On dry days, the boys' gym class walked to the nearby Bois de Boulogne, divided up into two teams, and played football in a narrow, grassy clearing close to Porte de Boulogne. Years later, in 1989, I searched for the clearing, but the noise and concrete of Autoroute 13, built long after my time at ACS, pushed me into a northerly and fruitless search. Luckily, in 1995 memory told me to imagine the autoroute and its racket not there, and my instinct for playing touch football in the "Bois" took me northeasterly along a bike path to the unmistakable clumps of evergreens flanking the old clearing.

Woods formed the sidelines of our field in 1951; jackets or sweaters thrown on the ground marked the end zones. One day, when our team sputtered and its captain was so desperate he asked if anyone had a play, anyone at all, John and I allowed as how, yes, we had a play. In spite of our unequal athletic skills, genes had produced brothers who complemented each other in one vital sandlot department: John could throw farther and I could catch better than most of our contemporaries. In pickup games on West Lawn Avenue in Madison, we were not permitted to be on the same team. At ACS, still feeling like outsiders, we grabbed the opportunity.

The boys at ACS didn't know what hit them. Even French onlookers sensed the change in this already curious American encroachment on ground where Merovingian royalty had hunted for wild boar twelve centuries before. Suddenly it was West Lawn football, based on the titanic long pass, the inventive use of irregular sidelines, the exploitation of disbelief in the defensive backfield. John faded back, bought time, and heaved. I ran down the sideline, not very fast but experienced in the use of trees, trash cans, and sharp cuts back to the center of the field at a prearranged distance. Touchdown. We connected for three more touchdowns that afternoon and redefined offense for the rest of the season. We also began to make friends, join clubs, and hold our own academically.

I was glad to find some common ground with my schoolmates. When several of them first asked me to accompany them to the snack bar at the American embassy after school, I happily accepted; I craved a hamburger and wanted to be one of the guys. But I never became a regular or one of the guys. The massive size of the embassy, the name-dropping among many in the snack bar crowd, the conspicuous wealth, and the pride of position in the American Cold War hierarchy all reminded me of our differences.

Forty-five years later, these differences resurfaced. I found the *Life* article about students at ACS in the issue of 7 January 1952, titled "'Quel Babes!' U.S. teenagers transplant their own way of life to Paris." Gordon Parks took the photographs: young Americans on the rear platform of a bus, at a sidewalk café on the "Champs," listening to jazz at the Vieux-Colombier, teaching Sunday school at the American Church. According to the article, American teenagers in Paris came from families that had servants, didn't mix much with French teenagers, and preferred American food. They hung out at ACS, the American Church, and the embassy canteen; some went to the Left Bank to hear jazz.

I met a few ACS alumni from the early 1950s at the fiftieth anniversary celebration in Paris in June 1996, where, to my delight, I was asked to give the keynote speech. One of my contemporaries cautioned against stereotyping all ACS students; a few were Francophiles, wore berets, drove Vespa motor scooters to school, and hung out at Montmartre joints where Yves Montand and Edith Piaf sang. Another alumnus, however, confirmed *Life* and my memory. He recalled how he and his friends felt superior and showed off; after all, "America saved Europe, didn't it?" They read every French sign of anti-Americanism as pure envy. They did not want to mix with the French nor with Franco-American children, whom they regarded as "odd and borderline." Although their parents put the Latin Quarter off-limits because it was full of Communists and libertines, his group would sneak away to cabarets there, Aux trois Maillets one of their favorites. He was surprised to hear me say I had felt like a foreigner among such students at ACS.

I felt less and less foreign among Parisians. Not as sure of myself as most Americans, I was more willing than they to let Paris behave "in accordance with its nature," as the Polish poet Czeslaw Milosz wrote in "Bypassing rue Descartes" fifty years after his first visit there, "shy, a traveler, a young barbarian just come to the capital of the world."

Late one rainy December afternoon, I left the embassy for the bus stop in front of the Hôtel Crillon. My bus for boulevard St-Germain had pulled away, the kind with the open platform in the rear where the conductor cranked out tickets and pulled the bell-cord to signal the driver. I ran after the bus, gained on it in the heavy traffic in spite of slick cobblestones, and pulled myself onto the platform, helped up by several passengers. They had started shouting encouragement during my long run, and they cheered as I climbed safely aboard when the bus drew even with the massive statue representing the city of Brest. When the conductor scolded me, they told him to pipe down. I was elated. I had made it and was heading home.

I did not have to sneak into the Latin Quarter, and feeling at home there became a source of pride. So did having a French friend named Jacques and parents who were neither cocky chauvinists nor disgruntled exiles. I always knew I was an American abroad. Nothing made me French. But Paris and Europe gave me a new point of reference, a source of comparison and cosmopolitanism. The process of correlation stirred up ambivalent currents about what sort of American I might become back home. Gen. Eisenhower, Pope Pius XII, and Goose Tatum all had a hand in this.

Like almost every American boy of my generation, I idolized Gen. Eisenhower. An unalloyed war hero, he stood for what I had been told were the major lessons of the Second World War. The war might have been prevented had the political leaders of Britain and France not appeased Hitler at Munich in 1938. To defeat the Axis, the Americans had to intervene, and the Allies had to concentrate on Europe. Victory by our combined forces required shrewd and diplomatic leadership by an American general. In Paris I applied these lessons to what I understood of the Cold War, as if Stalin had replaced Hitler. So did the governments of the United States and Western Europe.

Boys and statesmen took for granted that proven military heroes must fight the Cold War. Almost everyone except the Communists welcomed Eisenhower's appointment as NATO's Supreme Allied Commander Europe in December 1950, for they expected him to do what he had done best during the Second World War — emphasize the European theater, move things forward, boost morale, improve relations between military and civilian leaders, and build international cooperation. Returning to active service from the presidency of Columbia University, he did all of this in the seventeen months of his command, part of which coincided with my time in Paris.

After arriving in January 1951, Eisenhower immediately assured French leaders of American support for NATO. He graciously accepted President Vincent Auriol's offer of land for SHAPE's permanent headquarters near the village of Rocquencourt about twelve miles southwest of Paris. The quickly assembled one-story structures were Cold War functional, a dull style implying long hours and short meals, unlike the antique gentility of other French buildings in NATO's life, such as the Astoria Hotel, École Militaire, Palais de Chaillot, Fontainebleau. In July, with the French president at his side, Eisenhower asserted that the purpose of the new headquarters was not to wage war but to build a "Pax Atlantica" that would "lift from the hearts of men the fear of cell blocks and slave camps." A few months later he opened Shape Village, which would house the families of NATO personnel and had, according to the *New York Times*, "plumbing fixtures to satisfy most American tastes."

Reconciling American tastes and French realities was Eisenhower's toughest job. While proclaiming support for NATO, French governments hit many snags. The Western military buildup that began with the Korean War increased the rate of inflation, threatened the output of consumer goods, and widened the dollar gap as French dollar reserves declined. Morale in the French army was low, in spite of the National Assembly's attempt to raise it by reinstating the soldier's daily ration of wine. Public opinion resented poor wages, weak currency, unemployment, and the bias toward guns at the expense of butter. French leaders argued that these conditions would worsen without substantial increases in American military aid, nor would France be able to meet NATO schedules for rearming additional divisions for European security when it must also fight Communism in Indochina and maintain order in its former colonies in North Africa. French leaders had subscribed to NATO's "forward strategy" of defending Europe as far to the east as possible, which meant on German soil, falling back if necessary to the main line of defense at the Rhine. But the French stalled at what Washington deemed essential for the eventual success of this strategy: the rearmament of West Germany and inclusion of German troops in the common defense.

Eisenhower and Ambassador Bruce dealt with the French far more diplomatically than most American politicians would have done. Although stronger back home than in Paris, the loathing for the French that I encountered at ACS had seeped into the American consciousness from various sources. Grandfathers and great-uncles who had fought in France in the last year of the Great War told stories of incompetence and greed in the host country. The French collapse of 1940 and allegedly poor showing in Indochina and Korea seemed to prove that the French would not and could not fight when the chips were down. De Gaulle's wartime haughtiness toward Roosevelt and Eisenhower still rankled, as did his Cold War declarations of French and European independence from "les Anglo-Saxons." The neutralism preached by *Le Monde* and other publications after the war struck many Americans as typical French defeatism and unwitting support for Communism. Americans accused the French of being soft on Communism, both in France and in the French Union, which many of these same Americans would break up because of its wicked colonialism. The French were petty and small-time, unwilling to Americanize their economy. They ate frogs and snails, gave wine to their children, no longer went to church. They were rude, arrogant, and oversexed. They did not bathe enough, and, worst sin of all, they did not like Americans.

Backed by Bruce and Europeanists in Washington like Marshall and Acheson, Eisenhower did much to dampen such hostility and reassure the French that the Pax would not be as Americana as they feared. He admired Jean Monnet, architect of the Schuman Plan for European economic integration, and he also became a staunch advocate of the finally unsuccessful French plan for a European Defense Community that French leaders presumed their country would dominate. He sometimes appealed to French moral sensibilities. In January 1952, elected by the Académie des sciences morales et politiques to the foreign associate seat once held by Gen. John J. Pershing, Eisenhower referred to the "just and moral" purpose of safeguarding peace and freedom. He recognized France's "glorious heritage" and said the world again looked to France for "leadership and vision." (Praise for the French could go too far for some Americans. When the MSA proudly announced in March 1952 that, thanks partly to American aid in the form of machine tools, the French had developed the Mystère jet fighter that could outperform the American Sabre jet, the Pentagon denied the unfavorable comparison.)

Only after leaving France and plunging into presidential politics did Eisenhower reveal his misgivings about French qualifications to help preserve Western civilization. His offhand remarks in August and September 1952 about atheism and moral debility in France lost him many friends there. When I saw him hand over command of SHAPE to Gen. Matthew Ridgway, however, Ike was still very popular indeed.

Buses transported students from ACS and Paris American High School to the change-of-command ceremony at SHAPE on Friday morning, 30 May 1952. Today the old SHAPE compound is occupied by a computer company and belittled by suburban sprawl. In 1952 I stood about twenty yards to the left and rear of the small platform from which Eisenhower and Ridgway faced members of the press in a grassy area outside Eisenhower's modest office. The French defense minister, René Pleven, stood to Ike's left. The crowd was small. I looked over the heads of about fifty seated civilians. Behind the platform, a group of NATO officers included Field Marshal Viscount Montgomery (deputy commander), Gen. Alfred Gruenther (chief of staff), Marshal Alphonse-Pierre Juin (commander of land forces, Central Europe), Adm. Robert Carney (commander of naval forces), Gen. Lauris Norstad (commander of air forces), and Lord Ismay (secretary general). Beyond the platform, I could see a small French military band sporting berets.

The sky was overcast, the air cool, the ceremony brief and unpretentious. Eisenhower, dressed in winter uniform with green jacket, thanked his staff and said the coalition was moving ahead with both humility and high courage. Ridgway had replaced Gen. MacArthur as commander of United Nations forces in Korea a year earlier. Now, succeeding Eisenhower and dressed in summer tans, he pledged to defend liberty and the other "finest values man has recognized," and he paid tribute to Montgomery and Gruenther. The former and the new supreme commanders stood at salute while the band played "The Star-Spangled Banner" and "La Marseillaise." It was moving. It was over.

Watching this ceremony gave me none of the discomfort I had felt in the snack bar at the American embassy. I forgot the imperiousness of schoolmates and my suspicions about American self-interest. I forgave Eisenhower for leaving and for being a Republican. I was thrilled to see top brass and national flags. I believed in these war heroes, their values, NATO, America's right to lead the alliance. I knew history was being made before my eyes. I could see the Cold War clearly again after I had earlier seen its eclipse in Rome.

In April, during spring vacation at ACS, Dad took the family to Rome, where he wanted to look at documents in the Vatican library. Had he said we were going to Germany, I would have balked at the foreboding overtones of Nazis and the Iron Curtain. But Italy sounded different. The Roman baths at Cluny had reminded me of pictures in Dad's study in Madison and those viewed through the stereoscope in his parents' house in Haskell. I thought this Vespasian must have been something special to have public urinals named after him. I loved vacation, trains, and spaghetti. My hunch that it would be a great trip got a big boost when the train made an unscheduled stop in a tunnel between Switzerland and Italy, the lights went out, and an Italian passenger shouted, "Banditi di Texas!"

We had rooms at the Pensione Rubens on via Borgognona, very near via Condotti and Piazza di Spagna. Dad had stayed at the Rubens on previous visits to Rome in the late 1920s and early 1930s, when he had watched Mussolini speak to huge crowds. We toured for a couple of days, Dad imitating Mussolini on a balcony in Piazza Venezia, to our delight, but overdoing churches: Santa Trinità dei Monti, San Pietro in Vincole, Santa Maria Maggiore, and San Giovanni in Laterano, not to mention St. Peter's and the Sistine Chapel. It was Easter season, and Rome was full of priests, monks, nuns, and pilgrims. Priests seemed determined to bless everything in sight. One of them, seeing us seated in a café, shook holy water on the Coca-Cola cases stacked against the wall near us, giving us a wink that he might also have intended for the Italian Communists, who had warned that drinking Coke caused impotence.

One morning my brother and I said we wanted to explore the Forum while Dad was in the library and Mom went shopping for silk scarves and small leather boxes. Dad gave us a guidebook, skeptical that we would give it much use. After six months of exploring Paris, often without Dad, John and I resented the professor's insult. We got our revenge by pulling his leg that evening. We said we had played café soccer and drunk Cokes all day. We watched his disappointment build, let him start scolding our generation for insufficient intellectual motivation, then let him have it with a ruin-by-ruin account of the Forum. His eyes widened, his sheepish grin conceded our triumph. He would underestimate us in the future, but never again that badly.

John and I located remnants of the Temple of Vespasian and of arches, wells, walls, more temples, earliest Rome on the Palatine Hill. On that warm spring day I paused longest to gaze at ruts left in ancient pavement at the northern end of the Forum by countless chariots and carts. I had not felt shivers like that since my maternal grandmother showed me, on a hot summer day, the depression in the ground near Paint Creek on my uncle's ranch in Haskell County where she had lived in a dugout during her family's first year in West Texas in the early 1880s. Both moments took me elsewhere in a flash. Looking back on them after thirty years of teaching history, I think of what Albert Camus wrote a few years before his death: "A person's work is nothing other than a long voyage to rediscover by the detours of art the two or three simple and lofty images that first gained access to his heart."

The Vatican librarian, a Jesuit scholar who esteemed Dad's work, arranged an invitation for the family to attend an audience with Pope Pius XII. We were all slightly embarrassed by the prospect, for we did not know the ritual, and my parents feared we were usurping places that ought to have gone to Catholics. But it emboldened me to think how I could boast to Catholic friends back in Madison and to hear Dad remind us of how his father had blessed the pope during the American presidential election campaign of 1928.

Granddad always drank a couple of shots of whiskey in the evening, and he didn't care who in Prohibition knew it. He was a dyed-in-the-wool Democrat, and as for religion, well, he blamed Grandmother Post's recurrent bronchitis, and eventually her death at age eighty, on her having been baptized by total immersion in icy Mule Creek one January a few years before he married her. In 1928, when Granddad joined the regulars on the Haskell courthouse steps wearing an Al Smith button, one of the cronies admonished, "Henry, you're not going to vote for Al Smith, are you? Why, he's not only a Wet, he's a Catholic!"

"Hmph," Granddad snorted, "I'd damn sight rather see the pope in the White House than a blasted Republican." The family's tradition of toleration helped me get through the day.

On Monday, 14 April, we arrived at the Vatican at the appointed time and place, joining others who would attend the audience. Officials ushered us in groups through ornate corridors and antechambers that reminded me of Versailles. Our small group was the first one to proceed. In our vanguard were U.S. Marine Gen. Lemuel C. Shepherd Jr. and members of his staff. A hero of the war in the Pacific, where he had commanded the landing forces at Guam in July 1944, Shepherd had recently been named commandant of the Marine Corps. He was touring NATO's Southern Command, which included the U.S. 6th Fleet but not the Vatican's Swiss Guards.

The guards had not been warned. When we entered the room where they normally impressed visitors with condottiere professionalism, they were lounging about in yellow-orange-black-striped uniforms that looked like puffy pajamas. One of them saw the marines and shouted a command. The guards jumped up, frantically grabbing long pikes and plumed helmets, and came to attention, ignoring the helmet that was kicked clattering across the room during the commotion. Shepherd returned the salute and cruised through. My brother and I exchanged a look that said, "These guard guys are great Three Stooges' material." We almost cracked up but bit our lips and followed the marines.

About a hundred people were gathered in a large rectangular room that contained an inlaid marble floor, paintings depicting the life of Christ, wall-coverings of floral design, a crucifix near the public entrance. My family was taken to the front rank to join Shepherd and other dignitaries, again the librarian's doing and our embarrassment. Shepherd and his staff occupied the center of the row, while we withdrew toward the end farthest from the door the pope would enter. Dad had said that any Catholic symbol you had with you during the audience would be automatically blessed by the pope, so I had ten rosaries in my pockets for Madison friends.

Pius XII entered without fanfare, wearing glasses and dressed simply in white, a jeweled cross hanging from his neck. He walked along the front rank, pausing for a few words with every person and more with Gen. Shepherd. He gave Shepherd a box of rosaries for distributing to American troops, and the general passed it to his aide who passed it on down the line until it reached a lowly major. I watched the pope carefully. When he reached me I somehow knew he wouldn't mind my just shaking his hand instead of kissing his ring. A slim man with a narrow face and dark eyes, he took my hand and asked where I came from. "Madison, Wisconsin," I replied, almost forgetting to add "Your Holiness" because he had started a friendly conversation and, I suspect, because some ancestral Protestant voice reminded me that all believers are priests. Years later I would learn about the politics of the Vatican during the era of fascism, the concordat that this man had negotiated with Nazi Germany in 1933 when he was papal nuncio, the failure of the Catholic Church to preach against the extermination of the Jews, the Church's justification of virtually any form of anti-Communism. In April 1952 I sensed only the age and power of the institution.

After the audience, Mom showed her typical compassion for the weaker team or the wallflower at the dance. "Boys," she said, "let's go over there and meet that marine general."

Gen. Shepherd had seven rows of medals on his chest and looked lost. When we approached him, he beamed, held out his hand, and said, "Come on over here and tell me about yourselves, boys." After a few minutes he asked us whether we were going to be marines. During the war, I would have cried an enthusiastic "Yes!" But now John and I mumbled something like "I guess so" and didn't know what to say next.

Shepherd broke the silence. "Well, boys, would you like my autograph?"

When we returned to the Pensione Rubens, I emptied my pockets, and there were the rosary beads and Gen. Shepherd's autograph. "Geez," I said to my parents, "Gen. Shepherd is peanuts compared to the pope."

To this day I regret having said that, for Shepherd was the kind of hero many men of my generation still wish they had become in the "good war" they feel cheated to have missed. I meant no disrespect for him or the marines. The audience and our front-row status had certainly increased my respect for Dad, who wore no decorations, but I don't think that's what I meant either. I must have spoken from some gut recognition of historical irony.

Paris had already encouraged me to distinguish between Old and New Worlds, between twelfth-century stained glass and twentieth-century copies, between venerable institutions and ephemeral events. Rome drove home such dichotomies and heightened my regard for the older part of each of them. While we were in Rome, SHAPE conducted exercise Venus de Milo, a high-level staff study of a hypothetical Soviet attack in the Baltic region. In Rome, far removed from SHAPE's suggestive anachronism, ruts in the Forum and ritual in the Vatican completely eclipsed the Cold War. Powerful historical forces predated American exceptionalism and NATO. They excited the imagination without making any reference to America's moral responsibility for world peace. They took you far back, against the current of any political faith that points to the future and uses history to prove that the best is yet to come. Such forces could make even the most magnificent Americans feel lost. They said, "I am the original. Remember that."

On a rainy Saturday afternoon in Paris late in October 1995, I went looking for any sign of the old Palais des Sports, #8, boulevard de Grenelle. There I had seen Goose Tatum and the Harlem Globetrotters play on Wednesday, 11 June 1952. Every American kid who loved basketball longed to see the Globetrotters, and before television brought them into our homes the only way to see them was in person. I had gone alone to the game, the sole sports nut in the family and by now eager to add solitary experiences to my mental library. I paid 1,500 francs for my ticket, about $4 at the official exchange rate, one month's allowance from my parents, who did not change dollars on the black market. Splurging on a good seat paid off, for I sat in a box at midcourt. After making one of his twisting, laughing, airborne, impossible baskets, the Goose came loping up my side of the court, his head up in the rafters and his long arms seeming to celebrate and flail and embrace all at the same time. Our eyes met. He stopped in front of the box and shook my hand, enveloping it with the tenderness of a big man and the joy of a happy one. I floated home.

The Globetrotters did not look lost, and the Cold War was far from my mind. I gave no thought to the absence of Negroes, as we said then, from professional basketball, nor to the hypocrisy of defending freedom abroad while condoning segregation at home, nor to the Globetrotters themselves playing to white Americans' stereotypes of black Americans. I was proud that the Globetrotters were Americans, pleased that the French crowd loved them, and determined not to wash my right hand because Goose Tatum had shaken it.

In 1995 the Palais des Sports was gone. I found only a small, tidy garden in front of a low wall with a plaque on it. It was a memorial, stating that the Vélodrome d'Hiver had stood at this spot (in the Palais des Sports), where over 8,000 Jews whom the French police had arrested on 16–17 July 1942 were incarcerated "under inhumane conditions" before being shipped to their deaths at Auschwitz. According to the Jewish document center on rue Geoffroy-l'Asnier, no photographic trace of that appalling internment has been found, save a picture of two empty buses parked outside the entrance to the Vélodrome d'Hiver on rue Nélaton.

I had read about the "Vél' d'Hiv" but never connected it with the Palais des Sports. The discovery shook my trust in Brodsky's dogs. There will never again be any way of faithfully recalling a happy boyhood experience in that place without visualizing its older past or remembering my wartime introduction to Nazi genocide. The neighborhood bully had called my friend Rich a "kike," and Dad had told me this behavior had something to do with why we must defeat Germany. Memory leads you to history, and sooner or later going far back in European history will carry you forward to the war that brought out the worst in Europe and the best in America.

ACS, the change of command at SHAPE, the papal audience: I packed these up with rue St-Julien-le-Pauvre for the trip home late in June. During the past nine months, the fragments of Europe from my home in Madison had come together with scenes from Paris, opinions about politics, images of history. I don't recall having a central principle or coherent scheme for connecting all these clusters with what I had known back home. The differences between Paris and Madison were too great for that. Resistance was a subconscious riddle, not a plan. I do remember feeling older, proud to have adapted to Paris. I had survived a riot, learned to speak French, proved myself at school.

None of this would have happened without my mother. Paris reunited my family, ending one chapter of its history and beginning another. Against all odds and expert professional opinion, Mom had made a miraculous recovery. No one explained to me how she had won her long and painful battle in Europe, apparently immune to Communism. No one promised me that her war was over, that she would not become a casualty of the Cold War after recrossing the Atlantic to America, that my war was over. I would help her rebuild her strength against relapse. I loved her as much as any adolescent boy could whose mother was back in his daily life after a long, dismaying absence. Leaving on the boat train for Le Havre, I was eager to return to Madison, see my friends, show off Mom. I was also sorry to leave Paris, which had become my home away from home.

I suppose having two homes leads exponentially to ambivalence about a lot of things. I was proud of America's leadership in the Cold War yet offended by its superiority complex. I looked up to my country for aiding Europe, to Europe for healing Mom while restoring itself. I admired many Americans abroad but did not feel at home in our embassy. I feared Communism but still viewed bullies as Nazis. I knew the Cold War required urgent measures and might last my lifetime, but I saw ancient objects that had survived countless struggles. American civilization could win wars and promise a bright future, but it could not reproduce medieval glass or replace European historical memory. I was an American, but I could get into someone else's shoes. I carried two of everything — homes, identities, histories, sources of memory, senses of time. I was turning into a teenage Cold War agnostic.

## CHAPTER 3

*The Home Front*

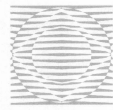 We sailed for America aboard the *Queen Eliza-beth*. The distance seemed shorter and the ocean friendlier than before Paris. I faintly regretted not needing the French I had worked so hard to learn. John and I met an Englishman who preferred our company to that of his own younger children. He showed us how to sneak out of tourist class and find the cabin class bar, where he bought us ginger beer while drinking ale. He was emigrating with his family to Illinois, unable to make a decent living in his homeland since leaving the British army after the Second World War. We told him about the Midwest, unable to separate information from promotion, proud that he would soon see the Statue of Liberty. On the dock in New York a customs official looked at Dad's detailed list of declarations and certified our baggage without opening anything. "If I can't trust a professor," he said, "I can't trust anybody."

Our neighbors in Madison welcomed us home warmly. I found places in my bedroom for my French winter coat, small roulette wheel, Swiss wristwatch, ACS yearbook, colored pencil sketches of French and British men-of-war, autograph of Gen. Shepherd, rosary blessed by Pope Pius XII. I gave the other rosaries to Catholic friends, whose grateful awe elevated my social status indefinitely.

Bits of Europe and memories of Paris escorted me through the 1950s as I tried to establish my own identity in a generation that attended high school while Dwight Eisenhower was president, hydrogen bombs were added to the armories of America and the Soviet Union, and the space race began. These forces worked on my generation during the rest of the decade, a period of high tension in the Cold War and of greater social anxiety than one would gather from recent nostalgia for the Eisenhower years. The greatest influence on me was having a mother again and hoping to hold on to her.

"Hi, Mrs. Post!" kids in the neighborhood shouted if they saw her in the yard or walking to Napper's Grocery on Monroe Street two blocks west of us.

Hearing those magical words in the summer of 1952, I felt as though she had just returned triumphantly from the war like dads and big brothers in 1945. Mom's gentle touch with people made her a big hit. Within days of our return, she was waving to neighbors and trading staples. She soon rejoined the bridge and reading clubs that had never gotten over losing her. She became a member of the Madison Theater Guild and acted in several of its productions; in *Jack and the Beanstalk*, performed for grade schools, she played Jack's mother and drew raves from youngsters in the neighborhood. She joined the League of Women Voters and solicited donations for the Mental Health Association. She whipped up outfits that won first prize at a university costume party, Dad a western gunfighter with handlebar mustache, Mom in a white Victorian dress with a black velvet choker and a red rose in her hair.

Mother transformed our house at 2313 West Lawn Avenue. John and I did not get the private entrance she had mentioned in Paris, but we were not bold enough to bring girls home anyway. The fireplace and surrounding beams were stabilized with jacks and joists, oak floors refinished, rugs cleaned or replaced, furniture re-covered. Mom hung Postimpressionist prints (Cézanne, Braque, Gauguin) in the dining room and put her new French crystal in the china cabinet. She revolutionized the kitchen with a new stove and fridge, a fresh coat of paint, and the French habit of buying ripe produce for immediate consumption. Outside, she planted herbs and revived the small wildflower garden that we had neglected in her absence: ladyslipper, jack-in-the-pulpit, lily of the valley, trillium. Upstairs, she sorted through dresses and shoes she had left behind years before, gave much away, and added things she had acquired in Europe, such as the shapely brown suit from Paris and, from Italy, a blue silk scarf and Florentine leather jewelry box. She hung over her bed the picture she had bought in Paris of the young woman sewing.

My parents slept in twin beds, the fashion they had adopted in the 1930s. I knew by then that fashion did not deter sex. Still, during our first winter back in Madison, I was astonished when Mom asked John and me whether we would like to have a little sister. "No!" we pleaded, later relieved to learn that she and Dad had decided not to. She was forty-one and Dad fifty, ages John and I considered too old for new parents and the upper limit for sex. It embarrassed me to think of them entwined, naked and undignified. I occasionally saw them that way through their open bedroom door when I came home late on a weekend night and they had fallen asleep in one of the beds.

My innocent accomplice in this domestic form of sex education was Barbos, who slept on an old towel between parental beds. We bought him as a puppy a few weeks after arriving in Madison, fulfilling our Parisian decision to add a dog to the family because we had grown used to having a pet and had been devastated by Kotik's death under the wheels of a delivery truck on rue St-Julien-le-Pauvre a few weeks before we left. We named him Barbos, honoring M. Makeev who had suggested the name because it was commonly given to dogs in Russia. Half Black Labrador and half Golden Retriever, Barbos was affectionate, smart, and loyal. He quickly became a family member with full rights and privileges. Among the duties he accepted in return, he would welcome John and me home at night, padding over to the bedroom door, nosing it open and waiting for us at the top of the stairs, his tail softly thumping the floor.

Mom taught Barbos how to swim until instinct took over. They drove to Willows Beach on Lake Mendota, west of the university campus. At first Barbos would cling to Mom's back as she swam a slow crawl; soon he was paddling confidently alongside her. Their relationship in the kitchen flourished, a source of cheer as she displayed a flair for everything from southern fried chicken to béarnaise sauce. "Barb', tu veux?" called him to lick a pot, and "tout de suite!" bought her a minute to open a can. She gave up trying to prevent Barbos from urinating on the chives she planted near the back porch. "Just wash them," she advised us, and guests at dinner parties had no idea why she had the lushest chives in town.

The clang of Barbos's metal identification tag inside pots, the laughter at dinner parties, the inviting decor downstairs, the diffusion of my mother's fragrance once limited to her closet, the spontaneity of her humming: this was home, and I cherished it. Home continued the story that had begun in Paris, two boys and their father living with the woman they had almost forgotten how to love as they grew accustomed to masculine loneliness. Mom reminded me of the best of our Paris with her bilingual playfulness, strong hands kneading dough for French bread, slim figure making plain clothes look elegant, fine sense of timing for changing the subject or mood. Now both of my parents were European. So was I, my identification with Europe locked into place by interdependent histories of war, homecoming, and reconstruction.

Nothing felt more like home than talking to my parents in their bedroom during breaks in my evenings' homework. Mom would put down whatever she was reading to look at drafts of my essays, unsplitting infinitives, demanding possessive with the gerund, encouraging me to listen to the words I wrote, saying "Bon!" when we finished revising something together. Dad would look over his glasses (usually from a detective story) to answer questions, crack puns, or comment generally on the state of the world. Barbos, happily dozing at the center of the family, would fall in and out of dreams of chasing rabbits.

Nothing threatened my sensation of home more than seeing Mom eat bread and buttermilk and go to bed early. This did not happen often, maybe once every three months at first and every six by the time I finished high school. But that was enough for me to recall her depressions in Paris, and that awful memory overlay my memories of war. So did Madison's reminders of loss and loneliness. The large storage box in the attic, which I had grown too big to climb into, had been a solitary refuge of mine during the war. One of the signature themes on WHA, the university's radio station, was the "Barcarole" from Menotti's opera *Sebastian*. Whenever I heard this soothing piece, I felt miserable, though I could not remember the precise wartime moment when the music had imprinted sadness. I did not discriminate between the origins and the echoes of unhappiness.

Living with Mom in Madison deepened my affection and diminished my fears, but I was not sure her recovery was permanent, no matter how favorable the signs. Before Paris, I had not known we would see her again. After Paris, I wondered whether we would lose her again. I continued to think in terms of war, past and present. Mom was vulnerable, and I must help protect her. Against what? was the question, and the best I could do for an answer was whatever had caused her collapse years before. Hitler was dead, and the neighborhood bully had graduated from high school and moved to the other side of town. Yet there was something threatening about the Cold War, its mood of hostility and suspense reminding me of the atmosphere during the Second World War. There would always be the danger of bullies outside, I supposed, and again there were apprehensions at home. Dad, John, and I may have done something wrong then, and from now on we had to get it right. I did not believe Mom's self-prescribed therapy of buttermilk and rest could turn back every attack. I did not know whether I had grown strong enough to defend her. If she suffered a major relapse, I might have myself to blame.

I believed I had been more hurt than Dad or John by Mom's absence and that I had become more sensitive than they to her moods. Looking back now, I feel certain that she knew I needed her explanation for leaving us after the war and her reassurance she would not leave again, that she knew I forgave her for not being able to give me either. And I think she forgave me for being more eager to please than she needed. Memory warned me to be watchful, cautious, ready to keep peace in the family in order to avoid pain. I presumed I should not ask her about her time alone in France and Switzerland nor burden her with more than understated allusions to my insecurities about high school, sex, and growing up. I complained less than the average teenager about doing chores. I felt wretched if I disappointed her, such as the time she asked me to paint the storm windows and I worked so sluggishly that she gave up on me and hired the job out.

From time to time Dad warned John and me to treat Mom gingerly. The minefield was still around us, and Dad's cautioning reinforced my solicitude. Unwittingly, the males in the family laid mines themselves. We did not give Mom enough credit for her very real strengths, above all her resuming the role of spouse and mother without making excuses for her absence or trying to reform us. We tended to view certain of her emotions, such as anger or sorrow, as ominous forewarnings of relapse. I can remember the anxiety in Dad's voice when he'd beg "Honey, *please!*" if Mom blew off steam even half as much as any of the rest of us. We did not allow her to be normal, and she was strong enough to pardon us for that.

My father was not easy to confide in about matters of the heart. Compassionate and generous toward others, he hid his own deepest feelings. He hugged us rarely and awkwardly; he did not want to be seen weeping when he learned that his mother died the day before we were to arrive in Haskell after a long trip by car in the summer of 1953. "Keep a stiff upper lip" and "don't step on your lower lip," he would say, but there were times I wish he had forgotten lips and simply asked what was on my mind, with no homiletic strings attached.

I needed to break through the long silence about Mom's breakdown and leaving. Dad had not confided in me then, and he refrained now, like a friend's uncle who would say nothing about fighting in the Battle of the Bulge. So I did not reveal my own fears and bad memories. I never told Dad how much it had hurt me not to invite my grade school girlfriend, Mary, over to our house because I didn't know how to tell her I had no mother there.

Dad's aloofness left unintended sores. We talked about high school, but he rarely read my essays, and he told me not to complain about any grades that were lower than I thought I deserved. We shared perennial frustration over the failure of the Red Sox to win the American League pennant, but only once did he come to watch me play first base for Sylvan Estates in the Madison summer league.

Yet there was an unspoken bond of affection between father and sons who had held together after the war. To her credit, Mom understood this. Dad, John, and I often looked back on those years for things to laugh at: Dad's consulting the *Encyclopedia Britannica* the first time he had to do laundry; his forgetting the cube steaks on one of our frequent Sunday drives to Devil's Lake State Park where John and I clambered over granite outcroppings while Dad read the newspaper and prepared lunch; Dad's weekly stew of Spam, onions, and kidney beans; his scolding me for ducking John's snowball that broke a window. We recounted adventures with pyrotechnics, which had resumed after Mom left, Dad having forbidden fireworks when they began to upset her during the war.

We recalled the graduate students who had occasionally looked after us boys. Most of them were veterans doing graduate work on the GI Bill, "best generation of students I ever had," Dad would say for the rest of his career. They treated John and me fairly, fed us well, and told stories about combat if we prodded long enough.

I loved talking with Dad in his study or on outings in the countryside west of Madison, where he taught me how to drive and took Barbos to run full tilt along gravel roads past tidy farms. Barbos would keep up with the car—a 1952 Chevrolet, replaced by a 1954 Dodge—until distracted by farm animals, squirrels, or skunks. He never ran away from a skunk, and we had large cans of tomato paste on hand at home for the deodorizing that he ruefully accepted as penance. Dad's study smelled of pipe tobacco, leather chair, old books. Among the pieces of Europe he added after our return from Paris was a small panel of stained glass propped against a southern window. After Paris and Chartres, I felt more comfortable than ever before in that scholarly room. I no longer used it as my depot for paper, scissors, and pencils. Mom remembered better than I how my childhood supply runs had gotten on Dad's nerves, and now she wisely insisted that John and I establish our own studies in our bedrooms.

Dad was happier with his work and less impatient now that Mom was home. I could visualize him as a medieval abbot, his preferred historical role so long as his abbey were worldly enough to have a large library and an enviable wine cellar; the Cluny of Peter the Venerable, not the Clairvaux of Saint Bernard. I loved browsing through Dad's library and listening to music with him. The authors' names were exotic and seductive — Rabelais, Aquinas, Machiavelli, Gibbon, Sabatini, Spengler, Chaucer, Anatole France. One evening, when I complained of flu symptoms, Dad handed me *Canterbury Tales*, marking a chapter and saying, "Here, go to bed and read this one." It was "The Miller's Tale," just the right medicine. On the radio's *Bell Telephone* and *Firestone Hours*, Ezio Pinza, Rosa Ponselle, and Jussi Björling were frequent guests; when Dad sang "Non piu andrai" from *Figaro* while shaving, he wanted to sound like Pinza. On the phonograph, we both tired of Tchaikovsky's *1812 Overture*. He welcomed discoveries I made among his old 78s, such as Sibelius's Symphony no. 5, Respighi's *Pines of Rome*, and D'Indy's *Symphony on a French Mountain Air* (all of which, now that I think about it, evoke landscapes and folk themes), to which he added Bach and Beethoven.

Dad would speak through clenched teeth while smoking his briar pipe, removing it to exclaim "By Jove" or "Egad!" (the latter borrowed from his beloved Major Hoople of the comics) or to stab the air to make emphatic points. His most emphatic were reserved for Senator McCarthy. "I hope that bastard tries to take us on," Dad fumed one day after returning from a faculty meeting about the man's assault on universities. That McCarthy never seriously attacked the University of Wisconsin, while other fine centers of learning around the country caved in, remains one of the ironies of the era named for him.

Wisconsin was probably America's best public university in the early fifties. Its faculty talked with each other, ate lunch together at the University Club, belonged to "dining clubs" (some of which combined town with gown), took teaching seriously, pitched in to help a dedicated and ethical dean of the College of Letters and Science (Mark Ingraham) uphold ideals of academic freedom and liberal education. It did not occur to most of the faculty to mix only with colleagues in their own disciplines. They were intensely proud of the university and loyal to it, not embarrassed to attend football games or sing "On Wisconsin." John and I did not yet know what we would do with our lives, but we naturally assumed the Wisconsin model awaited us anywhere if we became academics like our father.

Dad did not want to be a faculty politician and was a poor one. He never chaired his department, probably because he called a spade a spade and refused to compromise on matters of principle. Yet faculty and administrators respected him. He was a "scholar's scholar" (as I once heard him described), a popular teacher, and one of the charter group of faculty for Integrated Liberal Studies, an innovative cross-disciplinary program established after the war. During Mom's absence, some of his colleagues and graduate students had found him "very angry if not tormented," as one former student told me recently. The latter acknowledges he "must have hit [Dad] at the low point of his life" and remembers Dad's "constant concern for the well-being of his two sons, . . . doing things he had no aptitude for." In 1954 Dad wrote reassurances to this person, who had been wrongly accused of plagiarism by a senior scholar. "Don't be discouraged about history as a profession," Dad advised, "nor about historians. Every profession has its trials and its sobs." Don't try always to be "definitive" in your scholarship, he added. It's fun to do history and not necessary "to be either useful or definitive."

Dad was a man of contrasts. He had a brilliant mind, epicurean tastes, and a romantic streak. Yet he was also a realist with a common touch. He was steadfastly egalitarian, refusing to let academic degrees determine social rank, befriending the mechanic at the local Standard filling station as well as the president of the university. He was honest and everyone knew it, even his critics, even the banker who, when Dad said he couldn't make a monthly house payment in the late 1930s, replied, "OK, pay it when you can." His research in medieval law sounded esoteric and his articles were filled with footnotes, but his favorite themes were down-to-earth: What is the meaning of public welfare? What rights do governments have to defend the realm against external and internal enemies? What are the limits of reason of state? What duties do citizens have to fight for country? What obligations do rulers owe their subjects?

Dad often talked over my head, but I was inching up enough to know that he drew lessons and continuities from history. Like his Harvard mentor, Charles Homer Haskins, whose photo hung in the study next to the engraving of Saint Jerome, Dad respected law and institutions as foundations for civilized society. He would have fought in either world war if he had been the right age. He considered it his patriotic duty to oppose both Communism and McCarthy. Dad's lessons, authenticity, and joy in history were mine to acquire if I wanted them. I was increasingly aware that I did.

At the same time, I noticed how Dad's intellect could annoy Mom if, for example, he patronized her or responded more enthusiastically to a guest's remarks than to hers. After some of these occasions, she would say, "I'm just a cabbage," a deprecation that alarmed me because it was so untrue, so heartfelt, and so likely to signal one of her depressions. It was probably during these high school years that I began to consider the possibility that Dad was partly responsible for Mom's sense of intellectual inferiority, that, if this had been true from the start of their marriage, it may have done something to weaken her during the war.

After Paris, John showed more interest in discussing philosophy and writing poetry than in building model railroads. He got straight As at West High and was valedictorian of his class, his address entitled

"Must We Succumb to Fear?" His answer was always an adamant "Never!" That was his manner, a kind of bulldog determination never to be a coward. As a member of the high school wrestling team, he sometimes lost but never gave up. He worked at a pea cannery near Lodi one summer, enduring backbreaking tasks, overtime hours, low pay, and a painful leg injury, when he could have quit for an easy job in town.

John was tougher than I and more intellectual. I was envious on both counts, especially the first, for I was afraid I did not have his guts to fight real bullies. He envied my popularity and coordination. He remained less at ease socially than I and not as athletic, except for wrestling and canoeing, the latter thanks to a three-week canoe trip in Canada in the summer of 1953. Together we applauded the irreverence of Holden Caulfield in J. D. Salinger's *The Catcher in the Rye*, but John thought I was too deferential around home, and I thought him insensitive.

We did not really discuss what Mom's illness and absence had done to us. Both of us were oversensitive to criticism and dreaded the prospect of being rejected by girls. Our thin skin was part of the emotional inheritance handed down by years without Mom. Perhaps because of that shared legacy, John and I became more willing to acknowledge the other's achievements, less apt to attack the other's self-esteem with anything sharper than playful insults.

Being John's "little brother" at West High sometimes irritated me, and I welcomed the extra space at home and school in my senior year after he went off to Harvard in September 1954. But I missed him. In February 1955 I wrote him that the movie *The Bridges at Toko Ri* impressed upon me the futility of war. I was thrilled whenever he wrote to me, speechless when he brought me an issue of *Playboy* magazine at Christmas vacation; *Playboy* was only a year old but had already excited more teenage boys than *Lady Chatterley's Lover* ever would. He gave the family a recording of songs by Tom Lehrer, and we howled at the satires of Boy Scouts and atom bombs. John decided to major in history but talked about Plato. Although separation from him increased my self-reliance, I looked up to him and wanted to follow him to Harvard. By the time he returned from his freshman year I had chosen Cornell, or rather Cornell chose me, offering me a far more generous scholarship than Harvard and, fortunately, a trail all my own.

With John's encouragement, I got along well with his two best friends, John Brueckner and John Keene. During spring vacation of their senior year (1954), the three Johns and I drove together to Texas in Dad's new Dodge. He trusted us to break it in gradually, as cars then required, and to behave ourselves. We shared the driving, camped out at night, joked, sang, sermonized. We had nicknames for each other: Louis, Max, Charles, and Banana Boy. The last was mine, its origins now hazy but having some relation to my junior status on the evolutionary chain. We were earnest in our quest for manhood, but we took horseplay along for the ride.

In Texas we stayed with my maternal grandmother, Ada Fitzgerald Rike, whom the whole county knew as "Miss Ada." All four of us were over six feet tall; she called us "highpockets." Haskell, where both of my parents were born and raised, is a small town and county seat about fifty miles north of Abilene and a hundred miles southwest of Wichita Falls. Some of the Haskell boys, unused to lanky rivals from the north, called us "damned Yankees" and worse. A bunch of them followed us home in pickups to Miss Ada's one night after we had dated four Haskell High girls; she had fixed us up, unaware of provoking war. The boys walked slowly down the driveway toward the garage, where we waited in the dark, our hearts pounding in this odd Western. Without thinking, I took from the car's trunk the Winchester 30–30 Model 94 saddle rifle that a widowed aunt, my father's sister, had given me the year before. I did not hunt, had no ammunition, and my hands shook. John whispered, "Cock it." Darkness and the garage magnified the unmistakable two beats of the lever action. The bad guys stopped, muttered, and withdrew. Neither side publicized the confrontation afterward.

During visits to Texas, I hungered for stories of the old days of settling Haskell County and trailing cattle, but I also sought traces of my parents. I wanted to fill the large gaps in what little I knew about their youth, courtship, the Great Depression, and Mom's illness, gaps they seemed unwilling to close for me. Relatives and others held back, but not as carefully as they would have if Mom had been there with us; she usually went alone during the school year, leaving summer trips to Dad, John, and me. I began to find pieces of the puzzle that I will never be able to finish; my parents left no diaries and no correspondence except Dad's love letters before they married.

Haskell folks had always thought Dad "real different, you know, awful smart." Direct, too. On one birthday, he wrote to a cousin, "Today I am 9 years old. As I have nothing else to say, I will close." He experimented with gunpowder and built a small cannon, which burst in its test-firing just as Granddad stepped out the back door, a large fragment narrowly missing his head. Dad took four years of Latin in high school and loved to quote Virgil and Horace in the original. During the world influenza pandemic of 1918–1919, he contracted the virus and nearly died. I heard old-timers say, "Your daddy couldn't ride or chop cotton worth a durn" (heads shaking at this), "but you know what?" (heads nodding, eyebrows rising), in his senior year at Haskell High as the spindly center on the football team he had made the tie-saving tackle in a muddy game against Abilene, the eventual state champion, and in the 1930s he was one of the few sons of Haskell who had a steady job.

Dad's sister, who lived alone in San Antonio and treated John and me as if we were about five years older than our age, told us not to blame Mom for leaving. It was a good thing for all of us, Aunt Frances declared, that Mom went to Europe, because she stopped hearing voices on a mountaintop somewhere in the south of France the year before she taught school in Switzerland. My aunt said no more, but I had heard enough to know that unshrouding Mom's first year in Europe might help me understand the nature of her illness and solve the mystery of her recovery. What were these voices? Why had they seized her at home during the war, and what had released her from them on a mountain in France? I was afraid to ask Mom, Dad, or Miss Ada. So I began what became an endless search for clues of family history.

Haskell's traditions of "visiting" and storytelling came to my aid. "Your mama was the prettiest girl ever represented Haskell at the Stamford Cowboy Reunion," said her doting uncle Bud Rike, referring to the famous annual rodeo held in the next town to the south on the way to Abilene. "Coulda been a movie star, and she rode better than most of the young bucks 'round here." He called her "Dutchman." She was "Slouch" to her father; "Sunbeam" to her older brother, my uncle John; and "Katie" to her mother. Mom had been a tomboy, crabbiest when ordered to act like a "little lady," happiest when riding with her father, "Bunk," on his ranch east of town. Bunk had played the fiddle and taught Mom to jig on the front porch when she was a little girl. Miss Ada said Mom's way with people and horses came from Bunk. No one said a word about his drinking; I still believed he had just gotten sick and died.

Bunk passed away in March 1926, on Mom's fifteenth birthday. Her desolate anger had lasted for months and alarmed her mother. Mom would go out to the ranch with her brother whenever she could. There she would often ride alone, heading out in the morning with biscuits and bacon rolled up in a slicker tied behind the saddle, returning late in the afternoon, explaining neither why she had left nor where she had gone. Yet she was one of the most popular girls in Haskell. She had several suitors in high school and college. None swept her off her feet until Dad came home from Harvard graduate school one summer, dapper, worldly, and suddenly aware that the Rike girl had flowered like a rare bluebell.

They married in July 1935, the year Dad started teaching at Wisconsin and several years after Mom had graduated from Southern Methodist University and taken a job teaching school in the west of the county. Some of Mom's kin (not her mother or brother) had opposed the marriage because of a skeleton in the Post family closet and because Granddad Post drank and swore. Mom apparently became discouraged after moving to Madison with Dad and having two babies in quick succession, my brother in August 1936 and me only thirteen months later. She cried for no apparent reason during visits to Haskell during the war, and she would take us out to the ranch with Miss Ada so she could go riding. I remember seeing Mom trot up to the ranch house from the corral on Two Step, dismount to tighten the cinch, smile at me as she swung back into the saddle, lope a little, then gallop away toward Paint Creek, kicking up red dust and scattering grasshoppers.

As a teenager, I filed details away in my mind, faintly aware that I was revising the family history I had imbibed as a boy and that no one else in the family seemed interested in doing this. Much remained hidden behind silence and Haskell's courteous tonalities. I resented the secrecy and my ignorance, for this was my history, too, and the itch to know who I was got worse every year. I could feel Mom's story, our story, coming together around tomboy, losing her father, riding alone, and crying during the war. But I could not explain her voices or their disappearance.

It was easier to deal with lore about relatives and ancestors who had captured my imagination ever since I sat on laps. I worked steadily on the family tree. Like Miss Ada, Grandmother Rachel Ballard Post had been a graduate of a normal school and a schoolteacher before she married. A quiet and frail woman of strong moral character, she had given birth to seven children. The four who survived infancy had all attended the University of Texas. My father, the youngest, had inherited the lion's share of their mother's love of books. Her bookplate could be found in works by Thackeray, Dickens, and Wordsworth; Dad's in the novels of H. Rider Haggard and other purchases he had made in Austin. Rachel was not a shrew. She had tamed Granddad Post, as much as it was possible to, by her example of good manners, biblical virtues, and self-control, Ballard values since the progenitor, Thomas Ballard, had settled in colonial Williamsburg around 1650.

Granddad tried very hard not to use profanity around children and ladies, and he removed his hat to apologize. He went downhill fast after Rachel's death but stayed lively in tales told by others who quoted his incomparable similes: "he looks like a raccoon reachin' for a crayfish," "this whiskey will make those mesquite trees look like a peach orchard in full bloom," "he's excited as a feist in high rye," "churn-headed SOB." Granddad's father had fought at Shiloh, and a picture of Lee and his generals hung over Granddad's dresser. John and I were the first Yankees on either side of the family, but he adored us, forgiving mischief that he didn't tolerate from our cousins, all of whom were older — and envious, as they told us many years after he died.

I remember whiling away the hours on Granddad's front porch, drinking iced cistern water and listening to his tales about cowboying while cicadas droned from the chinaberry trees. He wore faded suspenders, sat in a cowhide rocker, and smoked a brown-stained corncob pipe. When Dad brought him some high-grade tobacco one summer, Granddad recalled the rancher who sent a sample of pipe tobacco to Texas A&M for analysis. "Keep working your horse," came the reply, "he'll be OK in a few weeks." Granddad grunted a lot between stories. When a grunt was followed by the declaratory sigh, "Well, here we are," I knew he had completed his revery over the last story and would soon search his memory for the next.

Dad reminisced about his father's outlook on travel in anything with a motor. He had bought two cars in his lifetime, one before and one after the First World War, his affluence due to success in banking and real estate, but he never drove over 20 m.p.h. for fear of tiring the engine. He was shocked that Dad had slept on an airplane. "What if it had fell while you were sleeping?" he wanted to know. Whatever the vehicle, Granddad would advise, "In case of emergency, leave a day early."

Rachel's brother, Uncle Tom Ballard, had been Granddad's best sidekick and, like him, a top-notch cowboy. He married Granddad's sister, Sarah; five of their thirteen children died in infancy. Eight of the twenty double cousins have lambs as headstones, sorrowful graveyard witnesses to infant mortality at the turn of the century. Uncle Tom died when I was six years old, but I vaguely remember turning still whenever he walked up to Granddad's or Miss Ada's front porch to visit. He wore a large black Stetson, his handlebar mustache had turned gray, and one of his thumbs had been severed in a roping accident. He used the calloused stub to tamp down his pipe tobacco midsmoke. I was impressed at an early age by men with pipes.

Miss Ada's father, "Wat" Fitzgerald, had been one of the county's most reliable peacemakers, better than the sheriff at settling disputes without bloodshed or dishonor. That finesse must have rubbed off on Miss Ada, who was Haskell's fourth grade teacher from the beginning of the century until she retired shortly after the end of the Second World War. Her double chin rippled on Sundays at the First Methodist Church when she sang "Faith of Our Fathers," and sitting next to her was as close to "having religion" as I have ever been. Her "cowboy stew" (called "son of a gun" or worse by cowboys) was made from "all the tender parts of the animal," she would say, and its odor alone would drive you from the house if you weren't ravenous. Although in her seventies and hobbled by arthritis, Miss Ada still helped with the cooking during roundups out on Uncle John's ranch. One day, his daughter, Anne Katherine, saw a horse kick up pieces of cow chip and dirt into the big pot of pinto beans Miss Ada was tending over a mesquite fire outside the corral. Unable to remove all but the biggest additives, Miss Ada calmly stirred the rest into the beans. "Don't tell your mother," she said to my cousin.

Uncle John had run the ranch since Bunk's death. I no longer wanted to be a cowboy, but that "red wrinkle," as Uncle John called the place, was dear to my heart. There, along with my brother and our cousin, John Sam Rike, I had learned how to ride, bulldog calves, dig postholes, load hay, kill rattlesnakes, dodge tarantulas, and predict rain. Helping Uncle John taught me a lot about teamwork, good name, and understatement. He never called anyone a liar or thief. "He finds things that haven't been lost," was Uncle John's euphemism for one ranchhand he would never hire again. Like Mom, he had a round face, long limbs, and sharp elbows. Like her, he rode easily and held the reins lightly with the downturned fingers of one hand as if about to stir his coffee.

People in Haskell often remarked on physical features I had inherited from one side of the family or the other. I was partial to genetic evidence of the kind of person I wanted to become. I hoped to inherit from both sides: the candor of the Posts and diplomacy of the Fitzgeralds; the similes of Granddad Post and euphemisms of Uncle John Rike; the courage and sensitivity of both sexes on both sides; cowboying and book learning; listening and telling; visiting and being alone. I presumed kinship, not conflict, between each of these pairs.

Madison, Paris, Haskell. If these places were people, they would not stay together for long at the same party. But they were stuck with me and could not leave. They told me stories about diverse communities, characters, and times. Time itself stretched out and looped around. I knew I was more than an observer of the present. I was part of a long and living story. I walked at the front of it amid footprints of many generations of heroes, victims, and churn-headed SOBs. The Left Bank, West Texas, the University of Wisconsin, the Second World War, my parents: this chorus guided me through the fifties believing in fair play, diplomacy, and the long term, all of which ran contrary to the nation's official version of the Cold War.

Events and Cassandras tried to drown out my chorus. In November 1952, a few months after we returned from Paris, the United States exploded its first thermonuclear device, and Eisenhower and the Republican Party won smashing electoral victories after accusing the Democrats of having pursued "immoral" policies. At the Yalta Conference in February 1945, the GOP charged, President Roosevelt had abandoned Eastern European peoples to Soviet domination, and thereafter President Truman's policy of containment left them captive to "Godless terrorism." Trying to disown the Democrats and their allegedly defensive strategy, the new administration's "New Look" emphasized the deterrence of further Soviet expansion by threat of nuclear retaliation and the liberation of subject populations by rolling back Soviet hegemony.

Although President Eisenhower and his secretary of state, John Foster Dulles, did not want to admit it, their strategy retained much of Truman's. Both administrations recommended deterring Soviet expansion with military power, economic strength, alliances, covert operations, psychological warfare, and negotiations. Nevertheless, there was something new in the content of the New Look and in the rhetorical zeal with which Dulles undertook it. First, Eisenhower and Dulles were determined to reduce the costs of defense by increasing airborne nuclear deterrence and cutting conventional forces. Second, the government thought aloud about waging nuclear war, with allusions to "massive retaliatory power" and going "to the brink" of war to pressure the enemy to back down even in a local crisis. Third, while avoiding what Dulles called "the taint of colonialism," the United States must intervene actively in the Third World, supporting anti-Communist regimes and forging regional alliances lest former colonial territories begin to fall like dominoes in a war that was global in its ideological and strategic dimensions. Fourth, even if the West could not physically roll back the Soviet empire, the United States would increase psychological warfare and covert operations in an anything-goes offensive that would give "captive peoples" hope for their liberation and prevent Communism from spreading anywhere else.

In contrast to these blunt leaders and blustery politics of the 1950s, my generation has been called "silent," as if we simply ducked and held our tongues while older legions made all the noise. In fact, we had a more dynamic collective personality than we have ever been given credit for. Our ambivalence offered us both protection and maneuvering room in an unprecedented state of war. Many of us were rebellious but not revolutionary. We neither believed everything our elders told us nor denied their remarkable victories against fascism and economic depression. Although less inclined than our parents to save for the rainy day, we did not discard their values of frugality and job security. We needed adults, their guidance and approval. We began to dissent without leaving home or renouncing institutions.

At the movies we rooted for James Dean and Marlon Brando,

young rebels who defied social convention, but also for John Wayne and Jimmy Stewart, who exemplified traditional values. We began to see weaknesses in World War II military commanders like the one portrayed by Gregory Peck in *Twelve O'Clock High*. That film made our "good war" more human without defaming its heroes; I silently thanked Gregory Peck for legitimizing mental breakdown. We flocked to *The Blackboard Jungle*, in which teenagers and rock-'n'-roll alarmed an entire community, but we also listened to Perry Como, Rosemary Clooney, and Spike Jones and his City Slickers. Some boys wore leather jackets and smoked; some girls were rumored to be "easy lays"; most boys and girls refused cigarettes and remained virgins. We still read Superman comics but adopted Alfred E. Neuman of *Mad* magazine as our countercultural chum, our homely champion of parody. In his magazine we could follow the adventures of Superduperman, Bat Boy and Rubin, and the Lone Stranger.

West High had excellent teachers and healthy extracurricular activity. Miss Kleinheinz (Latin) drummed conjugations into us and gave us exciting research projects, but she thought Neil Smith, Ed Ingraham, Tom Dean, and I went too far when we used rubber daggers in a skit about Cicero's retaliation against Catiline's conspiracy. Mrs. Steward (English) demanded clear writing and, thanks to my lessons from Miss Robertson at ACS and Mom at home, exempted me from a two-week section on grammar, letting me browse in the library instead. As Miss Krueger (math) handed out tough test questions, she would say, "All's fair in love and war, and this is not love." Mr. Butler (chemistry) admonished, "For safety's sake do as you oughter, add the acid to the water."

About 80 percent of my graduating class of 250 students went on to college, thanks to demanding courses, a largely middle-class student body, a midwestern ethos of academic achievement, and the aura of the University of Wisconsin. Our affection for UW climbed when the Badgers went to the Rose Bowl for the first time in January 1953 on the coaching of "Ivy" Williamson, whose twin sons were my classmates, and the running of Alan "The Horse" Ameche. Dad was impressed with the Badgers and chagrined that John and I sneaked into home games at Camp Randall Stadium, so he bought us season tickets for the following autumn.

Unlike John, I did not finish in the top three of my class, but high enough to win Dad's praise and a tuition scholarship to Cornell. My activities must have counted, though in those days most of us did what interested us, not what we figured would look best on our résumés. I sang in the glee club and boys' double quartet, acted in a play and an operetta. Too skinny for football, I played intramural basketball and second-string on the baseball team. My basketball teammates called me "birdman" because of the way I flapped my elbows running downcourt. I was elected president of the student government; "Pull for Post" read the signs that my creative campaign committee taped above paper towel dispensers in the rest rooms. One of my official duties, at a school assembly early in the fall of 1954, was giving coupon book #1 for school activities to Hiroyoshi Yamamoto, a Japanese exchange student whose goodness touched even classmates who had lost family in the Pacific. The European war touched us through refugee classmates whose accents were Slavic, Baltic, or German.

The acting I owed to Mom's inspiration. I played a rustic factotum (Mr. Kimber, really a man of *no* work) in Moss Hart and George S. Kaufman's *George Washington Slept Here* in my junior year, a pompous count (Berezowski, chief of the secret police) in Victor Herbert's *The Fortune Teller* a year later. In the former, John played Uncle Stanley. At curtain call we walked on from opposite wings, linked arms, and faced the audience, the most thrilling moment I remember sharing with him in high school — with our parents, too, who beamed at us from several rows back.

I owed the presidency of the student senate to classmates who urged me to run. In my major campaign speech I advocated open meetings of the senate so students could observe and inform their representatives. Although I probably acquired this fondness for direct democracy from kin, it was also a reaction to the secrecy surrounding my mother's hospitalization and absence after the war. My willingness to preside over such a democracy must have come from adolescent dreams of importance but also from peculiar exigencies at home, where prevention of conflict had become one of my self-appointed tasks and where I had begun to think I might be a better diplomat than Dad or John.

My political success seemed to verify a social law that I was hesitantly constructing out of largely idealistic materials: you will be respected and rewarded if you are smart, honest, and decent. But I had not expected this to happen to me on a large scale, at least not when

I was sixteen. When it did, I tried to be myself but knew I would never be the same, for I had been noticed. Tough guys in leather jackets who had called me chicken in our sophomore year for refusing to fight one of their gang on the playground after lunch now greeted me affably. Girls showed interest. Teachers congratulated me on being the right one for the job. When I asked one of them to sign my senior yearbook, she said, "Good luck for your future. I'll vote for you in thirty years for president." The principal consulted me. School assemblies applauded my speeches. Friends declared, "You've got it made."

Did I? In my senior year I experienced attacks of anxiety more severe than anything I could remember. The worst hit me before speeches, dances, and performances of the double quartet. I settled my nerves for the operetta, perhaps because I was playing someone else, but not for these other events, where I had no alias. I didn't know what frightened me. I confided in no one, fought embarrassment and dismay alone.

I have two major regrets about my high school career: not being good enough at baseball to make the first team and not having room in my schedule to take speech in my senior year, which would have qualified me to act in the speech department's biennial play. The speech teacher and drama coach, Mrs. McCarty, had for years been looking for an Abraham Lincoln for Robert Sherwood's play *Abe Lincoln in Illinois*, and in me she thought she had found him. I have often wondered how fulfilling her wish might have changed my life.

I gave my parents little chance to advise me on relations with girls. Dad's interest in my sexual hang-ups was limited to platitudes like "be yourself" and "don't worry" and "you're a fine young man." Mom read my moods accurately. I knew I could confide in her, but I made only vague references, for the very idea of talking with her about sex unnerved me, and she did not pry. I had romantic crushes every year, none of them easy for me to advertise nor reciprocated enough to give me confidence. Long walks at night were my preferred and frequent source of solitude during high school, and some of the longest concerned girls. I was attracted to two types. One was like Mom, slim and graceful. The other, big-breasted and sultry, was not. The exception, short and perky, rejected me for the guy who had run against me for the student presidency and drove a shiny old black

Cadillac coupé. Years later she married a man who she said reminded her of me. Thanks a lot.

I spent many weekend evenings with friends commiserating over failed romances, debating religion, solving the world's problems, playing poker. We were not a gang, for membership fluctuated according to schedules and locales. We had no leader; we respected each other too much to care for hierarchy. They were ideal companions for someone who oscillated between wanting to belong and wanting to be alone. Their comradeship helped me survive ontological doubts, a mild case of acne, and large dance parties where I adopted a uni-step that was neither too fast nor too intimate.

In the summers I worked and played baseball. My jobs included moving books from the university's old library to the new, assisting an agronomy professor (Neil's father) in his experimental fields of clover and alfalfa, and driving a delivery truck for A. E. Mack Fine Foods, a grocery store on Monroe Street a few blocks east of home. At supper one evening, my brother claimed he saw the truck careening along a quiet street with me at the wheel looking like Thaddeus Toad.

Hoping to improve my batting average one summer, I made a solo round-trip by train to Chicago to watch my idol Ted Williams, the "Splendid Splinter," bat against the White Sox. He had returned from duty in Korea in the summer of 1953, hit .407 over the rest of the year, and was hitting around .350 in 1954 when I traveled to Chicago. On the train I recalled Dad's story about taking John and me to Fenway Park in the spring of 1940 for a doubleheader between the Red Sox and Yankees. At the age of two-and-a-half, I had gazed in the general direction of great players: Williams, Jimmy Foxx, Joe Cronin, Bobby Doerr for the Sox; Joe DiMaggio, Joe Gordon, Bill Dickey, Lefty Gomez, Red Ruffing for the Yankees. John and I grew bored and cranky, and Dad took us home after the first game. In 1946, when the Sox were on their way to the pennant, Dad's story, embellished with allusions to Harvard and Boston, had awakened my dormant affection for the team; so began my lifelong agony over the Red Sox and hatred of the Yankees.

In 1954, at a bus stop on the way from the railroad station to Comiskey Park, a drunkard shambled up to me and slurred, "Say, fella, did anyone ever tell ya ya look like Whitey Ford? Uh, ya gotta

The Home Front : 71

quarter?" I was insulted by the first question. Ted looked great in batting practice that day and in the game hit a double off the right-field wall. Back in Madison, my left-handed swing looked smoother, but its meager yield kept me batting down around seventh in the order, a splendorless splinter.

Apart from trappings of cultural rebellion, what was distinctive about my generation? I believe the answer lies in the impact language had on us as the Cold War politicized American life. As youngsters, we had assumed there was a close connection between language, morality, and reality. Television was too new to degrade language or uncover widespread hypocrisy. Teachers did not deconstruct language and tie it to the vested interests of the people using it. We had accepted what our government told us during the Second World War and the early years of the Cold War: Nazism and Communism were brutal, evil systems, and it was morally right to fight them in order to save democracy. We knew little, if anything, about our country's history of ideological name-calling inside its own house.

The presidential election campaign of 1952 was the first of our political consciousness. Its language assaulted us, no matter how our parents voted. We were told by Senator McCarthy that Gen. George C. Marshall was a traitor and by the Republicans that Democratic presidencies had committed twenty years of treason. The enemy now was apparently among us in high places. Treason was a crime. Twenty years was our lifetime. While we built our vocabularies, we became conscious of how language could accuse, polarize, dehumanize, and banish our own countrymen. When we argued about morality, truth, and patriotism, we enjoyed finding inconsistencies, uncovering hypocrisy, making distinctions between theory and practice, saying "bullshit" when we thought a statement bore no resemblance to facts or common sense. But beneath the surface of this verbal give-and-take we had to weigh moral choices in a grotesque environment where "treason," "un-American," "pink," "soft," "enemy," "godless," and "massive retaliation" were everyday words denoting crime and punishment. Our government was part of this divisive milieu, not above it.

Like some of my friends, I was what I now call a "Cold War agnostic." We agnostics questioned the means of fighting Communism, not the necessity. We doubted that the Cold War gave Americans sufficient reason to justify waging it arbitrarily against fellow citizens. We wanted the United States to remain the world's greatest power but believed this power obliged our government to consider negotiating with the enemy. Compared to most of my friends, I was more fearful of bullies on the home front, more critical of American swagger abroad, more sympathetic to France and Europe in affairs of the Atlantic Alliance, and more inclined to doubt Washington's version of affairs.

Opposition to Senator McCarthy was the central domestic commandment of my agnosticism. He made me feel ashamed to be from Wisconsin. High school arguments about McCarthyism could make or break friendships, even in families. The members of my family agreed about McCarthy all along, but some of my friends were not so lucky. I saw the Gary Cooper of *High Noon* as the only man in town who would stand up to McCarthy. (I discovered years later that Cooper, my favorite movie cowboy, had no such figurative intent.)

I repudiated McCarthy before it became acceptable to do so in Congress or on radio and television. He tore down American heroes and stood for attitudes antithetical to liberty: dissent is a political crime; liberalism is Communism; intellectuals and university professors are either Communist or soft on it; you are disloyal if you don't swear loyalty, guilty until proven innocent; you are un-American if you doubt the existence of God, the righteousness of the House Un-American Activities Committee, the cleansing effect of McCarthy's accusations, the legality of any form of FBI surveillance, or the fairness of the 1952 McCarran-Walter Immigration and Nationality Act, which did not include former Nazis among the subversives to be denied entry into the United States.

I considered such propositions more dangerous than the threat of Communist subversion itself. Young eyes read the Bill of Rights literally. Free speech and free conscience were rights of passage, means for declaring my own independence. I suspected McCarthy of using Nazi methods to deny those rights. He threatened my family because he would give us no room to think for ourselves, no quarter for talking with French Communists, no civil tranquility for Mom's continued recovery. His language had none of Dad's reason, Mom's kindness, or Haskell's courtesy. I admired Walt Kelly, the cartoonist of "Pogo," for having the courage to introduce a sinister McCarthy-like "Wiley Cat" into the hitherto benevolent swamp. I watched the army-McCarthy hearings in 1954 and cheered the senator's subsequent censure by his peers. Because my family did not yet own a television set, I camped out at a friend's house during the hearings, suddenly aware of how the new medium could expose fraud.

I was not eager to find fraud in high places, for I trusted leaders and institutions. I never forgave Eisenhower for not publicly defending Marshall, one of my boyhood heroes, against McCarthy's slander, and I preferred Adlai Stevenson to Ike, but I preferred Ike to Gen. MacArthur, in whom I sensed the same kind of rigid intolerance I saw in McCarthy and the same willingness to defy the Constitution. I tended to fault individuals, not institutions: MacArthur, not the army; McCarthy, not the Senate, in which I assumed student government presidents might sit one day; J. Edgar Hoover, not the FBI, which did find real criminals and spies; rogues in the CIA, not the agency itself, whose parent, the OSS, had helped win the Second World War. I believed in the American system of democracy, including the expansion of government during the New Deal and Second World War. Nevertheless, something about this system seemed wrong if it could give rise to McCarthy and condone his assaults.

My generation cheered when Stalin died in March 1953, only to hush a few months later when Soviet tanks cold-bloodedly ended the subsequent "thaw" in East Germany. Communism under Malenkov and Khrushchev seemed to advance at an alarming rate even without subversive help inside America. Although not an obsession, intimations of doomsday unnerved us. The "Doomsday Clock," which still hangs on the University of Chicago campus, was introduced in 1947 by scientists who had worked on the Manhattan Project during the war. In 1953, in response to America's first detonation of a hydrogen bomb, they set the clock to two minutes before midnight, the closest it came to nuclear midnight during the Cold War. In August of that year Dulles's presupposition of American superiority in nuclear weapons and delivery systems suffered a traumatic reversal when the Soviets set off their first thermonuclear bomb. My generation had been children when we celebrated the arrival of peace at the end of the Second World War. Now we knew we might live the rest of our lives under the peacetime threat of nuclear war, as if the Second World War had never really ended and was being prolonged indefinitely without our consent.

Like most agnostics, I accepted nuclear arms as a necessity for deterring the Soviet Union but feared that some of our leaders would rather die by the sword than be accused of conciliation. Dulles's nuclear threats, for instance against China in the 1954–1955 crisis over the offshore islands of Quemoy and Matsu, were not all bluff; he feared that never employing tactical nuclear weapons would reduce the credibility of America's threatening to use them. Gen. Curtis Le May, commander of the Strategic Air Command, personified the Cold War mentality that frightened me the most: fanatical anti-Communism, trigger-happiness with nuclear bombs, blind faith in the ability of the air force to devastate the Soviet Union, refusal to negotiate with the enemy. I could imagine this sort of belligerency causing war when compromise might have prevented it, and I remember arguing at West High that Munich might not always provide the appropriate historical lesson for the Cold War.

Respect for Europe was this agnostic's major international commandment. I did not take European anti-Americanism as personally as I did American affronts to Europe. I could visualize American policy from over there, where Mom had mended and I, like her, had found a second home. I viewed European recovery as postwar healing more than Cold War necessity. At the center of my Europe was France, not Germany, whose admittance to NATO in the spring of 1955 lessened but did not eradicate my wartime feelings of revulsion. In tenth grade, a few months after returning from Paris, I wrote a paper entitled "America Is No Santa Claus," explaining why American policy in Europe was as self-interested as it was altruistic. In other essays I questioned Dulles's preaching against European colonialism while he practiced expansion of American interests in the Third World; asserted the values of tolerance at home and modesty abroad; defended the French against charges of effeminacy after their disastrous defeat at Dien Bien Phu in May 1954; declared that all peoples, not just Americans, believe in freedom; and criticized the sort of American who sees our country as the world's only oasis of democracy, goodness, and God.

These attitudes exceeded what most Americans, agnostic or not, thought acceptable. I would not have been elected president of the student government had candidates' platforms included the Cold War. My ambivalence about American motives would have appeared unpatriotic, my love of France abnormal, my equating McCarthy with Nazism extreme. I would have been unwilling and unable to explain the wellsprings of my politics.

As I saw it, war still cast a double shadow. The thought of Mom's relapse was as dark as pictures of mushroom clouds; mental illness was as menacing as Communism. Yet things had changed since the war against Hitler. In spite of tensions at home, there was no pervasive gloom in our house. We still fought two wars, national and private, but I could now distinguish between them. I knew Soviet bombs could kill us all, but I did not attribute Mom's vulnerability directly to Communism as I had to Nazism ten years earlier. If she broke down, I would probably blame forces on the home front. Inside the family, I would find fault in Dad's insensitivity, John's indifference, and my weakness. Outside, the most dangerous bullies were those in the United States who might harm the innocent with merciless accusations and threats of banishment. McCarthy, not Stalin, took the place of the neighborhood Nazi of my childhood.

I did not expect McCarthy to come up the front walk looking for Dad and Mom, as Hitler had done in my wartime fantasies. But this hypothetical threat to the family's peace made it easier for me to call upon my memories of the war and the anti-Pétain riot in Paris to strengthen my will for resisting what McCarthy stood for. McCarthyism was brutish, and my family and country had everything to lose. Except for this case, resistance was a vague notion full of quandaries. Social conformity, friendships, sexuality, college preparation, the family's history and Mom's recovery, Cold War tensions: all of these concerns raised questions in my mind about vulnerability, loss, and doing the right thing. Doing the right thing came down finally to the biggest riddle of all. Who was I, and where was I headed?

I obeyed conventional codes of morality and dress. I belonged to student organizations and a circle of good friends. My peers respected me enough to reward me with confidence in my leadership. My high school politics were democratic and conciliatory. I heeded teachers, parents, and relatives. Mom was well, I was strong, and my war was over. I had a scholarship to Cornell. I had it made. That's how things appeared. On the other side of appearance, I was lonely, nervous, and afraid. Mom was vulnerable, I was a chicken, and my war dragged on. I could fail at Cornell. Nothing was assured.

At the time I suspected that appearance was too good to be true, and yet I did not want to lose hope. That left me struggling with skepticism. It meant ambivalence and frustration, but it was my way of resisting both delusion and despair. I was far more skeptical than most of my peers about the Cold War. My doubts drew strength from feeling at home in Paris, remembering the stained glass at Chartres, and thanking Europe for Mom's recovery. I could be critical as well as loyal. I was more determined than my brother to probe for evidence about the family's past, where I might find omens of Mom's cure and my future. In both politics and family I resented secrecy and distrusted the authorized version of events. Getting to the truth and demanding the full story were becoming acts of rebellion.

These were introspective shadows, not everyday cares, when I graduated in June 1955. I looked back with a sense of accomplishment and ahead with excitement. I prepared for my freshman year at Cornell, eager to leave home, while my parents packed for a year's sabbatical leave in Rome, apologizing for abandoning me. My emotional inheritance from the Second World War had adjusted to the Cold War. I loved my country and planned to serve in its armed forces. I would help contain Communism abroad and resist McCarthyism at home. But life, I knew, held deeper mysteries and truths than ideological conflict. Discovering these was part of what I romantically called "finding myself," and I meant to find a lot at Cornell.

CHAPTER 4 *From Cornell to Fort Sill*

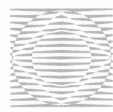 While I was in college, a decade nearly finished defining itself. The Cold War escalated, and Communism appeared to gain on the West. My mother flourished, and my father put his sons through the Ivy League. At Cornell I learned German, became an oarsman, discovered Camus, and fashioned a moral cause, one that combined military service with resisting oppression on both sides of the Iron Curtain. I was still defining myself when I left Fort Sill for Germany early in 1960, exhilarated to be independent and bound for Europe with the home front secure.

The intellectual atmosphere at Cornell was congenial to Cold War agnosticism. I occupied ground closer to the large number of moderate agnostics than to the small percentage of students on the Far Left who completely rejected American policy as imperialistic. Appalled at the thought of massive retaliation by either side, agnostics sought alternatives, from limited war to moral regeneration. We read books by authors who declared that limited nuclear war was feasible, such as Henry Kissinger's *Nuclear Weapons and Foreign Policy* and Robert Osgood's *Limited War*. We attended college symposia like the

Campus Conference on Religion, whose theme in November 1956 was "Power and Conscience." There I heard a Soviet scientist warn against the "ruling element's" unchallenged control over nuclear weapons in the United States and Soviet Union. Cultivating "universal altruism," he said, was the only way toward universal understanding. We sought out scientists and humanists on campus who had strong ethical sensibilities. At Cornell you did not have to be a physics major to recognize Hans Bethe, who had helped build the atomic bomb during the war and then became one of the most forceful voices for moral responsibility in science and government.

I feared nuclear Armageddon less than many of my contemporaries. In August 1957 the Soviets launched the world's first intercontinental ballistic missile (ICBM), and in October they used one to put *Sputnik* in orbit. This double first gave unprecedented bragging rights to Communism and to the Soviet leadership of the worldwide movement. *Sputnik* shocked me as much as anyone else, but watching it cross the night sky like a slow, inextinguishable shooting star also gave me goosebumps about the exploration of space. Perhaps I had an innate hunch that time was not running out, along with paternal assurance that history was here to stay.

Critics of the Eisenhower administration faulted it for allowing a "missile gap" to develop between the United States and the Soviet Union. They cited the government's own Gaither Report as evidence. The gist of the report was leaked to the *Washington Post* shortly after the humiliating fizzle of America's first public attempt to launch its own satellite on Pearl Harbor Day, 1957. Unlike the public and Congress, Eisenhower and I refused to panic. He was a fiscal conservative, he had confidence in America's deterrent power, he distrusted the arms industry, and photographic intelligence provided by U-2 reconnaissance aircraft convinced him that there was no missile gap. Ike was willing to buy more guns and less butter for a while and to support substantial increases in federal spending on education and science through the National Defense Education Act (1958), but he maintained the economic and military principles of the New Look strategy. What dismayed me was the insular hysteria behind demands for massive spending on missiles, early-warning systems, and fallout shelters for civilians.

*Sputnik* helped Nikita Khrushchev consolidate his victory in the internal struggle for power among Stalin's successors. The Soviet

Union, he claimed, could coexist peacefully with capitalist states, and Communism could triumph without war. After *Sputnik*, he boasted that the balance of scientific knowledge and military power was shifting in favor of the Soviet camp, a message intended to impress the Third World and China as well as the West. There seemed to be two Khrushchevs. The jovial one denied the inevitability of war and looked at home on a farm. The bellicose one threatened nuclear attack and promised to "bury" capitalism. I would have liked to believe the former.

I reluctantly watched the expansion of the Cold War into the Third World. If forced to choose between the strategic usefulness and political independence of a former European colony, I would usually have elected strategy, searching for justification in the balance of power, the frailty of neutralism, and the patterns of voting in the United Nations. But I did not believe that everything good for America was bound to be good for the world, and I felt uneasy when the United States intervened to defend "freedom" against national liberation movements that were not clearly on our side. I admired those characters in William Lederer and Eugene Burdick's *The Ugly American* who were not ugly at all, who helped native peoples cultivate their own freedom.

My map of the Cold War remained stubbornly Eurocentric, more than for the average agnostic. In the Suez crisis of October–November 1956 I supported Britain, France, and Israel, the latter out of mixed feelings of condolence and guilt for what the Jews had suffered during the Second World War. Solidarity among the democracies, I thought, took precedence over the decolonization that Asian and African states had demanded of the West at the Bandung Conference in April 1955.

During the Suez crisis, Khrushchev sent troops into Hungary to end the liberalization that had occurred there (and in Poland) after he denounced Stalin at the Twentieth Party Congress in February and dissolved the Cominform in April. Hungary's bid to leave the Warsaw Pact offered the best opportunity since the East German rising of 1953 to roll back Soviet control over Eastern Europe. Dulles referred to the irresistible forces of liberation in Eastern Europe, and the CIA used Radio Free Europe to encourage the Hungarian freedom fighters with whom I quickly identified. I was puzzled and disappointed by my government's failure to give them substantial help after all the talk of liberation, for I thought we could do so without leading to war with the Soviet Union. President Eisenhower thought otherwise. Because of the volatile atmosphere in the Suez crisis, in which Khrushchev threatened to launch nuclear missiles against London and Paris, Ike took all the more trouble to assure the Soviet leader that the United States had no intention of upsetting the status quo in Eastern Europe.

Concerning Berlin, however, I was in favor of conciliation. Late in 1958 Khrushchev issued his first ultimatum on the status of Berlin. Failing agreement among the four wartime allies in six months, the Soviet Union would sign its own peace treaty with East Germany and give that country responsibility for a demilitarized West Berlin. I believed we could negotiate with the Soviets over Berlin without repeating Munich. Appeasement remained the dirtiest word in diplomacy since Neville Chamberlain's caving in to Hitler at the Munich conference in 1938. I had absorbed its pejorative meaning as a boy but by now felt uneasy about simple definitions that presumed every Soviet leader was Hitler and every confrontation Munich.

I wanted the United States to remain the leader of NATO, but I took offense at American allegations that Europe did not carry its fair share of the burden and lacked the will to fight. Like my government, I rooted for European integration in the European Economic Community, created by the Rome treaty of March 1957. I was glad to see Germany in NATO and the Common Market, although Chancellor Konrad Adenauer was not an appealing figure and I assumed that many former Nazis lived in the Federal Republic. My fondness for France showed. I downplayed anti-Americanism there, although the neutralist movement of the late 1940s regained momentum by contending that Americans were as dangerous as Russians. I welcomed Charles de Gaulle's rise to power in 1958, rescuing the Fourth Republic from fractious politicians in Paris and rebellious French generals in Algeria and soon establishing the Fifth Republic with strong executive powers for the president. American leaders happily changed metaphors after June 1958: France, once effeminate, was now in strong masculine hands. Before long Washington was predicting that de Gaulle's nationalism would damage NATO. I disagreed; I knew France.

The European Left did not horrify me. I nodded agreement with professors who cited Tito's Yugoslavia as an encouraging example of national autonomy in the Communist world. Richard Crossman's *The God That Failed*, an anthology of essays by Arthur Koestler and other former Communists, led me to expect further cases of apostasy on the Left. I had met Communists in Paris of the kind who denounced the Soviet repression of Hungarian independence in 1956. I grew optimistic that social democratic parties, with their antifascist heritage, anti-Communist politics, and democratic principles, would prove healthy for Europe and NATO.

More fervently than most agnostics, I hoped the Atlantic community would be truly cosmopolitan, not dominated by American culture. That is one reason why I welcomed the infestation of the Volkswagen Beetle in America, that impudent, whimsical, European challenge to the Darwinian ascendancy of the tail-finned mammoths made in Detroit. Our Madison neighbor Stan Mailer bought a "Bug" in spring 1956, the last model with the small, oval rear window. He and I spent every weekend that summer driving the car around southern Wisconsin, seeking out auto mechanics just to see their faces when they searched in vain for the gas cap or engine.

The Bug was our symbol of rebellion, our badge of nonconformity. Stan and I had become good friends after John dropped model railroading. We were both outsiders of sorts in Madison, Stan much more than I. Neither of us looked sexy in low-slung Levi's. Neither of us owned a leather jacket or felt at ease around girls. Stan was reading *War and Peace* and could imitate the front end of a chrome-toothed Buick making a flabby turn. He drove all over the Midwest taking photos of steam locomotives and bewailed the national rot of rail transportation. I liked France, West Texas, and classical music. I worked on a section gang for the North Western Railroad, straightening rails, rebuilding roadbed, renewing grade crossings, making a note of rural gas stations for weekend jaunts. The regular gandy dancers nicknamed me "Stinky" the moment I let slip how embarrassed I was to ride home at the end of the day, reeking of sweat and oil and creosote, on city buses packed with clean office workers.

Stan and I found status in the Bug and rode it like lords of the manor. Stan's reputation as a misfit acquired respect as Bugs became fashionable expressions of disdain for American big business. My Europhilia no longer sounded like an alien disorder caused by too much exposure to history and Gothic architecture. Postwar Europe had arrived in the United States for everyman. The Beetle had character, great gas mileage, and a reasonable price tag. I felt vindicated.

These were sunny years for my family. Mom thrived in Italy during my freshman year, her letters brimming with confidence gained from learning Italian and exploring Rome on her own while Dad worked in the Vatican library. She traded language lessons with a Franciscan monk on days when the maid could serve as chaperon. "My friar's a scream," she reported while he was reading *Treasure Island*. "Pirate vocabulary is not designed for mass." She wrote often, her endearments a trilingual cornucopia of buttercup, coconut, sweet pea, turtle dove, clabber cheese, mozzarella, cauliflower, and several kinds of pasta. She sent me a sexy picture of Sophia Loren that I pinned to the wall over my desk.

Mom recalled good times together in Paris and Madison, missed me, and wished they could afford to fly me to Rome for Christmas. She always closed with love, from "devotedly" to "Je t'aime, kid." When I wrote that my self-esteem had taken several blows at Cornell, she replied, "Your ego will get kicked around quite a bit as you grow older, but don't let go of it; just sort of housebreak it the way we did Barbos so people can live with you comfortably." Could I pee on the chives? I answered.

I never saw Mom's own ego more vital than after her year in Italy. She discovered strengths in herself there, both intellectual and social, and these enabled her to find solid ground between humble housewife and modern feminist. If father and sons argued too long at the dinner table, she would restore order with one withering truth: "You all take yourselves too damned seriously!" She became a stalwart in the Theater Guild, helping with administration as well as acting. She continued to support mental health agencies and lent a sympathetic ear to two Madison friends of mine who suffered from depression. Both recall that she did them more good than any shrink. "I can hear her voice now," one of them wrote a few years ago, "slow and sweet and solemn in that gentle, even, kind of dreamy tone of hers."

The new Italian subdivision in Mom's cuisine made her a better cook than ever, and it helped me gain the weight I needed to become more competitive for promotion on the Cornell heavyweight crew squad, which I joined in my sophomore year. She gave me unconditional encouragement for college, telling me in one letter not to worry about being my father's son: "He is beginning to worry about being your *father*."

Home became a place for vacations, a haven in my new life of leaving, returning, and moving on. When John and I came home for summer and Christmas, Dad no longer warned us to go easy on Mom. She and I teased each other, watched old movies together on the television set that Dad bought in 1957 to ease her recovery from hysterectomy, traded news and gossip. Genuine friendship was developing between us, and I liked being with her.

But I doubted that the minefield had been completely cleared. I still heard echoes of Mom's illness in certain pieces of music and in the way she belittled her intelligence by calling herself a cabbage. Although she seldom ate bread and buttermilk, I occasionally saw the symptoms I associated with that old prescription: the downward stare, the indifference to conversation, the slow motions of a different world. Nor did she take many long walks, but I guessed that some of her outings with Barbos to the country or Willows Beach served the same purpose. My protests that she was intelligent had no apparent effect, and I wished Dad and John would try harder to buck her up.

I still did not dare ask Mom about her time alone in Europe. Winding that clock back carried too much risk, even though the likelihood of her suffering a relapse seemed smaller than ever. If she had gone to pieces, I would have ascribed immediate causes to the dormancy of mental illness and the family's inability to cure it. Like Granddad, however, I clung to my diagnosis of origins. Just as an icy baptism had started Grandmother Post's lifelong bronchitis, Hitler's war had weakened my mother permanently. She would always be vulnerable to bullies.

Italy was good for Dad, too. He brought home boxes of notes and pieces of crumbling mosaic given to him by an artisan restoring an ancient basilica in Ravenna. Dad advised me not to worry about grades at Cornell. "Just settle down and do a good job," he wrote; "just do as well as you can and let the future take care of itself"; and "rest easy about choosing a profession and just get a good general education." When I wished I were as intellectual as John, Dad replied, "Don't try to be an intellectual. Far better to do as you are doing, be intelligent."

I majored in history in large part because I looked up to Dad, and

I had him in mind when I chose the topics for term papers on law courts in ancient Athens and Saint Ambrose's debt to Cicero for moral precepts. (I had Mom in mind when I wrote on architectural settings in the paintings of Fra Angelico.) "History ain't easy!" Dad sympathized. "A lot of important historical development is dull stuff, but it has to be learned." "Don't get *too* involved in politics," he warned after I was elected president of my floor in a freshman dormitory, but by and large he admired my extracurricular activities and forgave the dent they put in my academic average.

John and I grew closer in the late fifties, one of the biggest dividends of my not following him to Harvard. I admired his rigorous analytical temperament, and deciding I could not equal it must have reduced the competitive friction between us. So did our acknowledgment of respective superiorities, his at camping and mine at rowing, which he had given up after his freshman year with the Harvard lightweight crew squad. We found it easier to share hang-ups and dreams. On the way east for my freshman year, we drove the family car into Canada at Sault Ste. Marie and crossed Ontario. We stopped in Blind River, a restless nuclear-age boomtown with muddy pickups and new storefronts after the discovery of uranium nearby. We camped beside lakes in the Timagami and Algonquin Provincial Parks, where the loons' eerie laughter brought back the loneliness I felt at Camp Manitowish on Boulder Lake in northern Wisconsin the summer before Paris. We took the New York Central's *New England States* home together for Christmases; John started in Boston, I climbed aboard in Syracuse around 8 P.M. After catching up on news, we slept fitfully between stations — Rochester, Buffalo, Cleveland, Toledo, South Bend, Chicago.

John's love of the outdoors deepened mine. Wilderness, more than anything else, assuaged our polar cravings for solitude and companionship. Twice we explored the wilds of Porcupine Mountain State Park on the shore of Lake Superior in Michigan's Upper Peninsula. Our happy band included the two other Johns of the 1954 trip to Haskell and Stan's older brother, Andy, a graduate student in English who had babysat John and me in the late 1940s and with whom we now discussed books. We rented "Section 17" cabin on the Little Carp (short for escarpment) River as our base, drank from the rust-colored stream, hiked through forests and above cliffs, and rehashed Hemingway's "Big Two-Hearted River" which was not far away. On the way home we watched for all-you-can-eat restaurants. We stopped at one in Minocqua, Wisconsin. It was named after Paul Bunyan, and so determined were we to live up to Paul's mythological standard that the proprietor stopped serving us after our fourth round. Since then, John and I have had many "coming out" dinners together after backpacking. We always follow this gluttonous rule: dine at all-you-can-eat restaurants only if you can make them regret their policy.

I was mowing the front lawn in the summer of 1956, shortly after my parents returned from Italy, when John came out of the house, wiping tears, to tell me Granddad Post had died. We lost the greatest storyteller in our lives, the cowboy who fathered the medievalist who raised us. Dad tried to hide his sorrow with platitudes about a full life and merciful death, but it didn't work. Before the end of the year, Granddad's old Edison phonograph arrived from Haskell, along with the heavy, waffle-thick records Dad had bought in the early 1920s. Among these were songs from Verdi's *La forza del destino* (Claudia Muzio singing "Pace, mio Dio"), Bellini's *Norma* (Frieda Hempel and "Casta Diva"), Donizetti's *Lucia di Lammermoor* (Arthur Middleton and others singing the sextet). Several old Victor recordings came as well, including Carl T. Sprague's authentic rendering of "Bury Me Not on the Lone Prairie," a truly mournful song that Granddad loved; he despised Gene Autry and Roy Rogers for abusing it in a major key. When Dad played these records in his study, I remembered hearing them when I was a boy and Granddad told tales of catamounts, Kiowas, and Saint Elmo's fire on the trail to Kansas. I heard no world of difference between Italian opera and cowboy songs.

At Cornell, students read books about hapless individuals struggling against the corporate system many hoped to join, such as Sloan Wilson's *The Man in the Gray Flannel Suit* and W. H. Whyte's *The Organization Man*. The more philosophical among us brooded over alienation and identity in modern society. I leaned toward those who described themselves as examples of Colin Wilson's *The Outsider*, not those who swore by the libertarian gospel according to Ayn Rand's *The Fountainhead*. Many female students followed the custom of the time, earning good grades but keeping a low profile in discussions and wearing the right clothes lest they offend potential husbands. Some, however, asserted themselves in the classroom, took strong political positions, and sought careers in business or the professions.

Antisocial Beats hung out at coffee joints in Collegetown, reading Allen Ginsberg and Jack Kerouac, scorning crew cuts, saluting their own authenticity with borrowed words from black jazz musicians like hip, cool, crazy, dig, square, groove, chick, pad, bug, joint, daddy-o, cop out. Beats acted as if they had discovered the secret of life. Crew cuts called them "turkeys."

We seldom questioned academic requirements, believing the university knew best what subjects we must study in order to become educated and find work. Some students demonstrated against the university administration for prohibiting alcohol at football games. Others used their wits, such as the guy who filled a hula hoop with gin and tonic and carried it playfully past the guards at the stadium gate. The technique spread. Until the authorities caught on a few games later, you could see hula hoops tilt skyward around the stadium, a free-thinking rite loose in an established church. The stunt was in the tradition of the legendary Hugh Troy, Cornell's most famous prankster. A student in the 1920s, Troy used a rhinoceros-foot wastebasket to produce tracks around campus after a snowfall. Bored with a desk job in the Pacific during the Second World War, he started notifying higher headquarters of the number of dead flies he counted on the flypaper in his office every week, and soon other units in the South Pacific were being asked for their "fly reports."

I was disturbed by the sympathy for segregation that I began to find in letters from Haskell as sit-ins shook the South. According to Miss Ada, some Haskell folks were saying that Mom's rebellious habit of calling black maids and handymen "Mrs." and "Mr." so-and-so was coming home to roost. I abhorred Governor Orval Faubus's use of the Arkansas National Guard to block the desegregation of Little Rock's public schools in 1957. I read Alan Paton's *Cry, the Beloved Country* and pitied black South Africans. But neither I nor the majority of my classmates were deeply committed to advancing the civil rights of black Americans. We took Jackie Robinson, Ralph Bunche, Ella Fitzgerald, Fats Domino, and jazz for granted. We were more concerned about civil liberties than civil rights, more interested in coexistence with the Soviet Union than racial comity in the United States.

I gradually acclimated to Cornell, its geographic isolation, preponderance of students from the New York metropolitan area, fraternities, tough grading. My freshman roommate, a Jew named Bob from Long Island, was brilliant in math and economics. He honed my skills at bridge, and we made pocket money by challenging all comers. Bob and I had long bull sessions about politics, sex, and religion. Although neither of us was devout, we agreed that no God worthy of the name would have permitted Nazi genocide and that we were not interested in heaven unless it admitted dogs. Bob would sing along to rock-'n'-roll radio stations while he did his homework, keeping time by tapping his desk. He knew this bothered me and tried to quit, but he was addicted, and I soon migrated to the library for serious studying. His favorite song began, "Well they often call me speedo but my real name is Mister Earl," followed by falsetto oohing, a mindless hallmark of the fifties that deserves more time on oldies' music stations than it gets.

While I was in the library one evening late in September, having forgotten the starting time for a meeting of residents on my dormitory floor, Bob placed my name in nomination for president of the floor. I arrived late to find I had been elected. This recruitment upheld my high school trust in leadership as a challenging reward for character, but my first foray into college politics turned out to be my last. I decided not to run for the presidency of the entire dorm. "I'm not the rah-rah! Joe College type," I wrote to my parents, feeling inadequate when I compared myself to the garb and affability of ostensibly self-confident preppies. A few months later, the pushy preppy who won was knocked unconscious by a smoldering amateur boxer from a Brooklyn public school who did not like being pushed.

I joined the drama club, hoping to continue avocational acting. After a few months I quit. I had neither the time nor talent to contend with people like Richard Fariña, an inscrutable guy who had befriended the already reclusive Thomas Pynchon and who later married Mimi Baez and became a countercultural icon in the 1960s. I made the freshman baseball team. The coach called me "Wally," after Wally Post of the Cincinnati Reds. After playing yet another season as backup first baseman, however, I resolved to change sports.

Giving up college baseball was an act of disloyalty to Ted Williams, for whom I had been playing since grade school, but breaking free of him and working on the railroad loosened me up at the plate that summer in Madison. For the first time in my life, I could see the ball all the way into the bat, and I stopped fearing good pitchers. After a few games I was batting cleanup; meanwhile, Ted had raised his average to about .345 after a miserable spring. Memory often replays my all-time best hit, against the best pitcher on the best team in the league. I bet correctly on a fastball from the left-hander who had been fooling me with curves, felt my bat get all of it, watched it sail over the right field fence, rounded first base with feigned nonchalance. Splendid at last.

One of the two Notre Dame students on my railroad crew that summer played on a team with a slew of Catholic wiseacres who crossed themselves a lot and slid with spikes high. The spikes really pissed us off, and batting against that bunch became a protestant act even for my Catholic teammates. My success at the plate soon stifled the Notre Dame boys' insults on the job, though I had considered it a badge of honor when they called me a "dumb egghead" because I admired Adlai Stevenson.

Baseball, politics, acting. When I gave up these extracurricular activities after my freshman year, I was conscious of discarding pieces of my high school identity and looking for the college me. I found a very big piece of that in rowing. I tried out for crew in my sophomore year, attracted by its fabled reputation at Cornell and encouraged by several good men in the fraternity (Phi Sigma Kappa) I had joined as a freshman.

Rowing was the quintessential amateur college sport in those days. No experience was required. All you needed were reach, strength, timing, and complete dedication. Because I was a novice, I practiced with the freshman squad. On our first, awkward day in the indoor rowing tanks in Teagle Hall, the varsity coach, R. Harrison "Stork" Sanford, came in to have a look at the new recruits. He had rowed for three great University of Washington crews in the mid-1920s and was now one of the most highly respected coaches in the country. After a few minutes he asked the freshman coach, Carl Ulrich, to switch me from starboard to port side, where the stroke usually rowed, the oarsman who sets the rhythm for the whole boat.

Many years later, an old ranger at the Aransas National Wildlife Refuge in Texas took my wife and me into a restricted area in search of whooping cranes, which he proudly called "my whoopers." As we approached a large field, many sandhill cranes took flight along with thousands of geese. The ranger told us to look closely at the wing beat of the cranes, noting that the sandhills' upstroke is much more rapid than the downstroke.

"Now, do you see any cranes with a slower upbeat, sort of the same as the downbeat?" he asked. We spotted a few.

"Those are whoopers," he said.

I thought of Stork, aptly nicknamed for his slender frame. "That's a stroke," he must have said to himself when he saw me on that first day I handled a sweep oar, my timing as natural as a whooper's.

Thanks to Stork's eye, I could compete with heavier oarsmen for a chance at the JV or varsity boat, for strokes weighed less than members of the "engine room" in the middle of the boat, and I was a light 175 pounds. Halfway through racing season in my junior year, I was promoted from the third boat to stroke of the JV, and as a senior I stroked the varsity in several races. My record was mixed, about as many losses as wins. Publicly, I could blame the losses on my not keeping the rate of stroke up as high as Stork wanted or on my forearms' tightening up. Privately, I was terrified that prerace jitters might be symptomatic of the nerves of a loser. The irony of my recently acquired confidence at baseball crossed my mind, but I did not know how to acquire it without giving up the sport.

I gave myself some credit for the JV's extraordinary victory in the Intercollegiate Rowing Association's (IRA) national regatta on Lake Onondaga near Syracuse, June 1958. It had been a disappointing year until then, a letdown after the 1957 varsity's undefeated season, which was capped by breaking the course record against Russia's best crew in the semifinals of the Grand Challenge Cup at the Henley Royal Regatta, then defeating Yale in the all-American final. With several alumni of that boat watching at Syracuse in 1958, we swept all three races: freshman, JV, varsity. "Hail all hail Cornell," wrote Allison Danzig in the *New York Times*. "Not quite the champion of all as a year ago, but never greater than today in all the history of its unsurpassed rowing tradition." In our three-mile race, the JV won by two feet, literally on the last stroke. We had trailed by two lengths with half a mile to go, but our low stroke until that point left us with the necessary stamina to row the last half mile at a virtual sprint, almost unheard of in long races back then. No matter how often I re-row that race, I never concede the possibility that our low stroke brought on the problem in the first place. Logic sullies legend.

I loved the ripple under the shell when we rowed powerfully and smoothly; the illusion of greater speed on an invisible medium after dark in late fall practices on Lake Cayuga; the fitness of body and clarity of mind during training; the exultation of victory in a state of utter exhaustion; the teamwork, comradeship, and egalitarianism of a sport that could ill afford pampered stars. I still dream, once or twice a year, that I am stroking an eight-oared shell. The boat sings, the old rhythm is there. If the motion awakens me, I wonder whether my wife suspects I have been dreaming about making love to another woman.

The quality of instruction at Cornell was high, the students bright, and the grading hard, especially for freshmen. An average of B+ put you in the top 10 percent of your class. Although narrowly missing election to Phi Beta Kappa, I completed the honors program in history, writing my senior thesis with Professor Eugene Rice on the historical thought of the French Renaissance political theorist Jean Bodin.

My courses covered the major branches of the liberal arts. The European emphasis I sought, along with the European background of some of my professors, nourished my hopes of returning to Paris and exploring the rest of the continent. My academic advisor was Theodor Ernst Mommsen, a medieval historian who wrote about Saint Augustine and Petrarch and thought highly of Dad's work. He persuaded me to take German, art history, and ancient literature and urged me to read fiction. "Historians should read novels," he declared. He struggled to overcome deep feelings of inferiority in comparison to illustrious forebears: his grandfather, the Roman historian whose namesake he was, and his maternal uncles, the sociologists Max and Alfred Weber. A Protestant, a liberal, and a humanist, Mommsen was profoundly shocked by Hitler's dictatorial and anti-Semitic policies. In the mid-1930s he immigrated to the United States, where he taught at Yale, Groton School, and Princeton before moving to Cornell in 1954.

The tips of Mommsen's starched shirt collars curled up, and he could not coordinate the swing of his furled umbrella with an awkward gait. Although shy, he liked to talk with students and could usually be found in his office beyond his scheduled office hours. He was a fine teacher, erudite but not stuffy, demanding but not intimidating. He invited small groups of students to his bachelor apartment, where he played records of Wagner, chain-smoked cigarettes, and labored nervously, with thick accent, to generate conversation among undergraduates who had never met a Central European intellectual nor listened to *Lohengrin* straight through. He never spoke of Germany as his true *Heimat*, with that word's comforting connotations of roots and identity. He was a lonely man.

When I saw Mommsen for what I could not know would be the last time, at his office in Boardman Hall in June 1958, he gave me an uncharacteristic pat on the back as he wished me a good summer. A month later he killed himself. When I heard the news, I knew instantly that he had been telling me a final good-bye. I wept as much as when Granddad died.

Mommsen's advice to me, combined with his expatriation and death, attached permanently to my memories of war. Why had so few Gentile intellectuals left Nazi Germany? What defense could humane letters muster against inhumane policies? What price would one pay for resisting, tolerating, or joining Nazis? Could an expatriate from such a regime ever go home again? Who was a good German? These questions about Germany contained moral dilemmas bound up with personal choices. I believed I would eventually find answers, that they would tell me more about Mom's collapse and myself.

In January 1958, shortly before the publication of *Lolita*, I registered too late to get into Vladimir Nabokov's enormously popular course, "Masters of European Fiction," which students dubbed "Dirty Lit" or simply "Nabokov." My everlasting regret was abated by taking a similar class with Robert Adams, who watched icicles drip under the eaves of Goldwin Smith Hall as he probed the meaning of the sign "Thither" in Thomas Hardy's *Jude the Obscure*. In history courses, I discovered Themistocles, humanism, appeasement at the Congress of Vienna, arguments from the Vatican and German Protestant Church condoning Nazism as a bulwark against Communism. Government Professor Mario Einaudi, son of Italy's postwar president Luigi Einaudi, stood for a liberal Catholicism in Europe. Greek history and literature (taught by Professors Laistner and Solmsen, both German expatriates like Mommsen) counseled me to seek freedom between excess and inaction. The economic and social benefits of sugar beets, according to Professor Edward Fox, helped France survive its nineteenth-century revolutions.

Requiring loyalty oaths as proof of American patriotism sounded like the European Wars of Religion, Robespierre, Hitler, and Stalin. From such examples of punishing freedom of conscience as a political crime, I drew parallel warnings about American orthodoxy that offended even some of my agnostic friends. I persisted, arguing that knowing the past would tell you a lot about what today's governments hide. Governments did not dare tell the truth, and I thought we had come to Cornell in search of it.

Reading my letters from college today, I find a moodier, more restless self than I remember. I was preoccupied with lacking and gaining confidence in just about everything: coursework, rowing, social life, my future. I worried about the apparent conflict between rowing and concentrating on my studies so as to pave the way to Phi Beta Kappa and graduate school. In the summer after my sophomore year I outlined this dilemma to Walter Prescott Webb, the distinguished historian of the American West who was staying with us in Madison for a few days. "Row!" was his advice, and I took it. In my junior year one of my professors advised me to drop crew if I wanted to do honors in history. I was grateful when Dad supported my doing both, irritable when he suggested that improving my grades as a senior would impress graduate schools. Throughout college I was frustrated by professors who gave me higher grades for reciting facts than for creative thinking, the kind of facts Dad called dull but necessary.

My dating was limited by strict training rules for crew as well as inexperience and timidity. During racing season, Stork, a bashful man who rarely cursed, advised the few married oarsmen, "Well, boys, uh, you see, well, just take it easy for a while." All of us were supposed to be in bed by eleven and to avoid dancing because it could twist finely tuned muscles the wrong way. Abstinence came easily for me. I studied best in the morning, disliked dancing, and was chaste except for an expedition early in 1956 to a brothel in Utica along with five other freshmen, two of whom had lost their virginity in high school and now shepherded the rest of the carload like veterans. Road companionship sustained my hope that I would pass my first test of manhood. But panic gripped me as I entered the dim bedroom. When my prostitute said, "Let's see Peter," I gulped, "Who?" Wise, sympathetic, and plump, she helped me undress, washed my privates, led me to bed, and did most of the work. I passed, just; enough to join in the general crowing on the way back to Ithaca but not so much as to conquer inhibition.

My crushes included a dark-haired senior at Emma Willard School in Troy, a Madison blond at the University of Wisconsin whose picture appeared on the cover of *Life* magazine as one of the most beautiful coeds in the Midwest, a language major at Cornell who translated Italian sources for my paper on Fra Angelico and smiled mercifully when I blushed at our contiguous work on footnotes, and, in my senior year, a Chicago girl about to graduate from Sweet Briar who lost interest when I said I could not imagine marrying until I was thirty. The Madison blond I put highest on a pedestal. The language major reminded me the most of my mother. At home, I mentioned all of them to Mom but never asked her why I felt so nervous around girls or how to traverse the expanse between kissing and sleeping with one. Few sons did ask their mothers this, but mine had a unique way of making young people feel at ease, and I should have taken greater advantage of it. I no longer thought my frustrations would burden her, but admitting lust would have mortified me. Time, experience, and friends would eventually solve my problem, I kept telling myself, even as I doubted they would.

It seemed as though I was "second string in everything," I complained in a letter home in the spring of 1958, "not knowing what I want to *be*." A boring course in international law dampened my interest in going to law school. I applied for a Woodrow Wilson Fellowship for graduate study in history. In my statement, I confessed that "being a member of the Cornell crew means just as much to me as doing honors in history" and that I did not regard my forthcoming military service as a distasteful interlude. I was turned down. That left the diplomatic service, I thought, in which I could combine my skills in history, foreign language, social diplomacy, and living abroad.

The Wilson rejection was a double blow. It damaged my high school faith that intelligence and honesty will be rewarded, and it insinuated that my intelligence didn't deserve the reward. I reconsidered the merits of having diverse skills and of choosing a career that would not recognize them.

Indecision over career was emblematic of the deeper mysteries I had hoped to bring to light in college. I saw the film *The Brothers Karamazov* on a winter's night in my junior year with Ted Buettner, a close friend and rowing companion. Later, shaken by the conflict between good and evil and unable to sleep, I took a long walk around freshly plowed streets north of campus. Next day, Ted told me he had been similarly affected by the movie. His walk had very nearly intersected mine, but we were glad they missed, for we both had wanted to be alone.

Somewhere between Ivan and Alyosha, Ted and I were searching for moral standards amid the contradictions we encountered in books, elders, and daily news. Unique to our generation's search was the thicket of opposites through which we felt our way: McCarthyism and anti-Americanism, reaction and revolution, Soviet hegemony and American self-interest, nuclear holocaust and disarmament, militarism and pacifism, social mobility and corporate straitjackets, education and anti-intellectualism, prosperity and materialism, democracy and segregation. These opposites blurred the line between good and evil. If we were "silent," it was because we were not certain where to redraw the lines that had been clear in our childhood.

Looking beyond college at that time in the Cold War, what values would we embrace, and what causes would break our silence? Our idealism had been fashioned by World War II and the Cold War. To our lasting regret, we had been too young to take up arms in the Second World War, which had begun to look like the last "good war." Some intuitive urge drove us to seek compensation for having missed the good fight that identified our parents' generation, to construct a tacit agenda for ourselves.

Although we could probably not end the Cold War, we would at least end the way our parents' generation had waged it. Many of us would repudiate the divisive and repressive language of McCarthyism. We would build upon the populist solidarity we heard in the folk songs of the Weavers and the Kingston Trio. We would demonstrate the wisdom of moderation, the sanity of peaceful coexistence, the compatibility between American ideals and political practice. We would accomplish something noble that had eluded our elders during the Cold War, something that would identify us as a new generation and put our footprints in history. Our cause, bigger than the Cold War, was as large as history and left over from two world wars. It was freedom, still a quiet abstraction for us but gathering momentum and waiting for outlets.

By freedom, I meant self-determination of the most fundamental kind. Nothing more clearly stood for this independence than the Hungarian freedom fighter and Albert Camus's rebel. Like many students, in October 1956 I adopted the freedom fighter as my hero. I pinned on him my hopes for democratization in Eastern Europe, and I hated Khrushchev for brutally ending that dream. On 7 January 1957 *Time* magazine made the freedom fighter its "Man of the Year" for 1956, its cover depicting a woman and child behind him, all of them carrying rifles. Behind them waved the Hungarian flag with a hole where Communist symbols had been excised. Behind the flag were damaged buildings and the burning hulk of a Soviet tank. I believed *Time*'s statement that the fighter's "greatest triumph was moral; he demonstrated the profound and needful truth that humanity is not necessarily forever bound and gagged by modern terrorist political techniques." I idolized survivors who made their way to American universities in 1957–1958 and told stories that reminded me of escapes from Nazi-occupied Europe.

In a letter to my parents in November 1956, a few days after the Hungarian uprising was crushed, I expressed "some sort of inner identification" with the freedom fighters and hoped it would still be possible to build a free world "with idealistic materials." Hungary kindled my yearning to belong to a larger community, a brotherhood that resisted bullies everywhere. How and where could I join? I didn't know, and no one in power asked me for suggestions, but I was certain of the central truth governing this community — the right to be free.

I found this truth in the works of Albert Camus. The English translation of *The Rebel* arrived in college bookstores in 1956, and he won the Nobel Prize for Literature a year later. The book hit me hard. I had already read *The Plague*, his overpowering metaphor for resistance against Nazism, and I revered Camus for having resisted the Nazis himself. I saw that the French edition of *The Rebel* had been published in 1951, shortly before the anti-Pétain riot revived my wartime images of Nazism and resistance. While I had been learning to respect French Communists for opposing Nazis and Vichy fascists, Camus was breaking with Sartre and other French intellectuals who condoned Stalin's crimes and gave Communism all the credit for the liberation of France. In *The Rebel*, Camus's enemy is any revolution that results in the totalitarian power of the state ruled by one system of thought. Dictatorial control and the suppression of individual freedom had not died with Nazi Germany but lived on in the Soviet Union and could happen elsewhere.

I underlined these passages in *The Rebel*: "In the age of ideologies, we must examine our position in relation to murder"; "if we believe in nothing, . . . we are free to stoke the crematory fires"; "the moment that we recognize the impossibility of absolute abnegation . . . the very first thing that cannot be denied is the right of others to live"; "history . . . is one of the limits of man's experience, . . . but man, by rebelling, imposes in his turn a limit to history, and at this limit the promise of value is reborn"; the rebel is "a man who says no, but whose refusal does not imply a renunciation"; "if the individual . . . accepts death and happens to die as a consequence of his act of rebellion, he demonstrates by doing so that he is willing to sacrifice himself for the sake of a common good which he considers more important than his own destiny."

What a revelation! I had found a mentor who bridged the "good war" I had missed and the Cold War I would have to fight. Unlike Hollywood rebels of the fifties, Camus's rebel had a cause. His rebel defied alienation as well as autocracy; he could do good and ought to, no matter who said no. Camus's philosophy of moral responsibility and courage had roots in resistance against Nazism and offered lessons for battling oppression anywhere. He assured me that rebels against injustice need not be unjust themselves. You could fight against autocrats without becoming one.

Reading Camus was like an exceptional outing on Lake Cayuga when timing and power come together and rowing is life. Thanks to him, I understood that the Second World War would never really end, that my fate was bound up with resistance. Resistance was compatible with skepticism, indeed depended on it. It was OK to be ambivalent, Camus assured me, and human to hide anxieties behind confident appearances. Freedom needed solitude as much as companionship; I could serve the community and remain an outsider, slave to no one. I could have fears yet also summon the courage to conquer them, as I had done as an oarsman, pushing myself beyond my limits. The best skeptic was one whose doubt led to action. Agnosticism turned to faith at such moments; your riddle was solved.

Camus argued that history itself could be autocratic: states or ideologies could try to justify violence because it was a historical reality. That gave me all the more reason to study history for symptoms and antidotes. My definition of autocracy was expanding. It started with infamous bullies but went on to cover any dogmatic person or system of authority that claimed to know what was best for me while repressing my rights to learn the whole story and act according to my version of it. Like Dr. Rieux in *The Plague*, I felt I must side with the victims of repression and would be guilty if I did not. Maybe I could help form communities of autonomous individuals. Somewhere in these reflections I began to perceive what Camus meant by integrity. Somewhere out there I was determined to personify it by resisting and building; I did not know where or for whom.

I inserted a few of these ideas, and quoted Camus, in a paper on suffering in Dostoyevsky's *Crime and Punishment*. Professor Adams chided me for sounding "terribly authoritative, rather as if you'd lived a rich, full life, and were ready to sum it all up for posterity." Now that I have read thousands of undergraduate papers, I see Adams's point; I would grade down accordingly, as he did, and tell the student to cheer up and lighten the prose. Now that I am ready to sum up part of my life, I would like to tell Adams I thought I had a right to sound authoritative about suffering although I could not reveal why.

My childhood bubbled to the surface in literature, history, politics. I could easily cite Nazism as my symbol of injustice, but I said nothing about my mother's breakdown and what it represented. During the Second World War, I had invented the man I wanted to become, someone strong enough to resist anyone who wore jackboots, protect Mom, and help her recover. A fighter. Camus told me it was possible to become what I had invented. Possible, no guarantees, up to me.

And there was the hitch. I had also invented the kind of person I did not want to be, a nervous bystander afraid to defend the right of others to live. A failure, a loner who hid. I confessed to no one my feelings that losing Mom was partly my fault, yet that I was also a victim, like her. Sharpening my memories of the anti-Pétain riot of 1951, Camus encouraged me to overcome fear and guilt through action. But I might not act. I was still fighting the war, praying that the good invention would win. Memory had turned into metaphor. Childhood had given me a fuller life than my professor could have known.

While revising this chapter, I met the late Buck Ramsey, the cowboy poet and musician from Amarillo, Texas. When I told him I was working on my youth and Camus, I expected him to poke fun at the naive soul-searching of an Ivy League kid. Nope. He nodded as if remembering an old friend whom he hadn't seen for years. He had read Camus at about the same time and age as I, in the Texas panhandle, not upstate New York. I asked him why he liked Camus.

"Because he was different, challenging, European," Buck drawled, "and because I was searching for virtue and integrity. Camus made me see rebellion as a *positive* act, made me think there was no way to live *but* rebellion. His stuff seems dark and pessimistic, but he's saying you gotta go through that stuff for an affirmation of life. Besides, his pantheism appeals to the cowboy in me."

Buck's major poem, "And as I Rode Out on the Morning," is about a young cowboy's initiation into manhood. The prologue ends with these lines:

> And as I ride out on the morning
> Before the bird, before the dawn,
> I'll be this poem, I'll be this song.
> My heart will beat the world a warning —
> Those horsemen will ride all with me,
> And we'll be good, we'll be free.

Like Buck and his young hero, like Camus, I wanted to be good and free. Were these ideals compatible with military service in the most powerful nation the world had ever seen? I thought so. Service in the Cold War was personal proving ground as well as public duty, especially if I could serve in Europe. In a philosophy course at Cornell, Professor Stuart Brown, who had fought in the Second World War, asked what we would do if we were on patrol and triggered a "bouncing betty" antipersonnel mine. Would we yell a warning to our buddies and dive for cover, knowing the explosion would kill someone else, or would we fall on top of the mine before it bounced up, knowing we would die? I hoped I would have the moral courage to do the latter, the ultimate act of faith.

As a Cold War agnostic, I did not reject war if peaceful means failed to prevent Communist aggression nor seriously question the morality of military service. I subscribed to the principle of reason of state but not might makes right. I wanted my country to be as good as it had been in the Second World War, when I had entertained no moral ambiguities. I derived my sense of civic duty in great part from memory of that "good war" that had defined patriotism for my generation. I also took cues from my father, who cited Roman and medieval law in conversations about the duties and rights of American citizens. In my family, those rights did not include dodging military service even if you disagreed with the government.

In spite of military cutbacks under the New Look strategy, the military draft continued. Pursuant to nearly one hundred years of legislation designed to raise reserve officers in a manner consistent with democratic principles (notably the Land Grant [Morrill] Act of 1862 and the National Defense Act of 1916), all able-bodied male students at Cornell had to take courses and drill in the Reserve Officer Training Corps (ROTC), during their first two years of college. Military uniforms were commonplace on campus, the "Eisenhower jacket" worn by army and air force cadets. Students who spent the next two years planning to evade military service after graduation could be found from Left to Right. The Selective Service granted deferments for graduate school, marriage, and work in defense-related industries. Among the students who sought these, the biggest hypocrites were those, usually found on the Right, who lobbed armchair slogans like "America, right or wrong" and "love it or leave it." To paraphrase what Samuel Johnson said over two centuries ago about the owners of slaves, some of the loudest yelps for liberty in the fifties came from draft-dodging patriots.

In addition to military careerists, a respected vocational option in those days, many students decided to do four years of ROTC, receive officers' commissions at graduation, and then serve on active duty for six months or more, followed by time in the reserves. They reasoned that, if you wanted to serve, had to, or needed a paying job while deciding on a career, it was better to be an officer. My brother and I took this route. He decided on six months of active duty, I chose two years because that gave me more time to weigh options and the best chance for a paid trip to Europe.

ROTC cadets at Cornell came in many types, and throwing them together was a democratic strength of the program. I hung around mainly with fellow oarsmen but got to know other cadets in the army's classes and drills. My good friend Ted, navy, was a government major and Christian Scientist from suburban Connecticut. His religious principles clashed with conundrums we faced together in Professor Brown's ethics course and with Ted's need for medication to relieve a painful ailment that almost cost him his seat on the JV. Dick, army and electrical engineering, liked Camus and read poetry in the boathouse to calm himself before races. Don, marines, parried sarcastic references to his major in hotel administration with mouthwatering descriptions of the special dish he had prepared in that day's cooking class. Sometimes, like the drill sergeants he had encountered at boot camp, he would bark short commands like "steak!" or "shortcake!" to shut us up before practice. Dick, navy and premed from Cleveland, loved rowing more than science and raced on his Saturday Sabbath. Dave, army, from a small town in Maine, persuaded me that veterinary medicine was one of the toughest majors at Cornell. Ed, army, came from a small coal-mining town in eastern Pennsylvania, majored in mechanical engineering, and played guard on the football team. He looked like a safe with eyes. A superb leader, he exhorted those under his command to build what he pronounced "espirit dee corpse."

In army ROTC we studied American military history, quotes from great men, and the theories of Carl von Clausewitz. We learned how to march, shoot, take apart and reassemble the M-1 rifle, identify insignia, name weapons, estimate distances, use "night vision" to make out targets in the dark, identify sounds such as amalgam being squeezed between fingers. We memorized the Code of Conduct that specified the only information we should reveal if captured. The code had been drawn up after the Korean War, in which an alarming number of American prisoners betrayed fellow captives or gave the enemy useful information about U.S. forces. We read in military manuals that in some situations disobeying an order or avoiding conflict was the right thing for an individual or a nation to do. The officers and sergeants teaching us insisted that our training might save our lives in combat and would be useful in any career. We were more concerned with avoiding embarrassment during weekly drills in Barton Hall, annual parades in downtown Ithaca, and ROTC summer camp following the junior year.

With the army's permission, I arrived a few days late at summer camp in June 1958, delayed by the rowing regatta at Syracuse. The euphoria of victory evaporated at Fort Bragg, North Carolina. Col. Sam J. Rasor, deputy camp commander, wrote to parents informing them that the famous 82nd Airborne Division was stationed there. "During the six weeks the cadets will be here," he went on, "they will receive training of a practical nature which cannot be given during the academic year. . . . The primary objective of this camp is the development of leadership, which will be beneficial to our nation in the event of an emergency, and to the individual even though he may be engaged in normal civilian pursuits." Although I could never decide how practical that training was for anything but surviving summer camp, I think the colonel was right.

The forty cadets in 3rd Platoon, C Company, came from colleges in New York, Ohio, Michigan, Tennessee, and North Carolina. We traded stories, duties, dirty jokes, compliments, insults, regional prejudices, ambitions. We competed for leadership positions or protective anonymity. We got through KP, guard detail, predawn reveille, calisthenics, C rations in the field, bayonetting sandbags, finicky inspections, fatuous demerits, boring classes, high humidity, low evaluations, red mud, evenings at the Officers' Club or seedy bars in Fayetteville. Bayonet drill was the greatest anachronism of all in this age of nuclear war, but military training clung to it as a means of discipline and an ancient ideal. I excelled at it.

We survived humiliations. In gas-mask drill, the instructor started us out, "By the numbers, take your right hand. . . ." He paused, glaring at a cadet who was using his left. "Your *other* right hand, cadet!" We cleaned latrines in the barracks and dug them in the field, a great leveler that alone justifies public service in a democracy. Nine times out of ten I'll bet I can tell whether a politician, lawyer, professor, business executive, or cultural critic lacks this experience and needs it badly.

We noticed that troops of the 82nd Airborne were not tall but tough; I remembered seeing their former wartime commander, Gen. Ridgway, in Paris. Units of the 82nd gave spirited demonstrations of arms and tactics against an enemy we assumed to be Soviet, in reassuring contrast to pictures we had seen the previous summer of the 101st Airborne confronting racist mobs in Little Rock. I informed family that I was so impressed I might join the airborne. "Go ahead if that's what you want," Mom replied, but "'airdrop' would seem to be a better word for it."

Since ROTC camp reduced my normal summer earnings, I wrote to my parents about meeting expenses: Cornell's annual tuition and fees would increase to $1,250; living in a rooming house would cost $8 per week. But my buddies and I sensed summer camp wasn't a transient game before our last year in college when our drill sergeant announced that U.S. Marines had landed in Lebanon after a coup by

Arab nationalists friendly to Nasser had ousted the pro-British government of Iraq. "We gotta keep Lebanon from goin' Communist," the sergeant explained. "Our boys are flyin' the American flag, and you just might soon be doin' your push-ups over there with 'em!"

As I wilted in the July sun, listening to the professional soldier's characteristic blend of pride and hazing, I recalled the story about an Illinois farmer who returned home wounded after the first battle of Bull Run in the Civil War and told his wife, "Them Rebs is shootin' real bullets." The image of doing push-ups and dodging bullets in Lebanon was more frightening than threats of nuclear retaliation: Khrushchev's against American and European intervention in Lebanon; Dulles's against China's renewed bombardment of Quemoy and Matsu a few weeks later. At Cornell, I had felt uneasy about supporting my country "right or wrong" and wondered how much benefit of doubt I might have to give my government in crises where my service was expected. At Fort Bragg, I did not question the government's right to send me to the Middle East. I began to envision combat.

During my senior year at Cornell, I commanded one of the four army battalions, a prestigious rank that required me to return the salutes of hundreds of bemused cadets as we converged on Barton Hall. I was elected to the ROTC honorary society called "Scabbard and Blade," and my selection as a Distinguished Military Student indicated "a definite aptitude for military service," according to a congratulatory letter from the commander of 1st Army. In spite of such acknowledgments, I fended off the army's appeal to consider a military career. Allen Pasco, a senior at City College of New York whom I had befriended at Fort Bragg, was hooked. Early in 1959 he wrote to me that he could hardly wait to receive his commission, attend Ranger-Airborne School, and buy dress blues, first steps toward his career. Allen would die in Vietnam, executed by the Vietcong, his hands bound behind his back.

I did not know what I would do after my two years of active duty. Majoring in history, I was discovering, limited my options. Friends in "practical" fields had warned me of this all along, and recruiters for industry shunned applicants from the liberal arts. The army was more inclusive and provided a chart to help you choose a branch based on your academic major. Perhaps I should try Military Intelligence or Judge Advocate General, I mused. But opposite history in the vertical column of majors, only three choices were marked in the horizontal list of branches — artillery, infantry, armor. All cannon fodder. A longtime expert with fireworks, I chose artillery.

Portents were in the air as I finished college. In January 1959 Fidel Castro and his guerrillas seized power in Cuba, and Ho Chi Minh formally sanctioned North Vietnamese support of rebellion against the South Vietnamese government of Ngo Dinh Diem. Mayor Willy Brandt urged West Berliners to be courageous in what would be Berlin's "year of decision," and President Eisenhower, in his state-of-the-union address, declared that the United States and other free nations had the solemn duty to defend the freedom of West Berlin. Prime Minister Harold Macmillan visited Moscow in February, demonstrating more interest in détente with the Soviet Union than West Germany and the United States thought prudent. In March the West German government objected to President de Gaulle's apparent acceptance of the Oder-Neisse line as the permanent border between (East) Germany and Poland. In April, the tenth anniversary of the signing of the North Atlantic Treaty, foreign ministers of the NATO nations expressed unanimous opposition to the Soviet Union's unilateral threat to change the status of Berlin.

A month later the foreign ministers of the wartime Big Four began talks in Geneva on the German question. They soon recessed to attend the funeral of John Foster Dulles, which I watched on my landlord's television with other students who lived in the rooming house on Stewart Avenue. All of us were moved by the loss of a statesman whose indomitable spirit finally yielded to cancer, and I repressed the irreverent ditty my fraternity brothers had sung about Dulles's prevention of war with "parties, banquets, and balls." Political cartoons that spring depicted a befuddled President Eisenhower. An ambitious Vice President Richard Nixon would soon travel to Moscow. Hungry Democrats were determined to prevent him from returning to the White House after Ike left it.

I was graduated in June. On the list of recipients of the bachelor of arts degree, my name appeared three lines above that of Thomas Ruggles Pynchon, Walnut Ave., East Norwich, New York; I did not notice his then. I left Ithaca with my B.A., my commission as second lieutenant in the U.S. Army Reserves, and two years of active duty to begin in the fall. The decade that schooled my generation was coming to an end. Most of the older generation of heroes from the Second World War, having contained their former Soviet ally during the Cold War, were retired or dead. Their successors, many of them younger than our parents, were now assuming charge and debating the missile gap. I would be in the army when the new generation of leaders settled that argument in the presidential election of 1960. I would be stationed in Germany, I hoped, when the victors decided whether to carry on Cold War business as usual or tap my idealism and change the course of history.

I was physically fit, ready to serve, eager to return to Europe, curious about Germany. For two years I would not have to depend on parental support or decide on a career. I could put off organizing the disparate ideas and influences I had encountered at Cornell. The loose ends of learning did not have to be tied together for single-minded graduate schools nor extracurricular enthusiasms concealed. Orders and field manuals would tell me what to do from day to day. Everything and nothing I had learned up to this divide prepared me for what lay on the other side.

In September 1959 Khrushchev became the first Soviet leader to visit the United States, and my family scattered. My parents moved to Princeton, where Dad would spend the academic year at the Institute for Advanced Study. John was in the middle of his six-month tour of active duty at Fort Leonard Wood, Missouri, having obtained a master's degree in philosophy at the University of Wisconsin and then completed his officer basic training at Fort Sill, Oklahoma. I saw him at Leonard Wood and picked up the family's secondary car, which he had been driving, on my way to Texas. My orders were to attend the Field Artillery Officer Basic Course at Fort Sill for three months and then stick around for further training on the Honest John missile. Earlier orders had directed me to report to Fort Bragg after Sill. Appalled by the prospect of spending nearly two years at Bragg, I had written to the army's career management office in the Pentagon requesting assignment to Europe because of my interest in European history and languages. Reacting quickly and rationally, the managers changed my orders, assuring me of European duty.

Not due at Fort Sill until the end of October, I stayed in Haskell with Miss Ada. Although her joints were more arthritic than ever, her mind and memory were still sharp. We traded yarns in the kitchen and out back in the shade of her pecan trees. She was curious about Cornell, crew, and the Cold War. She listened intently with the wide-eyed curiosity of a college freshman, her head slightly cocked to one side as if nothing were final. We talked about religion more than usual. She must have been the most open-minded devout Methodist in Texas. She respected my religious doubts, although she told me, ever so gently, that it wouldn't hurt me or anyone else to pray from time to time.

Haskell also brought this recent Ivy Leaguer down to earth. After an early breakfast with Miss Ada, I would hop into Uncle John's pickup for a day of chores out on the ranch. As we leaned against the pickup during a break one afternoon drinking Dr Peppers that he kept in a milk can full of ice water, he said, "Son, you may not be the best help I've ever had, but you sure are one of the best educated." When Uncle John did compliment me, which wasn't often, it pleased me as much as Dad's rare praise for my erudition. A distant cousin on the Fitzgerald side remembered Dad as "the smartest young feller we had here in Haskell, but he didn't have no sense at all. He tried teachin' me long words and I tried teachin' him some sense, but neither one of us got very far."

I would sometimes watch the sunset with Uncle Bud on the sagging front porch of the house he had built for his parents in the 1890s. He hadn't painted it since their deaths in the 1920s, and all but the two rooms he lived in had been taken over by spiders and mud daubers. Uncle Bud, almost ninety, a bachelor, and the sole surviving member of his class at Texas A&M, still cussed Truman for not giving Stalin a "good whuppin'." He warned me to "watch out for them Communists" when I went to Europe, jutting his lower jaw as he accented the second syllable of the repugnant word.

I sought more clues about my family's history, and my relatives readily obliged now that I was a college graduate about to join the army. Miss Ada said she and Mom had both been tomboys, she of homestead necessity, Mom by choice. She remembered how her mother, Katherine Johnston Fitzgerald, a diminutive North Carolinian she called "Big Mama," had used a silver hairbrush while sitting on a nail keg outside the dugout near Paint Creek. The brush and a matching hand mirror were the only mementos of the gentrified upbringing she had left behind when her family migrated to Texas after the Civil War.

Miss Ada rummaged about in her cedar chest, sorting through letters and old photographs of stern hierarchies gathered on front porches. Of all the men in her life, her father and husband had the most noticeable crow's feet, telling me where Mom's sense of humor came from. Miss Ada showed me the love poem that Wat Fitzgerald wrote Katherine when they were courting in South Texas in the 1870s. It began:

> Dear Kate, I do not swear and rave,
> Or sigh sweet things as many can;
> But though my lips ne'er play the slave,
> My heart will not disgrace the man.

There was this from a letter to Ada's husband, Bunk, in 1915 from his best friend, who had progressed from wrangler to an office job in Dallas:

> Bunk, I am in captivity. I get so sore on these four walls that it makes me long for the sight of a real man in a slouch hat and a squint at the worst stretch of bad lands that God ever laid out of doors. I would like to lay flat on my stomach and swig a drink from some of the red gulches on Turkey Paint. I would like to have some red beans with chili pepper and a few hot sour dough sinkers with ashes on them right out of the oven but I realize that it is a long way to Tipperary but it is a good deal further to such angel food as mentioned above.

Having majored in history, I welcomed such documentary confirmation of what I had grown up believing about the Old West. It was neither as crass nor as fictional as it sounded. Its style and nostalgia harked back to the Old South. On the other hand, I gathered from story, rumor, and silence that the Old West had another side that was neither lyrical nor heroic. In my family, that side was epitomized by alcoholism. I learned, not from Miss Ada though I don't recall how, that Bunk had been an alcoholic and had died of pneumonia brought on by a binge. Now I understood why the Rikes were so uneasy about Granddad Post's drinking and indeed Dad's. They had a skeleton in their own closet, and they believed, as did most God-fearing Texans, that alcoholism was the inevitable punishment for even sipping the stuff.

I kept quiet about my moderate thirst. Nor did I reveal the conclusions I was drawing from this shadowy side of my heritage. There must have been a narrow line in the Old West between health and illness, grit and depression. Bunk must have felt somehow inadequate, or he would not have hit the bottle. Could there have been much difference between his alcoholism and Mom's mental illness, even if heredity were not involved? The origins of her breakdown seemed less mysterious, the family's secrecy more understandable.

Mom's recovery in France also gained a bit of reality. I drove down to San Antonio to see Aunt Frances, in whom Mom now confided more than she did anyone else on either side of the family. Aunt Frances told me Mom had started writing a novel in the south of France but had burned the draft and all her notes before we arrived in Paris. The writing, my aunt supposed, must have helped Mom get a handle on her feelings of inferiority. Still, she said shaking her head in astonishment, your mama's recovery was a miracle, no other way to put it, and none of the Madison doctors could explain it when y'all got home so she stopped going to see them, but something good up there on that mountaintop got into her head and shut up those voices, maybe it was what she hoped she would find in Europe in 1939, I don't know, all I know is it couldn't have happened in Madison or Haskell.

Back in Haskell, Mom's mountaintop appeared in my anticipations of Europe. If that's all Aunt Frances knows about what happened there, I figured, I won't find any better clues in Haskell. Yet Haskell got me to thinking about the family's peculiar dependence on Europe. It was a long way from the plains of West Texas to the lights of Paris, but the journey was necessary and liberating in one way or another. Dad had started going to Europe in the 1920s, a bachelor set free to gratify his appetite for continental cuisine and medieval culture. Hitler had prevented Mom's first trip in 1939. When she finally made it over ten years later, trying to escape the apparently incurable oppression brought on by the war, something there freed her, as if in recompense for America's liberation of the Old World.

What did I need in Europe, and what sort of freedom awaited me there? Like Dad in his bachelor years, I needed time on my own for new experiences in old lands. Unlike him, I would see what military service abroad had to do with finding myself. But Europe meant more to me than that. Ever since the war, I had blamed Mom's illness on Nazi Germany; since Paris, I had credited her recovery to Europe, especially France. These inferences supported my Cold War agnosticism, my decision to major in European history at Cornell, and my request for military assignment to Germany. Perhaps living in Germany would give me a new start, not as dramatic as what France had given Mom, but a way to silence my own insecurities. Could I imagine the plot of Mom's novel and solve the mystery of her recovery over there? Perhaps not. But I could at least come closer to understanding her medical history by learning the parallel European story of collapse, liberation, and reconstruction, a sequence that contained moral lessons for me.

There were justifiable limits to what I could learn about family from relatives, whose silences no longer exasperated me. But I remained no less determined to fill gaps in my personal rebellion against secrecy, ignorance, and authorized versions of the truth. I was drawn to history because it enabled you to fill gaps, retell stories, and wonder how things might have been kept from falling apart. The more I learned, the more my family's recent history looked like European history.

At Miss Ada's, I thumbed through *The Armed Forces Officer*, a booklet issued to every new lieutenant as "a guide to the philosophy, ideals, and principles of leadership in the United States Armed Forces." I read that "nothing less than a gentleman is truly suited for [the officer's] set of responsibilities." Americans are "an altogether unregimented people, with a strong belief in the virtues of rugged individualism," and we rely on "voluntary group cooperation rather than absolute group loyalty." Except for ROTC and rowing, the virtues that had mattered most to me at Cornell were intellectual and cosmopolitan. The booklet gave fair warning that the army's ideals resembled those of my southern ancestry, not the northern university.

Officer Basic Course (OBC) 5 at the United States Army Artillery and Missile School (USAAMS) began on 2 November. Fort Sill was established in 1869 as Camp Wichita, a cavalry outpost in Indian country. Its old guardhouse, still standing, had held numerous chiefs, including Geronimo, who is buried in the Apache cemetery on the "east range" of the base. Renamed in 1870, Fort Sill became an artillery post after 1900. The School of Fire opened there in 1911. Its motto, *cedat fortuna peritis* (roughly translated, "skill is better than luck"), owed something to advances in technology and to the army's adoption of indirect fire following its effective use in the Russo-Japanese War of 1904–1905.

Two world wars and several name changes later, the USAAMS taught skills relating to an array of weapons. In 1959 these included the 105-mm and 155-mm howitzers; the 8-inch howitzer, which could fire a nuclear shell; and the enormous 280-mm atomic cannon. The army had also developed surface-to-surface missiles to carry nuclear warheads: Corporal and Redstone, each with liquid fuel; Honest John, with solid propellant. A few years earlier the Defense Department had blown the whistle on the army's development of intermediate-range ballistic missiles such as the Jupiter, signaling victory for the air force in the struggle over responsibility for this category. Undaunted, the army was working on plans for a 500-mile missile that would become operational in 1960 as the Pershing.

Classes on strategy and tactics taught us how the artillery had adjusted to nuclear warfare and would help transform the nuclear battlefield. We already knew that the defense of Western Europe began on German soil and that deploying tactical nuclear weapons in West Germany made up for the inadequacy of NATO's conventional forces. ROTC had taught us the new "pentomic" doctrine, in which self-sufficient battle groups (five to a division) would increase the army's mobility and, by dispersing forces, decrease vulnerability to the enemy's tactical nuclear weapons. At Fort Sill, we learned the defensive and offensive roles of pentomic artillery, nuclear and conventional: break up enemy forces as they concentrated for attack; create gaps in the enemy front that could be exploited by our own armor and mechanized infantry.

Or so it looked on paper. We did not seriously doubt that tactical nuclear weapons could destroy enemy units even though the army's own tests, which placed troops within a few miles of a small nuclear device in a western desert, had undermined that assumption. We did not dwell on how vague the line was between tactics and strategy in cases where tactical nuclear weapons were intended to escalate the conflict to massive retaliation; for example, early on against an overwhelming Soviet conventional attack. We did not probe the misgivings our instructors had about pentomic doctrine, that it was too biased toward nuclear warfare and impractical for conventional combat. The pentomic plan underlined the army's dilemma: the more the army tried to justify its importance under a president whose New Look strategy betrayed his old profession, the more it strayed from its own professional traditions, which did not descend from nuclear deterrence. Many of our instructors had served in the Second World War or Korea. They still called themselves "cannon cockers."

We studied map reading, organization, logistics, communications. Many of the best students in map reading — I was one of them — had done some backpacking or farming. We knew how to follow contour lines, determine altitude, and tell upstream from down. Business majors could look at an overhead chart and immediately grasp the geometry of lines connecting boxes that represented artillery units from battery on up the chain of command to battalion, group (at the division level), corps artillery. Anyone who liked logistics was suspected of being anal. In communications we played with field telephones, walkie-talkies, and wireless radios, none of these techniques having changed much since our childhood games during the Second World War.

In entertainment value and quality of instruction, none of these subjects came close to what Fort Sill taught best — gunnery. In the classroom and at spectacular demonstrations on the "west range" we learned the nomenclature and capabilities of field artillery weapons. We memorized types of shells, warheads, and fuses. We plotted range, trajectory, and powder charge. In "target analysis" we calculated the killing effect of air bursts, white phosphorous, and barrages. We fired 105-mm and 155-mm howitzers, once in a field training exercise during a norther that dropped several inches of snow and made us huddle around the warm orange burn of excess powder sacks that piled up behind the guns. Because I liked the noise, I did not use earplugs around the guns, and there has been a high-pitched ringing in my right ear ever since. We worked on the triangular relationship between the guns, the fire direction center, and the forward observer. The change to indirect fire before the First World War had increased the importance of the forward observer, who in effect aimed the guns by informing the battery how to adjust the direction of its fire. The battalion fire direction center, an innovation of the 1930s, coordinated reports from forward observers and gave orders to the firing batteries. Again, the fundamentals were handed down from the Second World War.

In that war and the Korean conflict forward observers were normally second lieutenants. Their life expectancy in combat, we were told, was only a few hours. We all knew the implicit message: second lieutenants in the artillery rarely survived bonehead mistakes.

My instructor in "observed fire," Capt. Richardson, loved his job and was good at it. "Nowhere else in America," he told us one day, "can you sit on your ass on a hilltop and have so much fun spending so much of the taxpayers' money in such a short time." We went on "shoots" equipped with binoculars, maps, map boards, rulers, pencils, erasers, colored pins for marking targets. We looked out on a barren rolling landscape dotted with the remains of vehicles or bunkers that served as targets. Our task was to identify targets assigned by Richardson (e.g., "two enemy tanks," "enemy reconnaissance patrol"), locate them on our maps by coordinates, and await Richardson's assignment of the "fire mission" to one of us. The chosen lieutenant would relay the target's location to the fire direction center and, after observing the two rounds fired by a training battery of 105-mm howitzers, try to bring subsequent rounds onto target by adjusting elevation (add or drop so many yards) and deflection (left or right so many yards). Unless you messed up badly, giving absurd coordinates or failing to see the first rounds, it was as much fun for us as for the captain, like being kids again.

Observed fire culminated in the "walking shoot," a legend in OBC. After each mission in this exercise, students had to discard a piece of equipment, from pencils at first to binoculars at the end. Walking between each mission also deprived us of a fixed reference point for gauging all targets. Richardson saved the last and toughest mission for me. We stood a couple of miles from where we had begun the shoot; all we had left by now was eyeball, memory, hunch, and luck. When the captain said, "Your mission, Lt. Post!" I saw him grin. The first rounds came in closer to the target than anyone had expected, and his grin disappeared. It reappeared when I violated a conservative rule about bracketing the target and creeping up or back to it. I ordered the guns to make one adjustment and "fire for effect," that is, fire final rounds to destroy the target. These rounds came in "short and long, left and right," a perfect result. Richardson said, "Lt. Post, you just stepped in shit and came out smelling like a rose." This was high praise for the army, leading me to believe I might have enough sense and luck to survive longer than a few hours in combat.

Beyond the basic course, I underwent training for assignment to Germany. In early December lieutenants on two years of active duty took a one-day "possible overseas replacement" (POR) course. We fired the carbine and ran through a "close combat course," crawling under barbed wire while machine gun bullets whizzed overhead and TNT charges threw dirt in our faces. In February 1960 I learned all about the Honest John: supersonic; "spin-stabilized" by small rockets mounted near the front of the main rocket motor; range up to about twenty-five miles; capable of firing fragmentation, chemical, and nuclear warheads; accuracy a problem because it was a free rocket, not a guided missile; fired from a launcher mounted on the chassis of a 5-ton wrecker; real wreckers used in the "mating" of the warhead and rocket motor; lacking in mobility because too heavy for air-lifting.

During the first two weeks of March, having obtained "secret" security clearance, I attended a course called "Honest John Nuclear Warhead Assembly." Classes were light on theory, heavy on practice. In fact, I think the army invented the "you don't have to be a nuclear physicist" school of thought. Using innocent mock-ups, I learned how to insert and twist a crank in a socket on the side of the warhead. If the green light flashed, the warhead was ready to deliver to the firing battery; if the red light shone, call in a "special weapons" expert. Easy. History majors could do it.

At Fort Sill, we quarried the English language for slang, nomenclature, and insult. We were "shave-tail" lieutenants, "cannon cockers" who used "barber poles" (aiming stakes) to "lay" our guns according to SOP. Our job in combat was to deliver "outgoing" mail; we would be SOL (shit-out-of-luck) if we received "incoming." We ate SOS for breakfast, looked forward to R&R, and noted how often things were FUBAR or SNAFU, remembering some of these acronyms from childhood.

The "naming of parts," as Henry Reed titled one of his poems about the Second World War, must have been devised by the gods of war to numb us mortals, like rum before battle at sea. Every weapon or piece of equipment had its biological chart with arrows naming parts. Among these was the "reverse shifter shaft lug latch plunger snap ring," the name more memorable than the function. Many instructors said "nucular," and one called turrets "turnts."

Our mistakes turned into anatomy lessons. "Don't stand there with your finger in your fanny and your mind in Tennessee." Or "Go to the bookstore and buy a five-by-eight inch piece of plexiglass. Take it to the post hospital and have the doctor insert it in your stomach so the next time you have your head up your ass you can see where you're going."

Bookworms, jocks, scientists, humanists, aggies, engineers, accountants, the lone black in our class, the Yalie grandson of Judge Learned Hand, the El Paso Mexican American, the rodeo broncrider from a town not far from Haskell, six-month and two-year and career men: no one was immune to chewing out. My turn came when I committed two sins before the major commanding the "Officer Student Battery." At our first inspection in ranks, I wore my belt the way I always had, with the tip pointing to my right. My left hand must have taken charge of belts back around the time I began throwing baseballs and shooting baskets southpaw while my right hand claimed handwriting and tennis. Nobody had censored this peculiar duo-dexterity until now.

"Christ, Post!" the major shouted, "you wear your belt like a girl! In this army you'll wear it like a man!"

A couple of weeks later he found an orange on my bureau during an inspection of our rooms in the bachelor officer quarters (BOQ) while we were in class. I reported to his office as ordered, not knowing why I had been summoned.

"Post, I'm tired of fooling with you!" he bellowed.

"Sir?"

"First your girl's belt, and now an orange on your dresser. You'll never make it in this army!"

After these reprimands, I believed that majors who doubted they would be promoted again were the most paranoid of officers. Nothing since then has changed my mind, but I still wear my belt his way.

After hours we shot pool on the base or in nearby Lawton, the jukeboxes playing a Marty Robbins song over and over again about a cowboy who is shot in an El Paso cantina. Many of the barmaids in Lawton were Germans who had married American soldiers over there and now appeared to be unhappy camp followers. Several lieutenants banded together for bull sessions in the BOQ, snack bar, Officers' Club or over Sunday breakfast of ham and eggs at the Golf Club on the outskirts of the base where we never played the game. Alone, I drove to Haskell for the weekend or hiked in the Wichita Mountains, whose wildlife refuge held buffalo and longhorn cattle, one of the breeds Granddad Post had trailed north in his youth through what was then called "Indian Territory."

I went to the post library, sometimes with Neil Rudenstine, a classmate in OBC 5, to listen to phonograph records of classical music. He had just finished three years at Oxford University on a Rhodes scholarship, and he loved Bach's suites for orchestra. Between records, Neil described his ideal of a liberal arts college. (It did not closely resemble Harvard, where he is now president, but he is trying to narrow the gap.) He introduced me to another recent Rhodes scholar, Richard Sylvester, a West Point graduate who was in an advanced officers' class.

Dick hosted impromptu evenings of conversation and music in his BOQ room. He and Neil had studied English at Oxford and knew Paris. They thought what Fort Sill needed most was a discussion group on Edmund Spenser called "The Faerie Queene Club." They turned down my recommendation to propose the idea to the major who was tired of fooling with me. Dick was one of the most humanizing forces at Fort Sill, as I told him ten years later when we became colleagues at the University of Texas and he explained why he had left the army for Slavic studies.

Cold War politics did not nag lieutenants at Fort Sill. After Khrushchev's visit to America in September, he and Eisenhower announced that negotiations on the status of Berlin should be reopened and that there was no longer any Soviet ultimatum on the subject. In December the leaders of the wartime Big Four agreed to convene an East-West summit in Paris the following May. Castro worried the CIA more than he did the army. The same can be said for Communist guerrillas in Laos and South Vietnam, the governments of which sent officers to Fort Sill for training, short men whom we saw in clusters at the post office but did not take as seriously as the taller NATO officers who mixed with Americans. No war threatened American interests, no emergency endangered our lives. Whatever our complaints about Fort Sill, many of us viewed active duty as a paid vacation and test of mettle before having to compete for jobs or graduate schools. We trained for nuclear warfare by learning lessons of conventional war. We played war the easy way, firing the taxpayers' money at harmless targets, taking the POR course without bloodshed. We prepared to fight Communism by enacting childhood fantasies of combatting Nazism.

In March I received orders to proceed to Fort Dix, New Jersey, for reassignment to Germany. I said good-bye to my relatives in

Haskell, where Uncle Bud repeated his warning about Com*mun*ists. Miss Ada gave me a pocket edition of the New Testament (King James version) and said she would pray for me. I drove to Madison to leave the car with John, who had resumed graduate study in philosophy at Wisconsin after his tour at Fort Leonard Wood. I took the train to Philadelphia and stayed with my parents for a few days in Princeton, where Barbos had recently passed an obedience course with higher marks than most of the pedigreed dogs.

Apparently unperturbed by the Cold War, Mom was thrilled that I would live in Europe for nearly two years, "just what you need." She hoped obeying orders was not too high a price to pay for the opportunity. The army would of course give me frequent leaves for revisiting Paris and just roaming around. "You could use a good old horse," she joked. I said I would buy a new Bug as soon as I could. She offered counsel she had learned from the French: don't be good, be wise. Dad fought back tears when he recalled saying good-bye to his parents in 1927 for his first trip to Europe. He assured me I would like Germany, as he had in the late 1920s, and he gave me the addresses of several German scholars whom he knew. "Fine universities in Germany," he said, "and be sure to visit Bamberg."

When they drove me to Fort Dix for my departure, I felt the butterflies of adventure, not dread. College and Fort Sill were behind me, an odyssey ahead. I was neither apprentice nor master. Although duty-bound, I felt astonishingly free. I was startled to hear both the idea and the uneasiness in Dad's voice when he said, "I hope there won't be war while you're in Germany."

*Cowboys before a drive, Haskell County, Texas, 1886.*
*Granddad Post is on far left; Uncle Tom Ballard is sixth from the left.*

*My grandmother, Miss Ada (Ada Fitzgerald*
*Rike) Haskell, 1944. Photo: Haskell Schools.*

*My parents, ca. 1938.*

*With Mom, 1942.*

*My mother, 1950.*

*#10, rue St-Julien-le-Pauvre, Paris, 1951.*

*With Mom and John (right), and guide, Paris, 1952.*

*The American Community School, Paris/Boulogne, 1952. Photo: ACS.*

*Ninth grade, American Community School, 1952.*
*I am standing fourth from the left. Photo:* ACS.

*Audience with Pope Pius XII, Vatican, April 1952.*
*Gen. Shepherd is to the pope's right; I am in the light jacket on the far right.*
*Photo: Vatican.*

*Mom and Dad,*
*Madison, 1954.*

*Dad and Barbos,*
*Madison, 1954.*

*With John (right) and our cousin John Sam Rike, Haskell, ca. 1954.*

*Madison West High baseball team, 1954.*
*I am standing second from the left. Photo: West High School.*

*Rehearsing for*
The Fortune Teller, *Madison, 1955.*
*Photo: West High School.*

*Phi Sigma Kappa, Cornell, 1957.*
*I am in the light jacket, back row. Photo: the* Cornellian.

*Cornell's* JV *champions, 1958. Photo: Cornell Athletic Department.*

*3rd Platoon, C Company,* ROTC *summer camp, Fort Bragg, North Carolina, 1958. I am the tallest person in the back row; Bo Roberson is fourth from the left in the back row; Allen Pasco is third from the right in the third row. Photo: Fort Bragg.*

*On Uncle John's ranch near Haskell, 1959.*

*Gen. and Frau Flörke with Antje, Giessen, 1961.*

*On stand-by alert, Grafenwöhr, 20 August 1961. Photo: Donald Kroeber.*

*In New York, about to board the SS* United States *for Oxford,
late September 1961. Photo: United States Lines.*

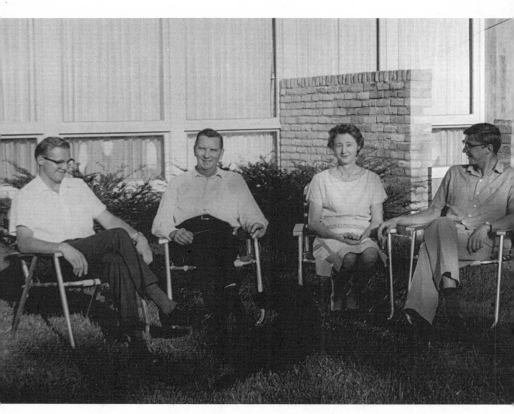

*The Posts, Madison, August 1963, with Barbos lying in the shade.*

## CHAPTER 5

*Honest Johns and Germans*

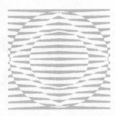 The flight from McGuire Air Force Base to Frankfurt took nineteen hours, with stops for refueling at Harmon Air Force Base in Newfoundland and at Prestwick, Scotland. Passengers sat facing to the rear of the propeller-driven Lockheed Constellation, a precaution in case of crash landing. Three years of rowing had accustomed me to backing forward.

I thought ahead to serving in Germany. The Cold War would be more challenging over there than on the home front, not the "good war" my generation had missed but our best opportunity to prove ourselves in uniform. In Germany I could reaffirm the European bases of my Cold War agnosticism: NATO was a partnership, Americans could be parochial and overbearing, social democracy was worth a serious try. Germany would give me a base for revisiting Paris and exploring Western Europe, not only a confidence-building grand tour but also a useful one if I decided to become a European historian. I could improve upon the year of German I had taken at Cornell. I would be at the source of music and literature I had discovered in college: Beethoven's piano concertos, Wagner's *Ring*, the novels of Thomas Mann and Erich Maria Remarque. By living with my old wartime enemy, I would confront enigmas that were both personal and historical. I could buy my own Bug.

Walt Whitman lamented that the "interior history" of the Civil War would never be written, meaning the ordinary stories of soldiers rather than the momentous accounts of generals and politicians. The next three chapters tell an interior history of a brief period in a forty-year conflict that Whitman would probably not call a war. These eighteen months witnessed dramatic political change in the United States and the last serious European confrontation of the Cold War. But lieutenants in Germany used small maps and seldom weighed grand strategy. I was preoccupied with day-to-day urgencies, preparing for inspections, delivering vehicles to the motor pool for maintenance, camouflaging positions on maneuvers. I marched to army manuals, military folklore, deadlines, and idiosyncratic commanders, not to the decisions of the National Security Council. This peaceful routine was broken only once, when the Berlin crisis escalated after the Vienna summit of June 1961 and put my battalion on unprecedented stand-by alert in August.

Returning to Germany in February 1996 helped me remember the ancient smells of the Cold War. I recalled how enthusiastically many lieutenants of my generation greeted the presidency of John F. Kennedy. We were proud of American strength in Europe and ready to experiment with his strategy of "flexible response." I counted on returning to civilian life as the "New Frontier" took shape at home, while some of my colleagues planned to further their military careers by going wherever the action was likely to be. Seeing Germany again also reminded me of the essentially moral questions that had prompted me to serve there. These connect my childhood with my career, and they reside on every floor where my memory wants to stop for something it knows is important.

During the Second World War, boys in Madison were just as eager to play Rommel as Patton and just as likely to fly a Messerschmitt as a Mustang in mock combat. We mocked Hitler, the goose step, and anything else we thought silly about the Germans, although we coveted German insignia in neighborhood bartering. I blamed Germany for starting the war, committing atrocities, and attacking my family. I knew our side was right and would win. There was no German question in my mind, no thought of an ambivalent German identity. Germans liked violence, started wars, murdered Jews, wounded my mother, and deserved to be punished for a long time. These convictions had survived the family's reunion in Paris in 1951 but had diminished during the fifties as I found bullies on the home front and West Germany joined the Atlantic Alliance.

My certainty about the German character disintegrated at Cornell because of Professor Mommsen. He represented the best of German culture. He was my ideal of the good German, his humanism the antithesis of brutality and collaboration with the devil. But living in America had not silenced the voices that hounded him. Was suicide the ultimate act of resistance for the good German? What sort of German would I have been under Nazism? I held this private conversation throughout my time in Germany. The longer I stayed, the more important Mommsen became and the more central Germany was to solving my riddle.

I landed at Rhein-Main Terminal in Frankfurt on 24 March, my mother's forty-ninth birthday. On the same day in Paris, Khrushchev warned the French to beware of West German "militarists" who were growing insolent. The United States formally rejected the Soviet claim that Berlin was a part of East Germany and produced Allied documents from 1944 declaring that postwar Berlin would be jointly occupied as an area separate from the other zones of occupation. Secretary of Defense Thomas S. Gates Jr. reviewed troops at the headquarters of U.S. Army Europe (USAREUR) at Campbell Barracks in Heidelberg on his tour of military installations in Europe. Campbell Barracks had been constructed in 1937 as the Grossdeutschland-Kaserne to accommodate the Wehrmacht's 110th Infantry Regiment. The carved swastikas beneath the two stone eagles flanking the front gate were — and are still — covered by the USAREUR shield that preserved the flaming sword of liberation from the wartime insignia of the Supreme Headquarters Allied Expeditionary Force (SHAEF).

I stowed my gear at the Rhein-Main base's "transient" BOQ and took a U.S. forces bus into Frankfurt for dinner. I began looking for traces of war, but most of the damage had been covered over by Germany's economic recovery. At a restaurant in the *Stadtmitte* (city center), I ordered Wiener schnitzel, cucumber salad, roasted potatoes, and Dortmunder Union beer. I chatted with the waiter, and my German worked! I was in high spirits all the way back to the BOQ, already having stories to tell my family.

I had orders to report next day to the 3rd Missile Battalion, 79th Artillery — 3/79 in army shorthand. A lieutenant from the 3/79 drove me to Giessen, about forty miles north of Frankfurt. We skirted the eastern edge of the Taunus Mountains, where Roman legions had constructed fortifications along the "limes," their northern line of defense between the Rhine and Danube Rivers. We passed Bad Nauheim, where as a boy Franklin D. Roosevelt had taken German lessons and Elvis Presley had just completed his military service. We skirted Butzbach, where an American army engineer, excavating for new barracks in the late 1940s, found Roman artifacts bearing numbers for cohort and legion identical to those of the American battalion and regiment that would now occupy the area. The country opened out into rich, broad valleys bordered by low ridges and roundtop hills with thick forests. On one of these hills, east of the autobahn, I saw the twin-towered ruins of Münzenberg castle, one of several fortresses with which Frederick Barbarossa, elected king of Germania in 1152 at Frankfurt, held the Wetterau depression between the Taunus and the Vogelsberg range to the northeast. In the fields, tractors or oxen pulled plows or "honey wagons" of liquified fertilizer, putrid beyond even a midwesterner's experience.

Giessen hugs the left bank of the Lahn River about twenty miles downstream from the picturesque medieval town of Marburg. Other towns with venerable castles, churches, and half-timbered houses lie downstream from Giessen all the way to the Rhine, their names evoking Goethe and Zeiss cameras (Wetzlar), Bismarck (Bad Ems), William of Orange and the House of Nassau (Weilburg and Nassau), and a German American settlement in central Texas (Braunfels). Within a few miles of Giessen are the ruins of Gleiberg and Vetzberg castles, Schiffenberg and Arnsburg abbeys.

Flouting these enchanting surroundings, Giessen was a drab small city of little historical or architectural interest even before the Second World War. Most of its old houses were demolished in December 1944 during two straight days of Allied bombing raids that destroyed two-thirds of the city. By the time of my arrival in early 1960, Giessen had rebuilt most of the downtown area in utilitarian concrete and glass to serve a citizenry of about 55,000. This number did not include the approximately 10,000 American personnel and dependents stationed there nor the hundreds of "expellees" from East Germany who lived in makeshift shacks, some of these along the northern side of Rödgenerstrasse as you drove northeast from the city center to the U.S. Army Quartermaster Supply Center and the 3/79 Artillery.

I did not share the conservative preferences of the city's major newspaper, the *Giessener Freie Presse*. Its editorial policy patronized Chancellor Konrad Adenauer and his ruling party, the Christian Democratic Union (CDU), and its even more conservative Bavarian affiliate, the Christian Social Union (CSU). The *Freie Presse* published articles on the injustice and impermanence of Germany's postwar borders with Poland and Czechoslovakia. It held that prewar Germany had been wrongfully divided into three parts. Thus, "Mitteldeutschland" (Middle Germany) referred to the German Democratic Republic, which the Federal Republic did not recognize as a sovereign state, and the territories lost to Poland after the war constituted the eastern third of Germany.

I had no doubt that Adenauer's government deserved much of the credit for Germany's recovery. His economics minister, Ludwig Erhard, prescribed government intervention to insure the welfare of society as a whole while letting market mechanisms determine prices and wages. This policy, combined with Marshall Plan aid, hard work, and the influx of over three million East German refugees to expand the labor force, had produced the famous "economic miracle" of the 1950s. In Giessen I saw the boom in new automobiles, highways, houses, radio-phonographs, and clothing stores.

When I had time to think about German politics, however, I rooted for the Social Democratic Party (SPD). Whereas some officials in Adenauer's government had been Nazi bureaucrats, the SPD had voted against the Enabling Act of March 1933 that gave Hitler dictatorial power and had gone underground to resist Nazism. I saw parallels between the SPD, the anti-Pétain demonstration outside Notre Dame in October 1951, Camus's philosophy of resistance and change. In 1959–1960 reformers like Herbert Wehner and Willy Brandt moved the party away from Marxist rhetoric and toward the political center, describing democratic socialism in pluralistic terms and pledging support for rearmament and NATO. The SPD's new menu agreed with my own appetite for liberal social reform, grass-roots democracy, NATO partnership, and a younger generation of leaders on both sides of the Atlantic.

Willy Brandt, the SPD's emerging star and mayor of West Berlin, reminded me of Senator John F. Kennedy, for whom I cast my absentee ballot in the Wisconsin presidential primary of early April, when Kennedy defeated Senator Hubert Humphrey in what proved to be a pivotal contest for the nomination. Like Kennedy, Brandt looked energetic and handsome in his forties, defied Soviet hegemony, and summoned the nation's youth to advance freedom. Organizing rallies of Berliners, speaking in cities and towns around West Germany, Brandt did not attract the older generation of conservatives. Nor did he try to win over countrymen of the kind who accused him of treason for fleeing Germany and living in Norway and Sweden during the Nazi period, or scrawled anti-Semitic slogans in Cologne and elsewhere during a virulent outburst in the winter of 1959–1960, or demanded the return of Germany's "lost territories." Aiming at voters between the extremes, Brandt used his party's new program to reach across lines of party and class more optimistically and more effectively than had any of its previous leaders.

I attended Brandt's speech at the Volkshalle in Giessen on 21 October, having recently voted in absentia for Kennedy against Nixon in my first chance to elect a president. Brandt had an enthusiastic audience, his party the largest in the city. Party officials distributed a leaflet entitled "Go with the Times, Go with the SPD." It contained a short biography of the mayor and a statement of his principles. On the cover was a photograph of Brandt taken in February 1959 at a dinner in Springfield, Illinois, commemorating Abraham Lincoln. Behind Brandt was a large banner quoting Lincoln, "A house divided against itself cannot stand." In his statement, Brandt affirmed that democracy was neither guaranteed by a constitution nor handed over like an invoice; it required incessant care and striving. In his speech, he asked Germans to stand united against Communism and declared that German freedom and democracy needed "the energies of the younger generation."

When I returned to Giessen in February 1996, Brandt was dead, and Helmut Kohl had been chancellor nearly as long as Adenauer held the office. The Social Democratic governments of Brandt and Helmut Schmidt had come and gone. Their innovative *Ostpolitik* (eastern policy), which improved relations with East Germany and the other Warsaw Pact countries, earning Brandt the Nobel Peace Prize, had been overshadowed by Kohl's adroit accomplishment of German reunification following the collapse of the Iron Curtain. Germany's younger generation was struggling to find work in a country where economic growth had stagnated and the rate of unemployment stood at a postwar high of over 10 percent. The German government was trying to send recent immigrants back home. I saw few optimistic faces, no quotes from Lincoln.

Only a handful of American troops remained in Giessen, none of them in combat units. Most of the remnants of American forces in Germany had been sent to Bosnia, where they cooperated with Russians. I took a long walk past buildings once full of Americans: Pendleton Barracks, Giessen Post Headquarters, Quartermaster Supply Center, and, across Rödgenerstrasse from the supply center, the BOQs and Officers' Club. Most of these areas were small ghost towns, their silence accented by a light snowfall. The BOQs and Officers' Club, built by the Luftwaffe in the 1930s and crowded in 1960, were almost empty now. No one checked my identification when I entered the gate to the supply center on my way to the area once occupied by the 3/79 Artillery. A military police van, the only vehicle I saw all afternoon, approached as I lingered near the bunker where we had stored nuclear warheads for our Honest Johns. Unperturbed by my civilian clothes, briefcase, and camera, the driver waved to me as he passed. A sign next to the empty parking lot outside the building that had housed most of the men in my battalion said "Exceptional Family Member Service."

Later, I stood outside the old battalion headquarters. The low winter sun appeared briefly, revealing a bird's tiny tracks in the snow where thousands of boots had trod for over half a century. The small, two-story structure had been built in the 1920s as the air terminal for Giessen, served by Lufthansa. In the mid-1930s the Luftwaffe took over the well-drained grass airfield, and the terminal became headquarters for, in succession, a flight training school, Bomber Squadron 155 from 1938 through the campaign against France in 1940, and a school for airplane mechanics. In June 1945 the Americans incorporated building and field in a large supply depot, which soon became the main supply center for U.S. troops in Europe.

The 3/79 Artillery arrived in 1958. Two other American artillery battalions were stationed in Giessen: 3/82 (280-mm gun); 2/92 (8-inch howitzer, self-propelled). All three were part of 36th Artillery Group (headquarters in Babenhausen, southeast of Frankfurt), one of three groups in v Corps Artillery. With headquarters in the I. G. Farben building in Frankfurt, v Corps was proud of its motto, "It will be done," and of its combat record in both world wars: in the first, the St. Mihiel and Meuse-Argonne offensives; in the second, Omaha Beach, liberation of Paris, Battle of the Bulge, Rhineland, Lahn valley, link-up with the Red Army on the Elbe River, liberation of Pilsen in Czechoslovakia. v Corps and vii Corps to its south reported to 7th Army (headquarters outside of Stuttgart), 7th Army to USAREUR (Heidelberg). The commander of USAREUR also commanded NATO's Central Army Group, consisting of 7th Army, the French 1st Army, and German units assigned to each. He reported to the commander of Allied land forces, Central Europe (headquarters in Fontainebleau, France). The German iii Korps, based in Koblenz, had responsibility for the sector to the north of v Corps; north of iii Korps were British forces around Paderborn. In the event of war, iii Korps would take orders from 7th Army, and 36th Artillery Group would probably support iii Korps.

The 3rd Armored Division covered v Corps's northernmost sector, stretching from near Giessen to the east and southeast. The corps constantly patrolled the inter-German border with units from the 14th Armored Cavalry Regiment based in Fulda. A small town east of the Vogelsberg Mountains, Fulda had given its name to an eighth-century Benedictine abbey containing the remains of Saint Boniface and to a historic route of invasion from the north and east. Soon after arriving in Giessen, I heard the term "Fulda Gap." Gap was a misnomer. It referred to an area of valleys between middling massifs, extending northeast from Frankfurt toward Kassel, Bad Hersfeld, and Fulda. NATO commanders expected the Soviets to pour armor through this gap early in any land invasion of West Germany, their objective to split NATO's forces and drive v Corps across the Rhine River. The Red Army would have rolled past Frederick Barbarossa's strongpoints in the Wetterau — including Gelnhausen, where Lt. Colin Powell commanded an infantry platoon in 1960 — and crossed the Roman "limes" east of the Taunus Mountains.

At staff meetings in battalion headquarters, we did not examine the discordant elements of NATO strategy. Planners in Washington, Paris, and Heidelberg might have viewed us as a "shield" that slowed the Soviet advance while NATO forces fell back to the natural defensive barrier of the Rhine, NATO's strategy in the early fifties, still heard occasionally in spite of its implication that West German territory would be lost if deterrence failed. Or we might have been considered part of the "trip wire" of conventional and nuclear forces that, according to New Look doctrine after 1953, would deter the Soviets for fear of escalation into massive retaliation by the United States. Finally, planners might have seen us in the "firebreak" composed of reinforced conventional forces that could counter "less-than-ultimate threats" without recourse to tactical nuclear weapons. NATO had added this corollary to New Look strategy in 1957. The addition complemented the Federal Republic's aim of contributing troops to a solid "forward defense" of conventional NATO forces close to the inter-German border, narrowing the Warsaw Pact's margin of superiority in conventional weapons along that front. The corollary and German planning antedated the emphasis on conventional warfare in the doctrine of flexible response, which replaced the New Look when Kennedy became president.

My battalion's combat mission was to help plug the Fulda Gap very close to the inter-German border, which formed the latest contour of Europe's ancient line between Roman civilization and Germanic tribes, or between Teutons and Slavs. Up close, the border was not an iron curtain. It had a mysterious aura about it, as if marking a malevolent forest in a Grimm's fairy tale. One day the battalion commander, Lt. Col. Phillips, led a number of officers north on the autobahn toward Kassel to inspect the top secret position assigned to us in case of a "general alert order." From there we would have launched nuclear missiles against concentrations of Soviet armor in the Fulda Gap. On the way, we passed a large sign that said, "Germany divided in three parts? Never!" In order not to call attention to ourselves, we drove in private automobiles and wore civilian clothes, both as unmistakably American as our short hair. When we reached our alert position, off a minor road about ten miles from East Germany, we stood around pretending to look at wildflowers.

We knew only the western tip of Eurasia. The forests looked darker to the east and seemed to crowd in on us. We could only guess the size of the hordes beyond them. According to London's infant

Institute for Strategic Studies, the Soviets had 20 combat divisions in East Germany, of which 10 were armored and the rest mechanized, with 6,000 tanks in all. The institute estimated that the Soviet army had a total of 35,000 tanks, that it could send an additional 135 divisions to Europe within thirty days after mobilization, that the other Warsaw Pact nations had 60 divisions under arms, of which about 5 were East German. For the defense of West Germany, NATO had 21 combat divisions, including 5 American (2 armored) and nearly 8 West German (2 armored) of the Bundeswehr's goal of 12.

In a conventional conflict between the forces currently stationed in the two Germanys, NATO had a reasonable chance of delaying a Soviet invasion. But NATO and American units in Germany were haunted by visions of an overpowering assault by modern Huns — Soviet forces that were already far superior in armor and could be reinforced by more divisions in thirty days than NATO could prepare in a year. Acknowledging what we would probably do if unable to stop a Soviet attack, the battalion convoyed south in April to practice crossing the Rhine going west. We crossed upstream from Mainz and a stone's throw from Oppenheim, where Patton's 3rd Army had crossed in the other direction in March 1945. In our case, boats were provided by a German engineer battalion.

The shield strategy, though not discussed by the 3/79 as I recall, was still very much alive in USAREUR's operational planning. USAREUR's annual history for 1960, portions of which have been declassified, contains a summary of "OPLAN 303" (August 1960) for a "general war situation wherein the NATO headquarters either failed to assume operational command or were materially delayed in so doing." In Phases I and II, D day to D+15 and D+16 to D+30, U.S. forces, "using nuclear weapons, would conduct a mobile defense east of the Rhine River with a view to achieving maximum delay as far east as possible." So far, when I read this in 1996, plans sounded familiar. I was shocked when I read on. If the Soviets "achieved a major breakthrough of the Rhine River defense line" during Phase II, the commander of USAREUR might order the execution of "OPLAN 304" for a "delaying defense and phased withdrawal across France to a final defense line based on the Pyrenees Mountains." I had been unaware of this link between the Rhine and the Pyrenees in 1960; if my battalion commander knew of it, he did not tell his lieutenants.

Nor was "staff call" a seminar on international politics. We did not study the division of Germany nor the volatility of Berlin in Cold War politics. Shortly after I joined the 3/79, Khrushchev called it "Hitlerite" for Adenauer to have declared, during a visit to the Vatican in January, that West Germany had a divine mission to protect the West against the Communist influence from the East. In April Western foreign ministers agreed on a plan for the May Paris summit: they would propose the phased reunification of Berlin and the two Germanys. Khrushchev renewed his threat to sign a separate peace treaty with East Germany that would end the Western powers' rights of access to Berlin. No one anticipated the tumult that began on 5 May with the Soviet leader's sensational announcement that the Soviets had downed an American spy aircraft (U-2) over Soviet soil.

For the next two weeks I followed the repercussions in *Stars and Stripes*, the major source of news for American forces in Europe. Things did not look good for our side. Khrushchev dismissed every tentative American admission of culpability with strong evidence and brazen threats. He viewed violations of Soviet air space as acts of aggression and warned that the Soviet Union would retaliate immediately against such acts with atomic bombs. The State Department fought back by stating that the Paris summit was being jeopardized not by the U-2 flights but by the Soviet reaction. When leaders convened in Paris on Monday the 16th, Khrushchev surprised them by calling upon God as his witness for having clean hands and a clear soul. The next day he canceled tentative plans for Eisenhower to visit the Soviet Union, demanded an American apology for the U-2 flights, and insisted that the summit be postponed for six to eight months. The summit collapsed on the 17th, infuriating Eisenhower and giving Khrushchev what even America's European friends viewed as a propaganda coup. Khrushchev rubbed it in. He called Ike a "fishy friend" for being hospitable in America the previous September in spite of knowing about the U-2 flights, and he expressed sympathy for Charles de Gaulle's having a "thief" as an ally. He asked the world press to "pull the ears of American imperialism." He warned West Germany that the Soviet Union had buried German militarists at Stalingrad and would teach that sort "not to start again."

On the first day of the summit, the Defense Department staged what it called a "communications readiness alert." Word leaked out and alarmed some American civilians. In Denver a family hid in their basement after hearing a local radio station, at the request of Lowery Air Force Base, notify fighter pilots to scramble. At an American air force base in eastern France, dependents prepared to drive to the Atlantic coast for evacuation in case the "non-combatant evacuation order" went into effect. USAREUR quietly implemented a state of "military vigilance." The day after the summit fell apart, Gen. Nathan Twining, chairman of the Joint Chiefs of Staff, assured a Senate committee that the alert had been successful and that U.S. forces were ready for any emergency. Upon returning from Paris, Secretary Gates told the press that the alert had been his idea and expressed surprise that anyone would question its wisdom and timing. The episode caused the Joint Chiefs to instruct American forces not to use the word "alert" for readiness tests short of actual alerts. I remember nothing more than a rise in the 3/79's collective blood pressure during the U-2/summit affair, the only such alert for us in 1960. We continued training as usual, our peacetime mission always to be ready for aggression from the east.

In college I would have criticized my government for using spy aircraft without congressional approval, bungling after the U-2 was downed, and increasing the chances of war. I would have argued that, if we did not want to repeat Munich, Paris was no improvement. So soon after arriving in Germany, however, my agnostic sensibilities were subdued. Although embarrassed by my government's blunder, I resented Khrushchev for shaming us and accepted spying on the Soviet Union as a strategic necessity. I was too busy learning my military job to be very critical politically. Doing things "by the numbers," even handling nuclear warheads, gave me tunnel vision. In the U-2 confrontation, I was focusing on details, not universals.

Many of these details came back while I walked around the battalion's former precinct on thin snowfall in 1996. Our workweek was officially forty-four hours but was much longer in fact. The battalion consisted of a Headquarters & Service (H&S) Battery and a Firing Battery. The battery commanders reported to the battalion commander, as did the officers heading the four staff sections — personnel (S-1), intelligence (S-2), operations (S-3), and supply (S-4). I was assistant leader of the Assembly & Transport (A&T) Platoon, part of H&S Battery.

The battery commander, Capt. Haggerty, tried to make the best of one of the worst jobs in the battalion, for H&S was a catchall involving thankless duties, most of the battalion's misfits, and no glory. Haggerty liked to clasp his hands behind his head and lean back in his swivel chair, talking around his cigar as he moved it from side to side in his mouth and trying to appear intrepid. If anyone wasted time attempting to do something flawlessly, Haggerty would snap, "Get the lead out. Jesus Christ was the last and only perfect person, and who the hell do you think you are?" Christ only knows, I would reply to myself when I was the target.

The A&T Platoon stored, transported, and "mated" the warheads and rocket motors for the Honest John missile. We carried disassembled warheads and motors on long-wheelbase 5-ton trucks. These pulled trailers onto which wreckers transferred the warheads and motors for assembly. Combat readiness regulations from 7th Army required us always to have one warhead and rocket "in a mated configuration." Jokes about intercourse got old.

We performed our tasks down near the edge of the old German airfield, sometimes coordinating with the Firing Battery to practice off-loading to their rocket launchers. From our small squad building, we looked west: across the large paved area where we parked trucks and trained, over the fenced security zone that contained the bunker holding the warheads, across the airfield and the Lahn valley to the hilltop ruins of Vetzberg and Gleiberg castles. In February 1996 the squad building was gone, the barbed wire and guard tower secured nothing, the bunker's shoulders slumped uselessly. Sheep grazed where Luftwaffe planes once taxied, where I held late afternoon soccer games during a precious few days when I commanded the platoon and improved its morale by assigning clear tasks and reasonable deadlines.

Our platoon sergeant, a weathered chain-smoker from Oklahoma named Wilkerson, had fought under Gen. Patton in the last year of the war. Many of Wilkerson's stories were at the expense of lieutenants, such as Patton's yelling into the field telephone, "Send me more lieutenants. They're going like hotcakes!" He told this one at least ten times during our exercise crossing the Rhine. When Wilkerson learned about my Texas heritage, he waited until the men were around for a smoke break before telling me the difference between an Oklahoman and a son-of-a-bitch is the Red River. Wilkerson and other members of the platoon taught me more military slang: boondocks, clicks (kilometers), five-bell flap, skoshi (small amount, from

Japan), barracks lawyer (soldier who habitually cites regulations), short-timer, when the balloon goes up (when war is declared), idiot-proof job (something even an ROTC lieutenant could do). As any good NCO must with lieutenants who are wet behind the ears, Wilkerson taught me a lot about our trade: human nature, vehicle maintenance, and the Honest John, including the trick of slapping the side of the nuclear warhead if the red light went on during the crank test. If the light then changed to green, you did not have to waste time calling someone in "special weapons"; "spooky weapons," we said. He was a fine sergeant.

The battalion's special weapons section, headed by Lt. Newman, organized instruction on maintaining the warheads and on the security of classified materials. Sometimes experts from ordnance units in V Corps or 7th Army would come to Giessen to brief us, such as when the 3/79 "converted" to a new warhead. I remember artifacts and rituals: test panel lights, small metal rings with bright cloth loops attached, "fire plugs," the meticulous keeping of logbooks that charted the health of each warhead. Once Newman asked me to take a sick warhead to an ordnance repair center near Kaiserslautern. My driver and I made the trip without mishap. While waiting for ordnance to remedy the problem, I wandered into the village church. Wearing fatigues and combat boots, I felt suddenly like a contrapuntal intruder when I read that the organ had been one of Bach's favorites.

The A&T Platoon frequently joined the rest of the battalion for classes in motor maintenance, protection against chemical-bacteriological-radiological (CBR) warfare, cold-weather operations, camouflage, and any other subject that higher headquarters deemed necessary. I taught some of these classes, assisted by experts and "teaching aids." The army had stringent rules to insure effective teaching, such as how to stand, hold a pointer, flip charts, use the appropriate field manual, follow an outline, ask questions, and so on. I violated all of these when I held a class for the enlisted men in the battalion on the Code of Conduct.

After the standard greetings, "Good morning, gentlemen!," "Good morning, sir!," the last moment in army classes when nearly everyone is awake, I departed from the materials provided by S-3. I had two reasons for doing so. First, many of the men knew that a captain in the battalion had been one of the very few prisoners of war in Korea to try repeatedly to escape. He was successful on his third or fourth attempt but had paid a fearful psychological price for his courage, and this in turn cost him promotions at the normal pace. I thought his example merited more than a routine class. Second, here was my first chance in the army to apply what I knew about history and philosophy.

Quoting from my copy of *The Armed Forces Officer*, I reviewed the faulty assumption that American soldiers would, if captured, show "collected [*sic*] courage, unified resistance, and inspired helpfulness one to the other." During the Korean War, according to the booklet, this axiom had "proved wrong, or rather, outdated by the Communist enemy who exploited the deprived and lonely state of the prisoner to serve his own ends." The enemy's methods had included "general inhumanity and seductive interrogations" and had prevented any means the prisoners might use to organize themselves for self-support and resistance. The Code of Conduct was designed to remove any doubt "about where the line of duty begins and terminates." Among its six principles, which had to be memorized, was this: "I will keep faith with my fellow prisoners. I will give no information or take part in any action which might be harmful to my comrades."

I had been trying for years to understand what had happened to American idealism since the Second World War, when courage, resistance, and solidarity enabled us to defeat Nazism. Though I did not say so in this class, I believed collective loyalty had been undermined by McCarthy and the language of treason. I talked about Russian and American history, Marxism, Communism, the Bill of Rights, and ethics. I left the lectern and sat down on the edge of the stage. Both gesture and word violated orthodoxies of military instruction and American Cold War dogma. I doubt that I appeared un-American to the men, but I must have reached their natural reserves of skeptical inquiry. Fewer men than usual for a battalion class fell asleep. More than usual asked questions and participated in the discussion that followed my remarks. Several men stayed around to talk after class, a rarity that delighted me. An officer from s-3 came in about halfway through the class in his capacity as supervisor of battalion education. Afterward, as he and I walked to the mess hall together for lunch, I asked him excitedly what he thought of the class. "Well, lieutenant," he replied, "that's one of the worst classes

I have seen in my army experience." That remark, more than any other humiliation or hassle, convinced me I did not belong in the army for more than two years.

Inspections and visits from higher headquarters unnerved officers more than enlisted men. Dreaded acronyms like ORI, TPI, AGI, and CMI meant teams of inspectors invading the battalion to grade operational readiness, technical skills, and maintenance, their eyes peeled for infractions, clipboards in hand. Commanders from 36th Artillery Group, V Corps Artillery, and V Corps dropped by from time to time. The trick for us was to make spiffing up look normal, and we relied on informers to tell us the idiosyncrasies of those who would judge us.

I recall the state of panic when we learned that a three-star general with a fetish for polished grease fittings would arrive the next day. We ran every vehicle through the motor pool and polished every grease fitting, abnormal for the fitting and for us. The battalion looked good to the general until Col. Phillips asked him if he would like to see the grease fittings.

"What?" the general asked.

"We keep our grease fittings polished, sir. Don't you want to see them?" Phillips repeated.

"I don't know what you're talking about. I've never heard of polishing grease fittings. That's a stupid waste of time, Phillips!" Wrong fetish, bad intelligence.

Field exercises were required of every combat unit in Germany, from a few days near the garrison to a month at a major training ground. Like other battalions, we had permission from German authorities to use a local area for field training exercises (called "FTX") and other small-scale maneuvers. Our turf was a few miles east of Giessen in a forest near the village of Annerod. There we practiced convoying and camouflaging vehicles, mating and delivering rockets in all kinds of weather and visibility, setting up security around our perimeter, simulating combat conditions. During my first such exercise, I took perimeter security seriously and checked guards in the middle of the night to make sure they were awake. Most of them were not, and I quietly collected rifles and a few personal items to make my point. Next morning, these men were so embarrassed that I took no disciplinary action, and they made allowances for my craftiness.

We used such outings to build up to our Army Training Test (ATT) at Grafenwöhr in northern Bavaria. It took us two days to drive to Grafenwöhr: autobahn south to Frankfurt, then east to Würzburg, skirting below its formidable Marienberg fortress that began life as a twelfth-century castle; then two-lane roads to Kitzingen, through a walled town farther east, across the Nürnberg-Hof autobahn about halfway between Nürnberg and Bayreuth. We carried our basic load of conventional and nuclear warheads with us. Signs on our trucks in German and English warned that they held explosives and live ammunition. We watched for the red license plates of the Soviet Military Mission, which was not permitted to snoop around military convoys; indeed, it was not allowed outside its Frankfurt compound for part of 1960, American retaliation for the Soviets' harassing our analogous mission in East Germany.

We observed strict "convoy discipline," officers scurrying around in jeeps and watching from bridges over the highway to insure the proper interval between vehicles. We avoided unnecessary chatter on our radios, which would displease not only Col. Phillips but also the American military security "spooks" who monitored our frequencies for inadvertent leaks. We divided the trip somewhere around Kitzingen, bivouacking on a grassy hillock. On my first trip to "Graf" in July 1960, I wandered away from the platoon to find a secluded place to sleep without a tent. My newfangled transistor radio, my graduation present of a year ago, picked up a station playing Mahler's First Symphony. I had been indifferent to Mahler before then, but that night I got hooked. Eternally; Mahler would like the choice of word. His heroic chords sounded sublime. They still remind me of the grove of trees where I lay awake in my sleeping bag and felt good to be alive, like the young wayfarer of the music who is close to the land and overcomes doubt.

Grafenwöhr, about forty miles northeast of Nürnberg and twenty-five miles west of the Czech border, was established in 1907 as training ground for III Korps of the Royal Bavarian Army and enlarged in the 1930s. Hitler visited there in 1938 to inspect bunkers similar to those being constructed on the "Westwall" line of defense against France; the copies at Graf were being tested for strength against direct hits. Mussolini came in 1944 to observe training of one of the few divisions he had left after the ss rescued him from detention by his former colleagues. Graf contained eighty-eight square miles of sandy and wooded terrain, the largest American training area in Europe. It included 7th Army's Combined Arms School, formerly named the Tank Training Center, which Senator Strom Thurmond toured in November 1960 and later praised in the *Congressional Record*.

After arriving in Graf, we put in a couple of weeks of training, then underwent a practice test to iron out kinks before the ATT. The training period was relatively easy. We had time for distractions. In contests to see who could inflate his air mattress the fastest, Sgt. "Tiny" Ritter, who had played tackle at Washington State, always won. We spent as many nights in barracks as in the field, and barracks meant showers, clean uniforms, and better food. But the practice test and the real thing were ordeals, each lasting three days, with a lot of pressure and virtually no sleep. The climax of these tests was firing the Honest John in "live shoots," which only Grafenwöhr was large enough to permit. If duties back at A&T's area kept me from going to the firing point, I listened for the telltale roar of the rocket motor and then monitored my jeep's radio for S-3's report on the accuracy of the shot. Accuracy depended on the condition of the rocket propellant, the precision of attaching tail fins to the rocket and of mating rocket and warhead, the meteorological section's calculations of wind and temperature, the S-3's translation of all this information into precise instructions for the Firing Battery, the firing section's skill in laying its launcher. We always came close enough to the target to pass the ATT.

My jeep driver, a sweet-tempered Jewish kid from the Bronx named Karp, did a lot to ease the agony of endless demands from captains and majors who always seemed to get more sleep than I did slumped over in my front seat. The army must have been Pvt. Karp's first trip outside the Bronx. I taught him how to drive the jeep, where Germany is, and what evergreen means. He squirreled away food in every cranny of the jeep and kept a thermos full of hot coffee. Whenever I was exhausted, cranky, or discouraged, Karp came to the rescue. His smile was somewhere between Mona Lisa and Alfred E. Neuman, and his accent alone was enough to cheer me up. "Hey lootenen, wannacuppa coowoffee?"

I remember the dust, the mud, the penetrating cold of a damp German forest even on a summer night. I remember the remains of villages forcibly abandoned during the expansion of Grafenwöhr in the 1930s and the signs warning you to watch out for unexploded shells from as far back as the Second Empire. I remember how much space is needed among trees to park and camouflage a long-wheelbase 5-ton truck, a 5-ton wrecker, a jeep. Work became instinct. I still automatically size up forests wherever I hike.

I came all too close to a tragic accident. In August 1960 I was attached to the test team at Graf that graded v Corps artillery units during their practice and real ATTs. I left the team at the end of August, after giving a practice ATT to an 8-inch howitzer battalion, the 3/18 Artillery. A few days later, in its ATT, the 3/18 loaded an incorrect powder charge in one of its guns and overshot the firing range. The shell landed amid bivouacked troops of the 3rd Armored Division, killing eighteen and wounding over twenty-five, the worst postwar training accident for U.S. ground forces in Germany. When I heard the news, my sorrow combined with relief that I was no longer on the test team. Had I been there, I might have been the officer examining the battery in question, and I might have missed the mistaken powder charge as innocently as did the officers on the test team and in the 3/18. In the artillery, you began to assume that powder charges and aim were not dangerously wrong, so you fudged on the rules that required visual verification of each piece by battery officers and test teams. Those officers and I had fudged during the practice ATT.

My morale was highest while on special assignments or sight-seeing, lowest when I realized I was a flunky. Junior rank and paternalistic commanders conspired to deny me the experience commanding troops that I had expected. Military service gradually lost its compatibility with my ideals; perhaps Camus's tragic death in an automobile accident in January had been a bad omen. I began to include the army in my broad definition of autocracy, but rebellion beyond historical discussion of the Code of Conduct was useless unless I sought a dishonorable discharge. So I gave up hope of reforming the 3/79 Artillery and felt sorry for myself. In letters to family I complained about taking orders from officers who were scared stiff of their superiors or less intelligent than enlisted men. The army was "a mad display with no logic or common sense," an organization that "wastes more time, effort and wood pulp on more nonsense than all the faculty committees of the world." (I underestimated academic waste and nonsense.) In September I wrote to John that American military strength lay in arms, not men, so disenchanted had I become with the "blissfully ignorant Officers' Club set whose idea of a challenge is to beat the slot machines." One of my staff sergeants, saying good-bye to me the day before returning to the States for his discharge, had noticed the change. "After your first few months here, sir," he confided, "I thought you were the best junior officer in the battalion, but the army has gotten to you, hasn't it?"

My family knew they had a romantic wayfarer in military uniform. They responded sympathetically and wisely. John said I had the potential to be a fine leader, uncustomary praise from him, but that I must not let senior officers get under my skin; "make the best of it, take notes." Dad sent me a magazine article on the good life of Soviet officers stationed in East Germany. "Perhaps the Russians value 2nd lieutenants more than we do?" he wondered, but "be a good sport" and "use tact" and "doing well at flunky jobs can be its own reward." Mom thought I was "in a spot where, according to West Texas cowboys, you just have to 'lick salt.'" The army paid my bills, fed me, and made my decisions. "What more does a man want?" she asked. "Yes, I know: freedom to be a fool. You and your Pa!" She wanted me to tell her the Cold War equivalent of warriors' returning on their shields; "the Honest John missile sounds terribly uncomfortable." Miss Ada told me to "read the little book" she had given me, and she assured me army training was invaluable; "You don't see it now but you will be happy over it some day."

These letters did little to thicken my skin, and my reading of the New Testament was too casual for consolation. I was easily irritated by my lack of command and by criticism from superiors in the battalion. I was very slow to recognize the battalion as a complex but effective mechanism. It had quirks and failures, both personal and mechanical, but it worked, and I should have taken instructive notes on its bizarre personality, as John advised. I did my job but felt like an outsider.

The alarums and excursions over the U-2 incident worried Dad more than me. "You may be thinking of combat if things don't go right," he wrote. "We hope your service ends before any shooting starts. Of course a nuclear war would be disastrous for us all. . . . Better not to think about it." Miss Ada wished she knew "what it's all about, but it's going to cause trouble." Mom seemed unperturbed, assuring friends at the Institute for Advanced Study that her son was "protecting them from the Russians."

My mother prospered. She joined the Princeton community theater, in one play doing "the grandest ad lib you ever saw" when her stage door failed to open. She seemed more sure of herself at the institute than anywhere else. Asked to collect from the bachelor fellows during a charity drive, she discovered that they were never home "except to sleep, and I refuse to sleep with them even though I'm dedicated to the cause of charity." She wrote glowingly of Robert Oppenheimer, the institute's director, and was grateful his wife did not come calling the afternoon Barbos came home smelling of something fouler than a skunk. "Barbos loves it here at the institute," she wrote, "not only the trees but the research," such as devouring the roast beef in the groceries of their neighbors, Sir Llewellyn and Lady Woodward, he a distinguished British historian from Oxford, both of whom cheerfully accepted a compensatory roast and invited my parents to tea.

Mom hated to leave "this Princeton idyll" where she had many new friends and Dad "got so fired up in his writing." At the end of June they moved to New York City. While Dad taught in Columbia's summer school, Mom played tourist with delight, seeing plays and museums, taking the boat tour around Manhattan, and "mentally picking" five winners in the paddock at Aqueduct racetrack on 4 July, among them one shoo-in — Sword Dancer, "a beauty."

Dad did accomplish a lot in Princeton, thanks to the institute's tradition of lively cross-disciplinary discussion of each fellow's work. He found it tough to return to teaching during the summer, in part because he had slipped a disk in his lower back and had difficulty getting around even with a cane. He sent me clippings about Cornell's excellent crew season and Ted Williams's home runs in what we correctly guessed would be his last year of play; in June Ted hit one every seven times at bat. Dad's back gave out in Pennsylvania as they drove back to Madison in August, and he took the train the rest of the way, leaving Mom and Barbos to complete the trip by car. After her safe return in spite of engine trouble, Dad wrote, "Your mother is a great woman." I had never heard him utter such blunt praise at home.

Although I felt far away, I discerned changes in my parents. Dad was showing his age (fifty-eight), and Mom, nine years younger, was

the stronger of the two even by his admission. She did the hard physical stuff: long turns at the wheel, gardening, shifting furniture, looking for a bungalow house because Dad's back protested against
climbing stairs. I inferred she also did most of the hard mental stuff
about running a household, such as the decision to move. Dad's letters conveyed both admiration for her and regret over the passage of
time. Putting a new, smaller furnace in the old house, he reported
in October, left more room for bikes and model trains than John and
I had in the basement when we were kids. "Irony of life," Dad reflected. "I wish you could go back to boyhood and live again at
home." But I wanted time to get on with it, and my wishing looked
ahead.

John transferred from Wisconsin to Berkeley in August to continue work toward his Ph.D. The move gave him the necessary distance from home to take a fresh look at our parents as they aged
faster than we did. Dad had weaknesses, John wrote in September,
such as "occasional childishness and periodic impatience with the
general hang of things." On the other hand, John was beginning to
appreciate Dad's "unique faculty of being able to see other people
for what they are," and in this respect John and I were "standing on
the shoulders of a giant" who, at his best, could "balance emotion
and intellect." Many of Dad's sayings about people, drawn from his
study of history, used to bore us, but now they seemed "quite sober
truths."

John also thought he had discovered the source of Mom's mental
breakdown during the war. She had been adored by everyone in
Haskell and spoiled by many. After marriage and having children,
however, the daily plod got her down. Despair set in, followed by depression. "She had not bargained for the treadmill existence which
we all must face no matter how flashy our beginnings." Recently she
had told John she still had moments when she froze: she knew what
needed to be done but could not do it, and brooding over that irres-
olution led to general despondency if she were not careful.

I agreed with some of John's analyses, but my distance from civilian life was as telling as my distance from home. Dad's sober truths
about enduring military service did not give me much comfort, perhaps because they seemed to align him with my commanders. Pater-
nalism all around me, I sometimes muttered. John's proposed causes
of Mom's breakdown made sense but did not go far enough. In my

judgment, he should have considered the possibility that her despair had begun with her father's death and the certainty that the Second World War had pushed her depression over the edge. I did not make much of her recurrent episodes of freezing and brooding. I suspected John was exaggerating their significance along with her confiding in him.

In any case, I was now impressed by Mom's evident strength. Her witty disarming of military life seemed to brush off the Cold War, and it gave me more encouragement than did Dad's teachings about perseverance. I praised her for her "pioneer guts" after her drive to Madison. Nothing in her letters, or Dad's, hinted that she was anywhere near despondency. She sounded active and confident, as comfortable with intellectuals in Princeton as around horses at Aqueduct. She seemed to have found social and civic escapes from routine, a far cry from hospitalization, flight, or the lonely walks she had taken in Paris after reunion. The home front was secure, I thought, the minefield cleared. Mom did not need me there. If anyone in the family desperately needed escapes, it was I. In fact, as I wrote John, I planned to stay in Europe for a year after leaving active duty in late October 1961, using money I saved from my monthly pay of about $230. I hesitated to tell my parents this, for I expected Dad to protest that I should enter graduate school.

The U.S. Army depended as much on the Germans as they did on us. I arrived in Germany fifteen years after the end of the war, a period during which German-American relations progressed through several stages. After the Germans surrendered, American authorities began programs of reparations and denazification in their zone of occupation, and many Americans held all Germans collectively guilty for Nazi atrocities. A War Department orientation film for occupation troops in 1945 warned them, "Be alert, be suspicious. . . . You are up against German history. . . . The German people are not our friends. . . . They cannot come back into the civilized fold just by sticking out their hand and saying 'I'm sorry.' . . . Trust none of them. Some day [they] might be cured of their disease — the super race disease, the world conquest disease, but they must prove that they have been cured beyond the shadow of a doubt before they are ever allowed again to take their place among respectable nations."

The military government under Gen. Lucius D. Clay soon adopted a more benign policy as differences arose with the Soviets over implementation of the 1945 Potsdam agreements regarding postwar Germany. This second stage, bound to the beginnings of the Cold War, brought a dramatic improvement in German-American relations during the Berlin airlift of 1948–1949 and culminated with the establishment of the German Federal Republic in 1949, comprising the American, French, and British zones of occupation. In the third stage, 1949–1955, the occupation continued, and the republic's sovereignty was limited. Although the three military governments disappeared, an occupation statute gave Britain, France, and the United States control over military and security affairs; their high commissioners had the ultimate authority in civil matters.

The final stage began when West Germany joined NATO in 1955. Membership achieved Chancellor Adenauer's objective of German sovereignty and security as a member of the Western democratic community. The United States could also claim success for its German policy since the Second World War: prevent the resurgence of German nationalism, avoid a repeat of the German-Soviet treaties of 1922 (Rapallo) and 1939 (Nazi-Soviet Pact), use Germany's geography and manpower to contain Communism. The military occupation officially ended, ambassadors replaced high commissioners, and the German government willingly accepted restrictions that still kept it from being fully sovereign: Germany could not produce nuclear, chemical, or bacteriological weapons; the three Western powers could station troops in Germany (as allies, not occupiers) and retained the right to negotiate a final peace settlement with the Soviet Union. Bonn hoped its alignment with the West would eventually bring about German reunification. NATO and the Warsaw Pact each incorporated half of Germany without publicly admitting that neither side wanted the two halves to reunite.

By 1960 the United States and the Federal Republic were close allies. We assured the Germans that we would keep troops stationed on their soil. They pledged to muster armed forces nearly half a million strong for NATO's forward defense; these numbered approximately 260,000 by the end of 1960, the army's portion about 170,000. Relations between the two armies were good from the start. After the war, the U.S. Army had pushed harder than the State Department for arming Germany. American commanders admired former Wehrmacht generals like Hans Speidel, Erich von Manstein, and Adolf Heusinger and welcomed their views on how to delay a Soviet assault. After 1955 American military advisory groups helped train the first divisions of the new German force. Americans and Germans soon cooperated in staging maneuvers, planning joint operations in case of war, patrolling the inter-German border, and gathering intelligence.

The change from occupation to alliance also increased American and German efforts to promote what USAREUR called "community relations." These efforts had begun during the occupation under the auspices of local German-American clubs and advisory committees, which planned the first "German-American friendship week" in 1954. "America Houses" in German cities built up their libraries of American materials and sponsored events to bring the two peoples together. The Federation of German-American Clubs, supported by the U.S. Information Service, sponsored activities of many kinds. American military units held open houses, normally on Armed Forces Day in May. The 7th Army Symphony Orchestra played before enthusiastic German audiences around the country. In Giessen in 1960 the 299th Engineer Battalion built a bridge over a tributary of the Lahn River; the mayor cut the ribbon opening this *Freundschaftsbrücke*. To celebrate the start of friendship week in May, the mayor read a message of American greeting flown in from Frankfurt by pigeon.

USAREUR urged American troops to learn German. The goal was for 25 percent of officers and 10 percent of enlisted men to be able to "converse intelligently" in the host country's language. USAREUR's Troop Information Branch distributed a booklet, *Orientation Germany*, on history, architecture, customs, and countryside. A bulletin, *People-to-People*, advised Americans not to attract attention by flashing wads of bills, which would only validate Communist propaganda about Americans abroad. An excellent guidebook on German cities published by *Stars and Stripes* sought, in the editor's words, "to show Americans in Europe some of the wonders of the Old World only a short hike or a Sunday drive away from their temporary homes."

In fact, very few Americans ventured far from the "little Americas" in which they lived, and even fewer could converse in German. USAREUR had about 190,000 dependents of military and civilian personnel in Europe in 1960. The large majority of these lived in Germany, where USAREUR had built self-contained American communities in which you could go from cradle to grave without speaking a word of German. They included schools, churches, libraries, medical and dental clinics, banks, food markets, snack bars, department stores, barber and beauty shops, auto parts stores, gas stations, service clubs, craft shops, movie theaters, bowling alleys, athletic fields, rod and gun clubs.

If you did not want to learn German history and politics from good books in the post library, you could go to the newsstand and buy glossy American magazines with lurid cover stories about sadism in the ss or sex in the Nazis' Lebensborn program. In the Troop Information Branch's bulletin, *Germany East of the Curtain*, you could find a sketch showing facial similarities between Hitler and Walter Ulbricht, the German Democratic Republic's Communist leader; the caption read, "It was no great leap from Hitler to Ulbricht." For news you could read *Stars and Stripes* and listen to the Armed Forces Network (AFN) radio station or Voice of America. AFN played rock-'n'-roll, jazz, and Sunday concerts of the Mormon Tabernacle Choir. More popular among enlisted men than *Stars and Stripes* was the tabloid *Overseas Weekly* (called "Oversexed Weekly"), which published gossip and gripes. You could take your holidays at resorts run by the Armed Forces Recreation Center in the Bavarian Alps: Garmisch, Berchtesgaden (on Hitler's former property), and Chiemsee. Whether in the barracks, in family housing, or on holiday, you drank water chlorinated by USAREUR through its own "approved water systems."

Everyone knew German words like *Fräulein, Bier,* autobahn, Wiener schnitzel, *Dummkopf, danke schön,* and *macht nichts* (pronounced "mox nix" by GIS). Some Americans liked to collect linguistic oddities, such as words beginning or ending with "fahrt." Many Americans knew what John Wayne meant when, in a dubbed Western shown on German television, he ambled into a noisy saloon and drawled, "Was ist los in diesem Gasthaus?" But conversing intelligently in German was rare, and I doubt that more than 5 percent of officers could do so, far short of USAREUR's target.

My superior officers in the 3/79 viewed foreign language as a functional problem, not a cultural necessity. Because I was the only officer in the battalion who spoke German with some fluency, I was summoned for various tasks. I was a better diplomat with Germans than with my own countrymen. I visited the German engineer battalion near Gross-Gerau, west of Darmstadt, to help plan the joint exercise that ferried the 3/79 across the Rhine. In this, my first close contact with the Bundeswehr, the Germans were cordial, meticulous in their planning, adaptable to mishaps, and completely reliable. They made me look good, and I was glad they were on my side. I liaised with units of the German III Korps during combined maneuvers in the Westerwald, a heavily forested region northeast of Koblenz where the wind did indeed blow cold, as in an old German army song. In the ceremonies marking the end of the exercise, the Germans marched to our band and we to theirs; they played and marched better. If battalion headquarters had to discuss maneuver damage or highway accidents with local officials, I helped with translating. At the scene of one minor collision, the German driver of a badly dented car patted our truck's solid bumper approvingly and said, "Gut! Stahl!" (good! steel!).

Maneuver damage taught me something about the power of the German *Forstmeister* (literally, master of the forest). Proud and proprietary, the typical *Forstmeister* calculated damages based on the value of the tree (according to its type, size, and age) plus the number of years it would take to grow another of the same dimensions. You could not bargain with them, and they could embarrass you in higher places if you did not cooperate. I came awfully close to disaster because of our mess sergeant, whom I shall call "D" in case there is no statute of limitations on willful destruction of German trees.

As battalion mess officer, I was responsible for decorating the mess hall for Christmas. Knowing how Col. Phillips liked to sweep into the hall on special occasions and hang up his red-lined cape with a flourish, I told Sgt. D to find us a beautiful Christmas tree. I assumed he would send one or two men to a lot selling cut trees. Sgt. D, whose twin I would encounter several years later as Sgt. Minderbinder in Joseph Heller's *Catch-22*, disappeared for a few hours that afternoon with most of his kitchen crew. I was in the mess hall when they returned. I heard their "deuce-and-a-half" (2½-ton truck) pull up. They piled out looking triumphant in battle dress, carrying a magnificent spruce. Sgt. D had set up a perimeter defense in the Annerod forest while finding and cutting the tree. He turned aside my protest with his familiar pretense of having acted for the good of the men, "and isn't that what *you* want, lieutenant?" He had used the same argument a few months earlier after leading half the men in the chow line, their mess gear clanging, on a howling chase of a family of wild boar that stumbled into our area during a combat simulation maneuver in which we were supposed to practice "noise discipline" (army jargon for "keep it quiet"). "Good for the morale," Sgt. D had said then.

My superiors in the 3/79 did not regard military service in Germany as anything remotely like a grand tour. They never granted me a three-day pass and only grudgingly allowed the ten-day leave I requested in November 1960 to go to London to be interviewed for a Rhodes scholarship. Nevertheless, I saw a lot of Germany and met many of its citizens. Mobility was insured when I bought a new Volkswagen in April 1960: light gray, whitewall tires, sliding sunroof, flip-up direction signals European style, with which I returned the salutes of enlisted men who took the trouble to salute an officer at the wheel of his car. I paid about $1,200 for the Bug. Gasoline cost less than twenty cents per gallon on U.S. bases. The dollar ruled international finance and traded for four German marks. You could eat well for three marks, and the best seat in the house at the Frankfurt opera cost about twelve.

I attended concerts at Giessen's Stadttheater, once with a musically gifted enlisted man although I knew such fraternization violated the officers' code. I watched crew races on the Lahn and swam at the public swimming pool, where bikini-clad girls with hairy legs and stiff beehive hairdos avoided the water. With a handful of lieutenants who liked German food, I went to Köbes on Grünbergerstrasse for peasant omelettes and Dortmunder Union beer (my favorite label by now), or downtown to a restaurant called Schwaabs that specialized in Indonesian dishes, or to the Hessischer Hof, a solid middle-class eatery that served excellent oxtail soup and sauerbraten. (In 1996 Köbes was gone, Schwaabs had turned into one of the many Italian restaurants that have spread through Germany, the Hof carried on.)

I dated occasionally: a couple of the American schoolteachers who lived in the BOQ opposite mine; a German named Helga, who was a secretary at post headquarters, spoke fluent English, and was slim like my mother. I slept with none of them nor with any of the German floozies who hung around the Officers' Club and satisfied lieutenants whose uninhibited appetites I envied and disdained. Chastity was less a matter of choice than of confidence. I felt more sure of myself around women than I had at Cornell, but standing between us and bed were my nagging doubts about how to get there, what to do then, and whether eroticism was a good thing.

Giessen provided a good base for extramural trips. Within driving distance for an evening out with friends or dates were the May music festival in Wiesbaden and the opera in Frankfurt. I took weekend outings alone, needing privacy and the freedom to follow my nose. I reached Göttingen and the Harz Mountains to the north; Lahn valley and Rhine vineyards to the west; Heidelberg, Freiburg, and the Black Forest to the south. I ran into a spring snowstorm in the Harz Mountains and saw a locomotive chugging alongside the Rhine on Easter Sunday with rabbit ears chalked on its front. Outside the castle that has been in the Metternich family since 1816, I sat in the Johannisberg vineyard and looked down between rows of vines to the Rhine below. I heard *The Marriage of Figaro* sung in German, toured a small paper mill in the Black Forest, ate rhubarb pie with a German family in Ulm. I talked with a rowing coach on the banks of the Neckar River in Heidelberg who accurately predicted in May that Germany's national "eight" would capture the Olympic gold medal in August, the first time since 1908 that the United States had not won the event.

At a post-Olympic track meet in Frankfurt in September, I saw Armin Hary, the great German sprinter who had just ended American dominance of the Olympic 100-meter dash, and Bo Roberson, whose final broad jump at the Olympic Games won him the silver medal, only a fraction of an inch short of Ralph Boston's leap, both of them breaking Jesse Owens's Olympic record set in 1936 at the Berlin games. I had met Bo at Cornell, where he was the Big Red's finest all-around athlete, and we had been in the same company at ROTC summer camp in 1958. When I congratulated him at Frankfurt for his Olympic medal, his smile of thanks betrayed disappointment, too.

Heidelberg became a special retreat because of the hospitality of the Ernst family. Professor Doctor Fritz Ernst (German protocol stacks titles), rector of the city's celebrated university, knew my father and had visited us in Madison when I was a senior in high school. During my first weekend in Heidelberg, 30 April–1 May 1960, I helped Ernst prepare a speech he would give on Monday to commence German-American friendship week. He would share the platform with Gen. Clyde Eddleman, commander of USAREUR, and he asked me to accompany him as his military escort, an unconventional idea that would have astonished the American brass. Alas, I had to decline the honor because of duties back in Giessen.

Ernst took me several times to his *Stammtisch* (a weekly or monthly gathering of friends at the same table) at a *Weinstube* close to his home on the southwestern slope of the Heiligenberg across the Neckar from the city. In October he told me I was the first outsider ever to join his group on Herbst, the day of the local wine harvest festival. We drank week-old wine cloudy with suspended yeast. I met German academics of many backgrounds and disciplines, including a kindly botanist with a heavy Swabian accent and a deer-horn snuffbox. I felt more welcome in their *Stammtisch* than at the bar in my Officers' Club, for their ecumenical conversation and mutual respect reminded me of the faculty at the University of Wisconsin. Their example, like Dad's, suggested that my ideals might fare well in the academy if nowhere else.

A sympathetic American officer enabled me to see much of Bavaria in August, while I was attached to the test team that he headed at Grafenwöhr. Col. Woodward had a stocky build, flattop haircut, and sense of theater. When his phone rang with someone at the other end crying calamity, he would place the receiver next to a bell on his desk and ring the bell the number of times he thought the flap deserved (five was max), then growl in a slow bass, "That's worth [x] bells, don't you think?" He teased me for the "Ivy League style" in my portions of the team's reports, but he admired my interest in German history and culture. Using the passes he gave me when time permitted, I saw the lifelike thirteenth-century statue of the knight in Bamberg's cathedral and understood why Dad had urged me to go there. I talked about the Battle of Britain with a former Spitfire pilot whom I met in the futile return-ticket line at the Bayreuth opera's annual Wagner festival. I wandered through postcard villages on the "Romantic road" from Rothenburg to Donauwörth, walked the sixteenth-century Fuggerei quarter of Augsburg that has housed the poor to this day, and heard *Don Giovanni* at the Munich opera festival. I discovered a dislike for Bavarian baroque and hiked partway up the Zugspitze.

Touring the country, reading its history, and remembering Mommsen, I began to comprehend Germany's propensity for Faustian dualisms. Each side in the Cold War claimed it saw the dark, totalitarian half of Germany's split personality on the other side. But Faust's personality did not divide along the inter-German border. West Germans themselves debated whether democracy in the Federal Republic formed a veneer over persistent longings for power and autocracy or constituted a genuine beginning in German history. Here was the immediate German question, loaded with the past. Here I could use Camus as my moral guide.

I found evidence to support the veneer thesis. I met unrepentant anti-Semites. A Giessen family proudly entertained an American friend of mine using dinnerware embossed with the swastika. Refugees and others criticized Adenauer for renouncing forceful means for regaining the lost territories east of the Oder-Neisse line. Devotees of the Teutonic Knights and geopolitics blamed the United States for not joining Hitler in 1945 to defeat Slavic Bolshevism. Some conservatives still called it treason to have resisted Hitler. A veteran with sunken eyes gave me a steely gray look that said, "We could have won; we should have won." These were the Germans whose führer had wounded my family, the bullies who had driven Mommsen from his homeland, the knights of bereavement.

More often I saw democratic potential. Most Germans I met were hospitable, grateful for American aid, and willing to accept the subordinate role that recent history and Cold War politics had given their country. Even among these Germans, however, I encountered resentment of "Amis," as they called us. They were offended by Americans who swaggered and condescended as if still occupying Germany, like the soldiers whom my parents had seen throwing beer glasses against the walls of a Bamberg café in 1956. (My parents had gone over to the soldiers' table. Mom asked sweetly, "Couldn't you little boys find something better to do with your bottles?," and Dad gave them a quiet tongue-lashing. The soldiers apologized to my parents, not to the Germans.) I also noted a more general umbrage toward America's military, economic, and cultural ascendancy. But these Germans admired American ideals of freedom and self-rule. Many of them, particularly those from my generation (some of whom had been members of the Hitler Youth), acknowledged the moral necessity of examining the Nazi period honestly.

Years later I would clip a quotation from a speech Thomas Mann had made at the Library of Congress shortly after the war: "There are not two Germanies, a good one and a bad one, but only one, whose best turned into evil through devilish cunning." That became my view in 1960. I did not divide West Germans simply into good and bad. True, they had begun to think democratically about how to cope with the Faust that is in all of us, but I doubted that democracy had been given enough time to send down deep roots. Perhaps Mommsen had lost hope that Germany could send them deep enough to prevent another romance with dictatorship. Perhaps he could never forgive Germany for Nazism nor himself for leaving. What else could he have done?

What would I have done? As I contemplated that universal question, I was all too aware of my own uncertainties. I noticed some fading in my heroic images of defending Mom in Madison, fighting alongside French Communists to liberate Paris, joining Camus to oppose autocracy. Living in Germany gave me materials for new inventions of myself. Suppose, as a twenty-two-year-old German Protestant before or during the Second World War, I had decided neither to defy Nazism outright nor to be a mere spectator. That would have left me with four choices. The bully: I might have joined the ss. The skeptic: while rejecting Nazi doctrines of race and dictatorship, I might have joined the army because it was my patriotic duty. The "inner emigrant" (as Germans called it): I might have withdrawn into a small circle of family and close friends, offering some haven to them while weathering the storm. The lonely refugee: I might have been Mommsen.

I could not imagine enlisting in the ss, but I saw good Germans in the other characters. And I saw traces of these characters in my patriotism, Cold War agnosticism, dependence on solitude, and need of Europe. The good German and I were becoming more composite and more alike.

The comparison confounded my idea of resistance and intensified my interest in German history. I wondered whether any of these personalities would deserve Camus's praise for moral courage and rebellion. (I had not yet read his wartime *Letters to a German Friend*, in which he accused the German nation of serving power and injustice; after the war he said he had meant Nazis, not all Germans.) If not, I would have to abandon him as a moral guide, hate myself, or forget the Second World War, none of which suited me. So I concluded yes, Camus and I would find examples of courage and rebellion in Germans who, though they did not fight for the right of others to live, held fast to that right in their consciences. And I thought maybe not; conscience alone did not save Mommsen or overthrow Hitler. The historical testing ground I imagined for myself was doubling: not only fighting the "good war" for Mom and country against Hitler but also living in Nazi Germany. German history would tell me more about myself. I would learn how thugs got power and things fell apart. I had never believed this couldn't happen again.

I agreed with those Germans who regarded American power as a mixed blessing. Americans defended Europe and brought with them an optimistic can-do spirit. Among our nonmilitary exports, jazz did probably more than anything else to erode national barriers and leap over the Iron Curtain with fraternal tidings; the Voice of America *Jazz Hour*, announced by Willis Conover, reached millions in Eastern Europe. But we remained "magnificent provincials." We learned little about Europe's history, customs, and aspirations. The Officers' Club was a small, parochial island, reminding me of the American embassy in Paris in 1951–1952. At the club one evening, a captain asked me why I used the "strange European" technique of keeping the fork in my left hand to transfer food to my mouth. I said I thought this made sense and that the repetitive American shift of the fork to the right hand was strange. He looked at me as if I were a traitor. Americans like him, who treated even etiquette as a matter of political loyalty, considered it shady for Americans to date German girls, treasonous for Americans to praise the Social Democratic Party, insubordinate for Europeans to question American policy. To countrymen like him, the freedom to have affection for Europe and doubts about the Cold War was un-American.

In early November 1960 I wrote to my parents that many Germans thought of themselves as Europeans. This international consciousness was evidence of a "European spirit of change and optimism." America should regard Europe's integration and increasing self-confidence as a good thing for the West in the Cold War. I had never felt more European myself. Although I missed my family, Barbos, and American autumn, I needed Europe more. I required space to work on what the Second World War and Professor Mommsen and Camus had handed down to me, time to decide upon a career, freedom to be a fool. I knew Mom would understand because of what Europe had done for her, but I expected Dad to advise against prolonging my grand tour unless I attended a German university.

I applied for a Rhodes scholarship in part because I wanted to stay in Europe after military service. The chairman of Cornell's history department had written in March; he and his colleagues regretted my not winning a Wilson fellowship and urged me to try for a Rhodes. My faith in just rewards shot skyward. The office of the American Secretary of the Rhodes Trust, then at Swarthmore College, warned me that I would either have to come home for the state and regional interviews (if I got that far) or resign myself to the extremely slim chances of success applying in absentia. In the fall, however, the office arranged a compromise: I and two candidates living in Britain would be interviewed by an ad hoc committee in London, which would send its reports to our respective universities in the States.

On my way to London in late November I passed the serried forts of Verdun, the cemeteries and vineyards of Champagne. In Paris I sat in the park opposite #10, rue St-Julien-le-Pauvre, our apartment now a restaurant named Cris de Paris. I attended evening mass at Notre Dame and ordered shish kebab from our old waiter at Les Balkans. I felt centered, at home, embraced by memories. On postcards of Notre Dame I told my family I felt I had never left Paris. I found a room for $1.50 per night at the Hotel Navarre (called Hotel du Vieux Paris as I write this), #9, rue Git le Coeur, which had been dubbed the Beat hotel in the fifties because Ginsberg and his friends often stayed there. I saw *The Barber of Seville* at the Opéra Comique. I remembered enough art history and French to strike up a conversation with a beautiful young woman at the Musée d'Art Moderne. I was summoning the courage to ask her to join me for a drink as we left the museum when a car pulled up to the curb. She waved to the driver, smiled at me, said a soft "au revoir," got in, and they drove away. Her smile seemed to say, another time, another place. I was grateful to her and Paris for leaving me with more nerve instead of less.

At Chartres I thought of Dad as the afternoon sun scattered refractions of stained glass about the interior of the cathedral like confetti. In Amiens the cathedral organist began to practice while I sat in the exquisite Gothic nave. The small hotel where I spent the night had lace curtains, and the proprietor couple, who cooked and served in their small restaurant, beamed as I polished off a basketful of crusty bread and a platter of assorted cheeses after dinner. A weathered French porter helped me catch the channel ferry to Dover as it pulled away from the Calais dock. On the ferry I met an Italian named Ugo who invited me to visit him in Formia, where he lived with his blond Sicilian girlfriend and sold catamarans. In London I saw old Pierre Monteux conduct the Royal Philharmonic Orchestra in Beethoven's *Eroica* symphony at the new Royal Festival Hall. I introduced myself to Alec Guinness as he came out the backstage door to his car after playing T. E. Lawrence in Terence Rattigan's play *Ross*. Guinness treated me as if I were doing him the favor. After the Rhodes interview, I spent a day in Oxford, enthralled by its medieval colleges and catching Jude's longing to go thither.

I doubted I would get the Rhodes. Although I hoped I was the kind of all-arounder Cecil Rhodes had in mind, I knew it was a long shot because I had missed Phi Beta Kappa and could not attend the state and regional interviews. These long odds probably helped settle my nerves for the interview in London. Also, going through Paris had lifted my spirits, and the interviewing committee seemed to want a good conversation, not a grilling. Perhaps military service itself had been allaying my fears of failure. Nothing in the 3/79 frightened me like taking a final exam or rowing to the starting line of the IRA regatta, and the new H&S commander, Capt. Holman, had started giving me more responsibility and credit than was the rule with Haggerty. I felt surprisingly relaxed during the interview and enjoyed it. I rushed some of my answers and kicked myself afterward for what I might have said about French history and NATO. But what the hell, I thought with uncharacteristic peace of mind, I rowed my best.

I returned to Giessen by way of Amsterdam and the Rijksmuseum, for whose striking portraits by Rembrandt and Hals no amount of art history could have prepared me. It had been a great trip, I wrote my parents, recalling Mom's exuberant letters from Rome during my freshman year at Cornell. "I'm now doing what I have wanted to do for so many years." I wouldn't bet on the Rhodes, but the application process had boosted my self-esteem, and the leave had "done wonders for my morale — mine is the only smiling face in the battalion."

About a week before Christmas I stood in the basement of H&S Battery, appraising work on our holiday decorations, when the mail clerk handed me the telegram informing me I had won a Rhodes scholarship.

"I'm damned!" Dad wrote. Miss Ada presumed it was a victory for prayer, adding that I must also have been "using the butter knife correctly." John's congratulations were followed by a long reflection on his own search for meaning in life. He was still smarting from not having won a Rhodes two years earlier. I thanked him for the advice he had given me before the interview, and I tried to say he deserved to win and my timing helped me because I had applied after honors thesis, varsity crew, and experience in the army. Aunt Frances reproved, "So you are the guy who thought your Dad and John knew all the answers." I could hear and see Mom when she wrote, "Oh kid, we are so proud of you."

I was so high I volunteered to take guard duty on Christmas Eve. Congratulatory letters poured in. Word spread fast around the battalion and Officers' Club, and I began to notice the mixed looks of awe, envy, disbelief, and disinterest that follow Rhodes scholars wherever they go. I took stock, the most optimistic and least ambivalent moment of my life. Kennedy would soon be president. He and the country would need Rhodes scholars from my generation who believed they could make a difference in what Cecil Rhodes had called the "world's fight." We both looked forward.

Dichotomies withered and loose ends connected as I reinvented my best self. I would become part of a common cause. Military service in the Cold War was but a frustrating skirmish. My real fight was not in uniform against the threat of Soviet aggression. It was to resist the coalition of enemies that had been forming at home and abroad since my childhood — autocracy, ignorance, and chauvinism. I would fight as a civilian for their antitheses, guided by history. History was continuous, older and bigger than the Cold War. I could use history because it filled gaps, tested the imagination, had meaning and consequence. Nazism and McCarthyism, collapse and resistance, my mother and Professor Mommsen, Paris and Haskell: armed with these metaphors and memories, I would help Kennedy make history after I finished my degree at Oxford. If the mysteries surrounding Mom's illness and Mommsen's suicide were unsolvable, that would itself be a valuable lesson in skepticism for me to remember in my eagerness to improve the world. I prized my roots and was moved by my family's moral support. But now it was clear that unraveling my own riddle lay less in where I came from than in what I would do.

My professional community would probably be higher education or perhaps the diplomatic corps or another branch of public service. In any career, I would draw upon my experiences in Europe. I would keep my options open and prepare for altruistic combat by taking two years of study and travel. Mom didn't need me at home. There was no serious threat of war in Europe. The army would release me in time to start at Oxford in the fall. I had it made.

CHAPTER 6 *Maneuvers*

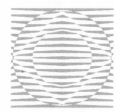 Recalling 1961 here will not resolve the debates among historians over Khrushchev's intentions, Kennedy's strength of will, or the likelihood of war over Berlin. I simply want to say this is how it appeared to a junior officer in a battalion of v Corps. This is how I remember it: before we knew there would be a Berlin crisis or, once it arrived, that it would be the war's last European showdown; before America changed its self-image forever by committing a generation younger than mine to deadly combat in Vietnam; before anyone on the planet could imagine that v Corps and Russian troops would one day cooperate to keep the peace in Bosnia.

I remember thousands of fragments. Sometimes these turn up haphazardly, answering impromptu signals that have no apparent design. Sometimes they accept conscious invitations to come help me teach, write, or review my life. In both types of recall, memory has proven more coherent than I would have guessed before I started this book. Most of the fragments gather under four objectives: completing military service, learning more about the Germans, studying modern European history at Oxford, finding love. These groupings are not recent inventions. I remember assuming, in my euphoria early in 1961, that they were complementary pursuits on my way toward the "world's fight" while Europe was at peace and my family could do without me. I remember believing that my life, like the public events that chart history, moved forward with purpose — until the Vienna summit of early June.

The year opened on an optimistic note with major liaison assignments and the inauguration of President Kennedy. During the week of 9–13 January I was attached to the Bundeswehr's III Korps in Koblenz. The commander of v Corps, Lt. Gen. Frederic J. Brown, wanted to improve coordination with the Germans, and the staff of v Corps Artillery, commanded by Brig. Gen. William Harris, had learned that I spoke German. In Koblenz I worked closely with Col. Wunderlich, commander of III Korps Artillery. A veteran of the Second World War, he recalled his ambivalent attitude toward Hitler as we walked along the Rhine one day after lunch, pausing at its confluence with the Mosel River to look at the Deutsches Eck, the massive stone foundation that once supported an enormous equestrian statue of Kaiser Wilhelm I.

Like the majority of officers in the new Bundeswehr, most of the officers I met at III Korps had served in the Wehrmacht during the war. One had a wooden leg; "I forgot the other one in Russia," he laughed. They seemed genuinely interested in my ideas for cooperation between our forces. Some of them complained about the uneven quality of their recruits, but I was impressed by what I saw. During a coffee break one morning in their headquarters, I walked over to the window to watch a platoon march by below. A major asked me how long I thought those soldiers had been in the army. "About four weeks," I guessed, thinking back to Fort Bragg. "Three days," he said, smiling at the implicit contrast between national learning curves.

I visited a unique German institution on a hill across the Rhine from Koblenz: the Schule für Innere Führung. The term "*Innere Führung*" means literally "inner (or internal) leadership." A looser and more helpful translation is "leadership and character training." The school was established in 1957 to instruct officers and NCOs in democratic values, the compatibility between democratic citizenship and military service, the subordination of the military establishment to the civilian control of the defense minister and the Bundestag. The school's founders had wished to prevent the Bundeswehr from becoming an undemocratic state within the state like the Reichswehr in the Weimar Republic. They had also sought to overcome the strong antimilitary sentiment among young Germans who deplored Germany's history of militarism and supported the Social Democratic Party's opposition to rearmament.

A portrait of Antoine de Saint-Exupéry hung in the outer office of the school's director, evoking loftier ideals than efficiency and obedience. That was a tall order for any military school but especially for German officers who had served in the Wehrmacht and now had to rebuild German military strength in a hurry. Back at III Korps, I did not ask officers for their confidential views of the school; later I wished I had. I am sure some would have objected to wasting the Bundeswehr's time on teaching citizenship. Even more would have blamed the Social Democratic Party for weakening the nation's will to fight. Probably all would have dismissed the party's charge in August 1960 that military leaders were interfering in politics when, in apparent violation of the principle of civilian control, they issued a memorandum stating that the defense of the Federal Republic required universal conscription, continued membership in NATO, and the acquisition of nuclear weapons.

My week at III Korps culminated in a small conference of German, American, and British officers. Col. Wunderlich asked me to translate his remarks into English, although he knew the language well enough to correct any serious errors. At the banquet on Thursday evening marking the end of the conference, all stood while the most junior German officer proposed a toast to President Heinrich Lübke. I wondered why everyone remained standing, until the German lieutenant-colonel on my left nudged me and whispered, "It's your turn." In my haste, fumbling for the correct German words, I raised my glass to "the new American president, John Kennedy." My blunder dawned on me as we began the first course — Eisenhower was still in office. I apologized to my table. "Don't worry about it," said the lieutenant-colonel. "Now we know you are a Democrat."

After a final meeting with Wunderlich on Friday morning, I drove back to Giessen along the Lahn River, my self-confidence raised more by his compliments than by the faint praise I had received from my superiors in the 3/79 Artillery during the past ten months. On Saturday I reported to V Corps Artillery headquarters in Frankfurt and spoke enthusiastically about the quality of III Korps and the prospects for collaboration with the Bundeswehr. I proceeded to Heidelberg for a weekend with the Ernsts. I delivered a similar message to them and to Professor Ernst's *Stammtisch*, my fluency in German having increased during the week with III Korps. In two weeks I would escort German or Austrian dignitaries at NATO's annual winter maneuver in Bavaria. I was in a groove, "lookin' good" in army talk.

Kennedy took the oath of office on 20 January, a few days after the Soviet government published Khrushchev's blueprint for the inevitable victory of Communism through peaceful competition and national wars of liberation. Robert Frost read "The Gift Outright" at the inauguration, saying his poem about the American land seemed appropriate because the new administration talked of "new frontiers." Kennedy pledged to defend liberty no matter how high the price, to fight against "tyranny, poverty, disease, and war itself." Throughout history, he said, "only a few generations have been granted the role of defending freedom in its hour of maximum danger. I do not shrink from this responsibility — I welcome it. I do not believe that any of us would exchange places with any other people or any other generation."

At forty-three, Kennedy was the youngest elected president in American history. I regarded him as an older brother who would listen, not a father who knew best or a battalion commander who treated me like a flunky. I forgave the president for sympathizing with Senator McCarthy in the early fifties; he had learned his lesson. In spite of my age and status, I knew I was included in Kennedy's broad conception of a unique generation. Although not sure what lay on the New Frontier, I and many other lieutenants in Giessen felt both justified and invigorated by this war hero's patriotic summons to do something for our country. Like the inaugural address itself, we focused on America's international role, not its domestic problems, and several lieutenants hoped the next frontier of their military careers would be in Vietnam. Among senior officers, most of whom had voted for Eisenhower in the previous two elections, Kennedy had support because of his brave combat record in the war against Japan and because he planned to improve America's conventional forces. The strong martial symbolism at his inauguration was evident in an unusually large military parade, including units of the 82nd Airborne Division in full battle dress with bayonets attached to their rifles. Lieutenants and colonels alike could agree with the editorial opinion of the *Giessener Freie Presse* (21/22 January): Eisenhower had probably allowed the initiative in the Cold War to pass to the Soviet Union, but Kennedy gave the impression he would not do so.

Kennedy's address reverberated throughout Western Europe on the eve of Exercise Wintershield II, NATO's largest land maneuver to date. I had heard horror stories about Wintershield I of February 1960, in which several captains and lieutenants from my battalion served on umpire teams in the field in bitter cold. "You'll have to go and you'll freeze your ass," they had warned me like fraternity brothers before hazing freshmen. I did have to go, but the weather turned unseasonably warm, and I saw the action from sedans and helicopters, the only lieutenant in 7th Army to be assigned as an escort officer.

Wintershield II took place in early February in northern Bavaria, in the area between Bayreuth (north), Regensburg (south), Nürnberg (west), Weiden (east). Although not the most likely route of a Soviet invasion, Bavaria contained the necessary maneuver areas and open spaces for an operation of this scale. The commander of 7th Army, Lt. Gen. Garrison Davidson, directed the operation. Like all NATO exercises, this one assumed defense against invasion from the Warsaw Pact countries and did not envisage counterattacking beyond the borders of West Germany. Hypothetically, the "Peoples Free Democratic Republic of Aggressor," believing it was "destined by history ultimately to dominate the world," had overrun Austria and southern Bavaria, setting up the "Tyrolean Democratic Republic." NATO, "an organization of democratic nations determined to protect themselves against the designs of Aggressor Imperialism," had taken up positions north of the Donau (Danube) River and west of a line running from Ulm southward to the Swiss border east of the Bodensee (Lake Constance).

Gen. Davidson's objective was "to enhance combat readiness by emphasizing continuous operations at all levels under conditions of the atomic battlefield." Both sides simulated tactical nuclear blasts against enemy concentrations and routes of advance. Both crossed rivers, called in air strikes, employed helicopters for tactical support, gathered intelligence through air reconnaissance and electronic surveillance devices. (Battlefield photography from satellites was only in the research and development stage; computers and lasers would come much later.) Both sides used psychological warfare, such as leaflets about typhus, unfaithful wives, and a fierce breed of lynx that prowled the forests. A thaw and rains caused many German rivers to flood. Several vehicles slipped into the Donau one night, their crews all surviving, some of them finding warm blankets and beds in the home of a German family. In Giessen, where the Lahn reached its highest level since 1946, the *Freie Presse* depicted Wintershield as a *Schlacht im Schlamm* (battle in mud).

In orientation material distributed to all units before the exercise, 7th Army warned that maneuver damage could hit Uncle Sam hard in the pocketbook and "alienate an ally in the NATO team for defense against the communist menace." German authorities had complained in the past about torn-up roads, haystacks used as bedding, the cost of operating on cows that had ingested wire and other military equipment. At the end of Wintershield II, actual damage was estimated at $3 – 4 million, by far the costliest such exercise in NATO's history and a shock to USAREUR at a time when Washington sought to reduce the flow of American dollars into Germany. Besides inclement weather and human carelessness, three circumstances were to blame. First, costs were rising along with the increasing land values and population of a booming economy. Second, the sheer size of the maneuver was unprecedented for NATO: approximately 60,000 troops and 15,000 vehicles, and 130 railroad trains to move armor and other heavy equipment. Third, Wintershield was planned as a showcase for some 500 visitors from NATO and neutral countries, including twelve four-star generals, thirty-six lieutenant generals, fifty-seven major generals, sixty brigadiers. USAREUR did not intend to waste this brass's time worrying about cows.

Gen. Hans Speidel, commander of land forces, Central Europe, came for a brief visit. After the First World War, Lt. Speidel had written his doctoral dissertation in history at the University of Tübingen comparing Prussia's recovery after 1807 — later to fight its "war of liberation" against Napoleon — with the military weakness of the Weimar Republic. In the Wehrmacht, he rose to the position of chief of staff for Field Marshal Erwin Rommel in France in 1944. He survived seven months in Gestapo custody after his name was linked to the unsuccessful plot to assassinate Hitler in July of that year. After the German defeat, Speidel became one of West Germany's most influential military experts, advising Adenauer to seek strong security guarantees from the Western powers. In a speech in Washington in August 1960, Speidel praised NATO's new strategy of shielding Europe from well east of the Rhine, with added strength from the Bundeswehr.

Speidel came to Wintershield at the invitation of Gen. Bruce C. Clarke, commander of USAREUR since October 1960, who had fought across France in 1944 under Patton. Clarke, Speidel, and a few other highest brass dined one evening in a U.S. Army railroad car near maneuver headquarters in Vilseck, on the southern edge of the Grafenwöhr training area. I was one of a small crowd of lesser folk who watched the arriving dignitaries gather outside the car. Having been encouraged by Professor Ernst to introduce myself to Speidel if I had the chance, I sent word (and Ernst's name) to the general through skeptical channels. Soon, surrounded by generals, Speidel and I were exchanging salutes, shaking hands, and discussing our mutual interest in history. "Nun, wir sind Kollegen!" (well, we are colleagues), he said, asking me to write to him. I said I would, saluted, and withdrew, feeling smugly older than my rank.

Guests and their escorts were comfortably billeted at Rose Barracks in Vilseck. The Guest Observer Bureau, its acronym GOB etched in my memory, provided briefings in English, German, and French; press tables; transportation; entertainment; green armbands; name tags color-coded according to native language (white for English, gray for German). I served as escort officer for two Austrians, Maj. Gen. Leo Waldmüller, commander of Austria's only corps (1 Korps), and Capt. (Baron) Johann Dreihann-Holenia, 35th Panzer Grenadier Battalion. Both had fought in the Second World War on eastern and western fronts.

In what we called a "sedan war," the Austrians and I drove to different sectors of the battlefield. They interviewed American, German, and French officers, the latter during a leisurely pause for lunch along the roadside. My guests, who spoke French, huddled with the French commander and his assistant; I struck up a conversation about Paris with a couple of lieutenants. One overcast morning I requisitioned a helicopter so we could survey the action north of Regensburg. After making several large circles, the pilot began to follow a river upstream. According to my map (I had aced map reading at Fort Sill), the river was probably the Regen, and we were heading east toward the Bohemian Forest and Czechoslovakia. I went forward to point this out to the pilot, remembering the exercise directive's warning, as if one were needed, not to violate the borders of East Germany and Czechoslovakia. The pilot, a captain with obvious contempt for lieutenants, looked down, told me I was wrong and to let him do the flying. Soon the Austrians confirmed my suspicion that we were approaching Czechoslovakia, and the general calmly reminded me of his country's neutrality. I hastened forward again, an edge in my voice as I asked the pilot to look at his map. He did so impatiently, then glanced down at the river, back at the map, ahead at the deepening ravines, back, down, back once more. He froze for a split second. "Shit!" he yelled, and banked steeply around to the west.

At a combined arms demonstration held on Sunday during a break in the exercise, my guests and I observed the latest in 7th Army weapons and tactics. A small drone flew by on photo reconnaissance. Helicopters, H-34s, landed troops behind a ridge, supported by fire from smaller H-13s. Artillery, mortars, and recoilless rifles pounded enemy positions. Infantry-tank teams attacked a hill. Atomic weapons fired conventional warheads: Honest John, 8-inch howitzer, also the Davy Crockett, a new lightweight rocket for use at battalion level with a miniature nuclear warhead and a range of just over a mile. Planes from the 50th Fighter Bomber Wing, U.S. Air Force, strafed and dropped napalm. The drive-by display of tanks and other vehicles included America's new main battle tank, the M60. All of this hardware prompted Gen. Waldmüller and Capt. Dreihann to describe the weapons that Austria purchased from countries on both sides of the Iron Curtain. Befitting Austria's neutral status, their comparative inventory came out about even.

Toward the end of the exercise the general asked me to take him to the large American Post Exchange in Nürnberg so he could buy blue jeans for his daughter. We dressed in civilian clothes, he and the captain sporting snappy felt hats. By now we were relaxed in each other's company. They sang Austrian folk songs in the car, and I joined in the refrains. After shopping at the PX, where neutrality did not apply, we drove around the rebuilding city. We stopped at Saint Sebald's Church, a Romanesque and Gothic reminder of medieval Nürnberg. The mood changed from convivial to somber when we arrived at the field where Albert Speer had orchestrated masses of flags and the faithful at the Nazi Party's annual rallies. I felt shivers as I looked at the remains of the platform from which Hitler had reviewed the SA and SS, not the thrill of discovery I had experienced in Haskell and Rome, but the shudder of dread. I did not ask Waldmüller and Dreihann why they had served the führer. They offered nothing.

In some respects Wintershield II was a dinosaur. It used pentomic organization and tactics that were never popular in the army and would soon be changed by the new administration's doctrine of "flexible response." A year later, in its annual historical report for 1961, 7th Army observed that "some of the experience gained during the exercise has been rendered obsolete by adoption of new organizations and equipment." Artillery commanders placed "too much emphasis on atomic fire support," not taking advantage of "the conventional fires that are available to them." It was "extremely difficult to inject realism in nuclear weapons play." Gen. Clarke agreed with 7th Army that, although exercises of this scope were useful for corps and division staffs, they failed to provide sufficient training for small units and individual soldiers. For these reasons, and in order to reduce damages of civilian property, Clarke directed 7th Army to do away with the "large scale free maneuver" in the future.

Probably the most successful outcome of Wintershield II was international. The exercise had no bearing on divisive issues in NATO, such as control over nuclear forces in Europe; President Charles de Gaulle's idea of a tripartite NATO directorate with equal authority among France, Britain, and the United States; and various proposals for establishing a multilateral force of intermediate-range ballistic missiles under international control. The good that Wintershield did for NATO was more tactical and temperamental than political. The weekly newspaper of v Corps (the *V Corps Guardian*) noted the versatility of the 11th French Mechanized Brigade and its AMX light tank. Seventh Army, in its annual report for 1961, praised "the outstanding manner in which several NATO forces effected coordination and mutual operations. The attachment of various military elements of one nationality to commands of a different nationality was extremely successful despite the language barrier and the differences in methods of operations. Continued emphasis on this interrelationship of forces should prove beneficial in the development of NATO."

I saw many examples of cooperation: the NATO members' national flags planted in the snowbank outside exercise headquarters, the reading materials and briefings for guests, the cooperation between units in the field, the daily contacts between participants and observers. After dinner one evening, the French pianist Jean-Paul Billaud, then serving in the French air force played for an audience of mixed ranks and uniforms. I remember Chopin, conversation over coffee, and "good-night" in different languages as we parted to walk back to our billets on crunching snow, a cold front having ended the thaw. The rapport of that evening lodged in my memory of Wintershield II. So did images that might have come from the Second World War: Speidel outside the railroad car, Austrians in Nürnberg.

In early March, arriving back in Grafenwöhr for three weeks of training with the 3/79, I wrote home that I welcomed field duty as a change from the paperwork and boredom of garrison. The welcome quickly wore out, thanks to two episodes of this trip to Graf that have clung to my memory like ivy. A blizzard hit us while we were out in the field, shredding camouflage nets, penetrating field jackets, glaciating helmets, and halting operations. Not a smoker myself, I stoked up a friend's extra pipe just to keep my hands warm, wondering how I would look to Dad, Granddad, and Uncle Tom Ballard. Even Pvt. Karp began to look worried, his face shriveled by the cold and his eyes betraying the premonition that his resourcefulness might not outlast the storm. Many of us had no more than six hours of sleep in three days. Olive-drab lumps of men clustered around generators, stoves, and vehicle engines. The battalion limped into barracks like refugees.

When we returned to Giessen a week or so later, I had an equally severe tongue-lashing from the battalion commander. Leading the A&T section of the convoy on the autobahn north from Frankfurt, I was so pleased with the platoon's good convoy discipline and the fair weather that I thought we could easily pass a line of several slow German trucks, surely an excusable breach of the army's rule against passing. Dumb move. The A&T Platoon, our 5-ton trucks and wreckers invincibly afile in the passing lane, backed up a queue of civilians, the angriest of whom were Germans accustomed to driving their Mercedes at breakneck speed with headlights flashing imperiously to clear the way of vehicles of lower class. Col. Phillips, flying over the convoy in an L-19 observation aircraft supplied by 36th Artillery Group, told me how scatological my decision was over the radio channel used by the entire convoy. When I checked into battalion headquarters later that afternoon along with other officers, there was no place for me to hide. Phillips, hands on hips, face only inches from mine, let everyone in the building know he had never seen such stupidity in all of his years of convoying. "No excuse, sir," I said, the lieutenant's wisest confession while blushing after sin, and I made a private vow never to let a boss get that close to my face again.

In those early months of 1961 I did not worry much about Berlin. In September 1960 the East German government had imposed restrictions on West German travel to East Berlin. Britain, France, and the United States had protested against this action as a violation of four-power agreements on Berlin. In October the West had rejected the Soviet reply that the German Democratic Republic had full powers over all territory under its sovereignty, including East Berlin, and therefore that the Western Powers were interfering in the internal affairs of a sovereign government. In December USAREUR noted that tension over Berlin had caused an increase in the number of East German refugees entering West Germany, nearly 16,500 during November compared to about 10,000 in November 1959. USAREUR also finished reviewing its contingency plans for reopening access to Berlin in case the East Germans closed the Helmstedt-Berlin autobahn.

The new year began calmly. Shortly after his inauguration, President Kennedy ordered American military leaders to avoid antagonizing the Soviet Union with unnecessarily tough talk. In February Secretary of State Dean Rusk stated that the change in presidents had not caused a change in American views on Berlin. The Democratic Republic ended its recent restrictions on travel, Khrushchev reiterated his position that Berlin must eventually become a free and demilitarized city. In March, in an apparent departure from his previous statement, Secretary Rusk announced that America was no longer bound to the concessions it had offered at the Geneva conference on Germany in 1959, such as reducing the number of U.S. troops stationed in West Berlin. Kennedy assured Mayor Willy Brandt that the United States would preserve his city's freedom. At the end of the month leaders of the Warsaw Pact nations renewed their claim that West German militarism was the major threat to peace in Europe. Neither of these latter two statements seemed to upset the status quo. Although the Soviet leader still threatened to conclude a separate peace treaty with East Germany if no international settlement of the Berlin question were reached, he issued no ultimatum about deadlines. All parties expected another summit conference to be arranged for discussing Berlin.

I thought more about Oxford than about Berlin. The French Line wanted American Rhodes scholars to sail to England on the *Liberté*, and Dad hoped I would, "in memory of our voyage to France in September 1951. Remember?" His letter with the French Line's brochure reached me in the field in Grafenwöhr, before the blizzard, and I did remember. I looked in my small shaving mirror and laughed to imagine that face in the first-class ballroom illustrated in the brochure.

I planned to ask the army to release me in Germany in early October, a few weeks before the end of my two years' service. I hoped to use my accumulated leave for a thirty-day vacation back home in Madison in September, saving money by flying both ways at the army's expense. I would then drive from Germany to Oxford, where the fall term began in mid-October. Neil Rudenstine advised me to put New College at the top of my list of preferences for placement at Oxford, one of the oldest colleges there although called "new" since its founding in the fourteenth century. Neil suggested that I ask the warden of Rhodes House, E. T. Williams, to help me obtain an early discharge. Williams "can do *anything*," Neil wrote. I did not yet know about the warden's distinguished military career in the Second World War as the youngest brigadier in the British army and Field Marshal Montgomery's chief of intelligence. (Williams, formerly a history don at Merton College, accurately predicted the weak points in the German and Italian lines before the battle of El Alamein in the autumn of 1942.) New College accepted me, Williams wrote in late January. Still confident the army would let me go in time for Oxford, I did not ask him to write to the Pentagon on my behalf.

I wanted to buy my mother some china before leaving Germany. Dad had done this for his mother thirty years earlier when he was in Germany as a graduate student, and making it a family tradition appealed to me. My wish contravened USAREUR's campaign to reduce the volume of dollars going into German coffers. In early February the Kennedy administration canceled plans, approved by Eisenhower late in 1960, to reduce the number of American dependents abroad. USAREUR, estimating that about half of its dependents would have to be sent home, bolstered the Pentagon's protest that the damage to morale would outweigh any savings in dollars. But the American government continued searching for other means to lower the mounting deficit in its balance of payments, of which West Germany alone accounted for more than 25 percent. Secretary of Defense Robert McNamara asked U.S. personnel abroad to reduce their annual spending by $80 per person. Washington wanted Bonn to pay some of the costs of keeping American forces in Germany and to assume a share of the West's spending on worldwide foreign aid. While these negotiations made slow progress, USAREUR announced that we could no longer ship our cars back to the States at no cost to ourselves, its Troop Information Branch entreated us to "dam the dollar drain," and Gen. Clarke began to extol the virtues of thrift.

Frugality abroad was not an American virtue when the dollar was strong, and just serving abroad seemed patriotic enough. My American friends and I continued to spend guiltless dollars on German culture, from the Frankfurt Opera's luxuriant production of Mussorgsky's *Boris Godunov* to *Fasching* (carnival) balls. My closest comrades were John "JJ" Rostenberg and Frank Linden. Our affectionate threesome lessened my need for solitude; perhaps also the Rhodes scholarship had given me more heart to be gregarious. A lieutenant in the 2/92 Artillery, JJ knew jazz, introduced me to the Oscar Peterson Trio's album *Fiorello*, and looked ahead to a career in business and local politics in Westchester County, New York. Frank, a captain and dentist at Giessen Post, drove his MG roadster with soft hands and heavy foot and aimed to be the best dentist in Montana when he returned home to Great Falls. We had our own *Stammtisch* at Köbes and ordered #19, an Indonesian dish, on the menu at Schwaabs. We faked indifference to the phallic symbolism and free love we encountered at *Fasching* bacchanalia in Giessen and Wetzlar on the eve of Lent.

In my letters home I griped about idiocy in the army and longed for "intellectual challenge." I was enthusiastic about Germany, Oxford, and liaison work, all of which gave me confidence and freedom from battalion control. My parents' letters to me were generally upbeat, full of details about the new house to which they moved in mid-January. Shortly after their move, they used their two sons as unwitting accomplices in opposing the construction of a neighborhood fallout shelter. It was a new neighborhood with young children, and many of the families wanted everyone to contribute funds for constructing a shelter. At the decisive neighborhood meeting, Mom said she understood their concern for their children, but her boys had left the nest. Dad then made a short speech that one of the younger fathers later told me was the clincher.

"I'm sorry," Dad said, "we aren't going to contribute money to the shelter. Our boys are away, and we have had a pretty good life. If the bombs start falling, I'm going down into our basement with a case of bourbon. But I'll tell you what. We'll give you our boys' rifles so that if my wife and I change our minds and run to your shelter you can defend yourselves against us in the civil war for survival."

The motion to build was soundly defeated. The meeting adjourned for a long evening of refreshment.

Mom wrote, "You must come home in September!" Knowing I missed Barbos, she assured me that the move and winter did not deter him from making his preferred rounds on the west side of Madison. She sent me the quarterly *Letter from Cornell* containing an item about my Rhodes award and an article by Hans Bethe on the need for public literacy in science, which he found lacking in spite of the Sputnik scare. She did not answer my query about what sort of china she would like.

Dad gave lectures at Indiana, Notre Dame, and Harvard and was elected a corresponding member of the Heidelberg Academy of Sciences, "the greatest honor I have received," he admitted with uncharacteristic pride. Mom sent a clipping from the University of Wisconsin student newspaper, the *Daily Cardinal*, summarizing a lecture Dad gave in an extracurricular series on political thought. He told students he saw little change in the theory of "reason of state" since the Middle Ages. Then as now, he argued, states used the "good deceit" to justify lying abroad for the good of the country, as the United States had done in 1960 in the case of the U-2 flights. "No civilized society can exist without some compromising with the devil for a higher end," he declared.

Twelve years later Dad would caution Archibald Cox, special prosecutor for the Watergate affair, not to misinterpret Henry de Bracton, medieval England's preeminent legist. When Bracton said the king was "under no man but under God and the law," as Cox correctly stated to the press, Bracton did not mean the king could be judged by courts of law; if the king violated his coronation oath to rule according to the laws, he could only be judged by God. "Not that Nixon is king," Dad added. In his reply Cox pled guilty to adopting the "vulgarized" interpretation of Bracton that "has come to epitomize the Anglo-American legal tradition which began to develop with Coke's quotation to King James and came down [to us] through *Marbury* v. *Madison*." Cox did not promise to drop Bracton's statement from any future arguments based on precedent, as Dad suggested.

My brother was tired of his "monastic life" at Berkeley and urged me to consider a career in public service, "one of life's highest callings." He reported that our parents expected me to come home before starting at Oxford. "Dad is saving a couple of bottles of great wine for when you and I are both home together. Can you make it? When? Do all you can to get back — Mom and Dad miss you a lot." John also advised me to write to our grandmother Ada to cheer her up; "apparently she thinks you are under fire or nearly so."

Miss Ada covered all the fronts. In Haskell in early February it snowed "flakes as large as a lady's hankie." Oxford "would be a better well rounded school if it enrolled more women," she replied to my description of the place. She wanted me to go out with "little Janes" in Germany, and "don't forget Granny who says 'Now I lay me down to sleep' every night for you." The more she watched the news on television, the happier she was to have voted for Kennedy in spite of his Catholicism. "I am still in love with Pres. Kennedy and the 'new frontier,'" she wrote. "He is young but is blessed with the know-how — it may be wrong some time but *do* and have *done* things is his motto."

Miss Ada remembered how I would tell her everything I had done after a long day on Uncle John's ranch, but now "Uncle Sam won't let you do that." She worried that I was "getting mighty close to Kruschef [*sic*]. . . . You just keep your shirt on. Granny doesn't think it will go so far as shooting & my prayer is that God will take care of all our boys & bring them home safely." God had always answered her prayers for me "in His own way." Uncle John was anxious about me, she reported, "and it helped him so much" to see my long letter to her that arrived the day after he took his yearlings off the fields of winter wheat.

I asked Miss Ada to tell Uncle John I wished I could do some cowboying with him; "I am very much attached to that land which I explored as a kid on horseback." I missed open country. And I did pray, I assured her, "in my own way."

By the time I dug out this correspondence thirty-five years later, my memory had equated 1961 with the Berlin crisis and coated the whole year with escalation. I assumed I would find evidence of increasing anxiety early in that fateful year on the front closest to Berlin, something to echo Miss Ada's grandmotherly apprehension. I found no such evidence in my letters and journal. "No problems on this side of the ocean," I wrote to my parents in early March. "Don't worry about Khrushchev, that's what I am here for," I reassured Miss Ada, certain he had grown less dangerous since the U-2 affair nearly a year ago. Had I minimized escalation for my family's sake? Or had I missed what was under my nose during those months, perhaps because I looked ahead to Oxford? Surely I would find proof of an intensification of the crisis in *Stars and Stripes* and the declassified documents of USAREUR. I did not. All of these sources convey a peaceful and positive mood of rising expectations. Kennedy would strengthen American leverage and leadership in the Cold War. I would finish my tour of duty, study at Oxford, and enlist in Kennedy's New Frontier. There my best invention would flourish, solving my riddle through some form of service to my country. The records give no clear sign that my country and I were in an eerie calm preceding a storm over Berlin.

The international barometer began to drop in the spring, although not enough for Washington or USAREUR to predict disaster. The Kennedy administration launched its new defense strategy along with a combative global policy, and I believed these initiatives were in good hands. Militarily, flexible response meant preparedness to retaliate against any level of provocation. Secretary McNamara emphasized improving the weapons, combat readiness, and mobility of conventional forces. The United States, he argued, must be able to win local wars without resort to the tactical nuclear weapons that, in NATO's doctrine under Eisenhower, virtually insured escalation to massive destruction. As USAREUR later summed it up, the new strategy held "that combat units would have to be tailored to meet specific situations, that their tactical mobility and firepower would have to be matched to the environment and to the enemy, and that their organizational structure would have to reflect the increasing probability of limited conventional war." USAREUR expected additional troops and improved weapons, many of which had been developed before Kennedy's election — for example, the M60 tank, the M113 armored personnel carrier, a new series of self-propelled howitzers, the Lacrosse surface-to-surface missile.

On 10 April Kennedy outlined the new strategy to NATO's Military Committee meeting in Washington. Six weeks later, in an extraordinary address to a joint session of Congress, he announced his "Freedom Doctrine," with moral and military echoes of NSC 68, the authoritative National Security Council paper of 1950. The United States could not stand aside while "the adversaries of freedom" took over "the world's newest nations." To fight this "battle for minds and souls as well as lives and territory," he asked Congress for a major increase in spending on defense: for greater civilian and military aid to developing countries, a more mobile and flexible army with additional reserves, new helicopters, and more marines. In addition, Kennedy announced a program to improve civil defense against nuclear attack and pledged that America would land a man on the moon before the end of the decade.

Much as I liked the sound of Kennedy's policies, I noticed the spring turn inclement for flexibility and freedom. The Soviets humiliated America in the race for space: in April Yuri Gagarin orbited the earth; in May Alan Shepard Jr. flew his capsule about 300 miles. The disastrous CIA-backed invasion of the Bay of Pigs in Cuba, coming on the heels of Gagarin's triumph, caused some Europeans — along with peoples in the developing nations — to question American methods in battling for the world's minds and souls. West German defense minister Franz Joseph Strauss criticized flexible response for undermining nuclear deterrence and increasing the danger of war on German soil because the superpowers could keep it from spreading to their own territories.

Above all, American policy in Southeast Asia boded ill for European security. Kennedy seemed more willing than his predecessor to hold back Communism where the French had failed. He considered sending forces to Laos, where the pro-Communist Pathet Lao were winning a civil war, but British prime minister Harold Macmillan and President de Gaulle helped talk him out of it. In May Vice President Lyndon Johnson, on a visit to Saigon, pledged American aid to the South Vietnamese government in its struggle against the recently established National Liberation Front (Vietcong), and the Joint Chiefs of Staff suggested dispatching American troops to South Vietnam — over 1,000 American military advisers were already there — to act as a deterrent against North Vietnam or China. The situation in Laos caused the Pentagon to postpone indefinitely an exercise in strategic mobility — airlifting a large force of American troops to West Germany — that the Joint Chiefs had proposed in September 1960.

Washington insisted that the United States could battle the Soviet Union around the globe and at the same time defend Europe. In April Kennedy assured Adenauer, who did not like or trust the younger man, that America would use force if necessary to protect the freedom of West Berlin. Secretary of State Rusk, addressing a conference of NATO foreign ministers in Oslo on 8 May, proclaimed America's determination to preserve Western rights of occupation and access in Berlin even if the Soviet Union concluded a separate peace treaty with East Germany. On 19 May Washington and Moscow announced that Kennedy and Khrushchev would meet in Vienna on 3–4 June to discuss various issues. On 20 May President de Gaulle visited Bonn to reaffirm his extraordinary friendship with Adenauer and his country's commitment to maintain the status quo in Berlin. When Kennedy came to Paris at the end of May on his way to the Vienna summit, he and de Gaulle agreed to meet with force any Soviet threat to Berlin, a solidarity reinforced by Kennedy's eloquent praise of France and by the French public's adoration of his charming wife. Privately, however, the French leader warned Kennedy not to intervene in Laos, and members of the NATO Council puzzled over Kennedy's entreaty that they concern themselves with the Communist threat around the entire southern half of the globe.

In Giessen that spring army life changed little, while my familiarity with Germany increased dramatically. The 3/79 Artillery shared in 7th Army's general improvement in both hardware and morale. We worked nights and weekends preparing for our Annual General Inspection ("annual nervous breakdown," I wrote to my brother) and passed it with flying colors. We received new and more powerful rocket motors. They were classified "secret," but many of their features could be seen in the latest toy Honest John on sale at the PX. As the battalion's intramural athletics officer, I was put in charge of the late afternoon exercise program that Gen. Clarke instructed USAREUR to begin, with less emphasis on calisthenics and more on dogtrotting; he recommended four miles in fifty minutes. The switch to aerobics seemed to pep us up as a unit, progress that I began to attribute to the Kennedy administration's fetish for fitness. I was promoted to first lieutenant, normally an automatic step after eighteen months of service, but Col. Phillips had already blocked the promotion of one of my fellow second lieutenants, and I was not sure what Phillips thought of me, especially after I screwed up that convoy. Although I had to admit Phillips was a good officer, I was not sorry to see him leave in May for another assignment. Nor was I glad, for he handed over command to his executive officer, Maj. Hayes, a skittish, thin-lipped southerner whose performance so far had earned him the title of "No Decision Hayes" among the enlisted men.

We participated in v Corps's training exercises: Spring Tonic in April; Helping Hand in May, a joint operation with the German III Korps, in which units of the 6th Brigade, 2nd Panzer Grenadier Division, occupied positions to the west of Giessen. The Germans of III Korps had better maps than ours, and their movements looked more precise. Standing among their camouflaged vehicles one day during an impromptu conference of officers, I remembered how often I had played war against the Germans as a boy, firing at them from behind stone walls and elm trees.

I had hoped to serve as a liaison officer in Helping Hand, but v Corps chose instead a captain who spoke poor German and lacked a feel for *Gemütlichkeit*. My disappointment subsided when I received a book about Austria from Gen. Waldmüller and Maj. Dreihann in thanks for my escorting them during Wintershield II. The U.S. military attaché in Vienna, in his letter transmitting the gift, noted their praise for my "language fluency, courteous attitude and accurate responses in providing a running orientation of the training." Attached to his letter were endorsements from each headquarters down the chain — 7th Army, v Corps, v Corps Artillery, 36th Artillery Group, and 3/79. I liked 7th Army's best: "Service with the forces of a foreign power requires initiative, professional competence, and diplomacy; and when performed creditably, enhances the prestige of our Armed Forces."

These letters are the closest thing to a ribbon or citation — or what the British call "mention in dispatches" — that I received in two years of service. Seeking various ways to define the Cold War, I recently inquired about decorations. An official at the National Personnel Records Center in St. Louis informed me that "there are no real 'Cold War' medals" for service in Germany after the Allied occupation ended formally in 1955. It was the war that wasn't.

Members of my platoon and the Firing Battery spray-painted vehicles, spit-polished boots, and wore red scarves for the parade marking German-American friendship week. "Jockstrap, blue sandals, and a light coat of oil" is what some of us called such frippery, but it lifted our morale and impressed the large German crowd that watched. German and American units drove in bright sunshine, the column preceded by one soldier of each nationality carrying the blue NATO flag. Each band played the other's national anthem after the last vehicle had passed the reviewing stand, where the dignitaries included military commanders, the mayor, and the rector of the city's Justus von Liebig University. It was the largest military parade in the history of Giessen's German American week, and feelings of solidarity ran high.

I had never been more aware of German history and politics. USAREUR post libraries reported William L. Shirer's recent book, *The Rise and Fall of the Third Reich*, to be in great demand, a good sign for America's historical literacy. As I read it, I became impatient with how often Shirer's map of German history showed roads leading directly to Hitler, as if signposted by a highway patrol of inevitability. This American version of Germany's national character was too simple, and I was beginning to think I could prove the point. Still, continuities in German history gave me pause, such as the Bug's origins in 1939 as the "KdF-Wagen" (Kraft durch Freude [strength through joy], a program to improve workers' morale with paid vacations) and the use of its chassis for the small German command car during the war.

Germans began to confront Nazism more than they had ever done since its defeat. In April the trial of Adolph Eichmann opened in Jerusalem. German television and the *Giessener Freie Presse* followed the trial. Adenauer stated that nearly every German felt ashamed of the Nazis' crimes. The city government of Frankfurt published a booklet refuting claims that most Germans knew nothing about Nazi brutality against the Jews during the war. "We have developed the art of forgetfulness to a masterful virtuosity," the booklet stated. Large audiences watched the brutally explicit television series *Das Dritte Reich*. Two major historical novels published in 1959 were widely read: Heinrich Böll's *Billard um halbzehn* (*Billiards at Half-Past Nine*) and Günter Grass's *Die Blechtrommel* (*The Tin Drum*).

I struggled through Böll's novel in German. One of the characters in it, who had been imprisoned by the Gestapo, says years after the war, "Every time I meet someone, I ask myself whether I would want to be handed over to him." That sentence shocked me then and shakes me still. In it Böll indicts the twentieth century and reminds me of my worst childhood nightmare. He cuts to the visceral moment when you decide whether you will resist. For over thirty years Böll has influenced my choice of friends and my judgment of politicians and colleagues. Like the character in *Billiards*, there aren't many people I would want to be handed over to. In every case, I also have my mother in mind.

Antje gave me *Billiards*. Frank Linden had introduced me to her. She was sensational: full breasts, provocative eyes and sensual mouth, suggestive voice. Not Mom. On our first date, 9 April, I took her to a chamber concert at the university — Purcell, Bach, and Telemann — and then to the Reehmühle, an old country inn near Giessen famous for its Mühlengeist, a flaming drink of unrevealed ingredients and unmistakable kick. A week later we attended the "artillery formal dance" at the Officers' Club. Her poise and beauty quickly melted the frigid reaction I had seen in senior and married officers whenever bachelor lieutenants appeared with German women. Col. Phillips came over to us more often than his southern roots and West Point manners required, complimenting Antje on her charm. When he did this after the last dance, Antje replied, "If I am so charming, why didn't you dance with me?"

I was smitten. Antje and I drove to Heidelberg the following weekend in my Bug. I remembered reading Remarque's *Drei Kameraden* at Cornell, a romantic story, with a sad ending, about a man, a woman, and an automobile. Failed romances, sad endings, and loneliness belonged to the old me, I assured myself. We stayed with friends of Antje's family. The son, studying theology in Hamburg, told me his father, a former staff officer, had studied tactics under Rommel at the war academy in Potsdam in the 1930s. Rommel had handed back one paper saying, "Your solution is like the girls of Provence, picture-pretty but impractical." That evening, on the balcony overlooking the glimmering city, I pictured how I would embrace Antje if our hosts were absent. Back in Giessen, I bought tickets for *La Bohème* at the Wiesbaden May festival but had to cancel at the last minute because Capt. Haggerty, now on battalion staff, insisted that I appear before him at 7 P.M. to make a statement about damage to a vehicle in the A&T Platoon. Later that evening I played rummy with Antje and her mother at their home, her stepfather having gone to bed. Antje called it the "La Bohème game" and accepted Haggerty's obduracy far more stoically than I.

A few days later we did make it to Wiesbaden for an evening of Stravinsky performed by the Brussels Ballet and choreographed by Maurice Béjart: *Pulcinella* (with Béjart himself in the title role), *Jeu de cartes*, and *Le sacre du printemps* (with Tania Bari). Afterward, Antje and I danced at the Von Steuben Hotel in Wiesbaden, a high-class watering hole for a nearby U.S. Air Force base. At the theater, the eroticism of *Le sacre du printemps* had stirred my desire to undress her and wrap myself around her stunning curves. On the dance floor, I was all decorum. At our table, I was in love, inexperienced, and unready when she told me that she was also dating another guy, a handsome, supercilious American officer in Giessen whom I did not like.

Three comrades threatened by a jerk, I silently lamented on the drive back to Giessen. My pessimistic voice said oh-oh, and my gut tightened: old warning signs for the loner still in me to expect the familiar pain of rejection and beware the unknown world of passion. I suddenly wished I were driving a Porsche at high speed, looking seductively at Antje, caressing her leg like a pro, heading for my place. I dropped her off at her place, gave her a light kiss good-night, and kicked myself all the way back to the BOQ.

My relationship with Antje's parents prospered, however, and led me deeper into German history. Her mother, née Rasmussen-Bonne, had grown up near Königsberg in East Prussia on an estate founded by her grandfather when he moved from Denmark in the nineteenth century. In 1935, the year my parents married in West Texas, she had wed a young officer named Gaudlitz, who came from Halle in Thüringen. He had served in the ground troops of the Condor Legion in Spain, Hitler's notorious contribution to Franco in the Spanish Civil War. After returning to Germany, Gaudlitz had transferred to an infantry regiment; his battalion commander was Lt. Col. Hermann Flörke. Gaudlitz, Antje's father, died on the Russian front in August 1941 when she was an infant. Two years later his widow married Flörke, whom Gaudlitz had asked to look after his wife and child if he fell. While Flörke was in detention after the war, mother and child scraped by on painting and selling buttons. In the 1950s Frau Flörke was one of the most popular leaders of Die Brücke, an organization of German and American women in Giessen.

Antje kept her father's name and loved her stepfather, who was born in 1893 in Hanover. Flörke had served as a junior officer on the western front in the First World War, and he remained in the Reichswehr during the Weimar Republic. He had fought on both western and eastern fronts in the next war, which he had finished as a lieutenant general commanding a corps against the American 1st Army as it pressed eastward from the Remagen bridgehead. He considered himself "lucky to have surrendered to an American, and a nice one, too." He was released from detention in 1947 and soon became head of the Labor Service in Giessen, German civilians who were employed by the American supply depot. He had retired by the time I arrived in Giessen but remained active in German-American organizations and was head of the local chapter of the Verband deutscher Soldaten (Association of German Soldiers).

Antje and her parents lived at 21 Wilhelmstrasse. When I returned for a look in February 1996, the large gray dwelling had been painted beige and converted into rooms for university students. The shape of the house and its entryway awoke memories of my first long talk with the Flörkes about Nazi Germany on the evening of 27 May 1961. We drank a 1959 Mosel wine and listened to Schubert's *Trout* quintet.

I noticed how Frau Flörke's gray-blue eyes could change in an instant from light humor to broody toughness. The general wore a bow tie and prefaced many of his remarks with "one must consider" and "one should not forget." We sat on the heavy furniture he had inherited from his parents — maroon upholstery, dark mahogany ornately carved in vine leaves and clusters of grapes, with eagles' heads at the front of the armrests. Among the photographs in the room was one of the Rasmussen-Bonne mansion in East Prussia and another of a grave somewhere in Russia with a steel helmet placed over the wooden cross. There was nothing militaristic about the room or the general, whose modesty hid much of what I gradually learned from his family, from men who had fought under his command, and from German archives. He had received one of the Wehrmacht's highest decorations, the Ritterkreuz mit Eichenlaub (Knight's Cross with

Oak Leaves), awarded to him personally by Hitler in August 1944 for exceptional valor during the unrelenting Soviet offensive of that summer. He had allowed his officers and men more initiative in combat than was the norm and had shown them more respect as individuals. Among superiors and subordinates he was known as a fine commander who cared for his men, and they remembered him with affection.

We talked about the Weimar Republic, anti-Semitism, Hitler's popularity, genocide, resistance. Gen. Flörke defined *Freiheit* (freedom) and *Geltung* (prestige) as political assets that Germany lacked during the Weimar Republic. He justified Nazi foreign policy up to the invasion of Poland, which, he had predicted to his battalion officers, marked the beginning of a long war that Germany would lose. We began disagreeing that evening over topics that we would debate for many years. He emphasized a nation's freedom from international pressures, claimed that his units in Poland and Russia had no connection with the Final Solution, blamed Hitler for bad military decisions, criticized the opposition movement against Hitler for betraying the state while it was at war. I dwelt on personal freedoms, indirect connections, military advisers, higher moral laws of resistance against tyranny.

Flörke admired my American heritage and sympathized with my Confederate ancestors who had fought for a "lost cause" in the Civil War. Widely read in military history, he could sketch Jackson's enveloping move at Chancellorsville, Lee's gamble at Gettysburg, Grant's strategy of attrition. He reminded me that Germany and Europe had much longer histories with powerful continuities. "One should not forget," he would say during discussions of Germany's strategic position in the center of Europe, that the Fulda Gap antedated the ancient Roman "limes," or that the German leader Arminius drew the Romans into a fatal trap in the Teutoburger forest (southwest of Hanover) early in the first century A.D., or that Louis XIV burned Heidelberg late in the seventeenth century.

Compassionate, cultivated, principled, a gentleman in every sense of the word, Gen. Flörke led me to refight the Second World War as if I were serving under him on the eastern front. I would have respected and trusted him as my commander. But how would we have behaved toward members of the ss and other Nazi organizations that followed the army across Poland and Russia? In the early sixties most historians argued that the army had almost nothing to do with the Final Solution, a position that has been revised by recent scholarship. Although I subscribed then to the accepted view, I knew that general orders for the invasion of the Soviet Union had included references to racial inferiors and that there had to be some overlap of authority near the front. Would Flörke and I have been able to separate military operations entirely from racial policy? If so, would we have protested to our superiors as we learned about the ss "action teams" and extermination camps? If unable to insulate ourselves from racial policy, would we have disobeyed orders to treat Jews and Slavs as "subhumans"?

Orders were orders, especially in the German military tradition, and I began to doubt whether I would have disobeyed. Resistance looked dubious for the skeptical good German I had been inventing for myself, and either self-deception or a guilty conscience looked inescapable. On the other hand, if I did disobey and faced trial by court-martial, Flörke was the sort of officer I would want to be handed over to. Germans like him were not oppressors simply because they served an oppressive system. I could envision Flörke and Mommsen discussing history and my mother and the general charming each other.

In Flörke, and in my contacts with the Bundeswehr, I saw examples of loyalty and courage that did not point toward blind obedience or mindless brutality. In the Federal Republic, perhaps democracy could for the first time in history become a German habit of mind. Membership in NATO might allow Germans to redefine *Macht* (power) so as to renounce unilateral hegemony and to redefine *Recht* (right) so as to abjure the territories lost to Poland and the Soviet Union. It was too early to tell. Meanwhile, my German question continued to grow more complex than my memories of war and Mommsen's example. I might have been Flörke?

Ambivalence about Germany reinforced my Cold War agnosticism. There were no guarantees that people serving a democratic system would behave democratically. The more I learned about Germany's Faust, the more I questioned Dad's statement that civilized societies must compromise with the devil, using deceit for reason of state. If they must, then with what consequences and within what moral boundaries? If Americans could recognize their government's flirtations with the devil, I thought, they might be less inclined to boast that Nazism "can't happen here," a complacency that Shirer's book inadvertently sustained. The devil could ruin civilized societies other than Germany, recruiting Fausts and bullies as needed. Americans were fighting a "good war" against Communism but had behaved badly when Senator McCarthy fanned the brimstone of our fear and our xenophobia. If we could allow the devil that much freedom in our own yard, could we not also give him opportunities abroad?

I saw more good in U.S. policy than I had in the fifties. I had been elected to the male elite of my generation at the height of American imperium. I trusted our government and believed in Kennedy and his well-educated advisers, men who fit Cecil Rhodes's ideal of civil servants and officers who would rule well. The president's popularity among Europeans made me glad to be an American. His doctrines of freedom and flexible response, I thought, did not upset the status quo but promised to restore America's rightful position of military superiority and moral authority in the struggle against Communism. Similarly, firmness on Berlin restated a prior commitment. There was nothing intrinsically wrong with an active foreign policy. American hegemony could prevent Europe from repeating Munich, and NATO fought for a worthy cause. I was proud to have helped both my country and the alliance when I escorted the Austrians during Wintershield II.

In spite of my enthusiasm for Kennedy, however, I felt twinges of agnosticism. The president raised not only my hopes but also the standards I expected my government to meet in waging the Cold War. I was not sure how he and his advisers, many of whom had fought in the Second World War as young men, would apply that experience now that my generation was in uniform. No matter who ran the government, wouldn't there always be an authorized and incomplete rendition of events? My map of the Cold War was European, not global; history and security concentrated for me in the Old World, not around the world's newest nations. I could visualize American hegemony and apply lessons of Munich far more easily in Europe than in Asia. But even in Europe, would the memory of Munich cause my government to misread Soviet aims and increase the risk of war for the sake of an image more than for Berlin itself? Had not Khrushchev become more bluster than bully? I could more readily justify the CIA's clandestine activities in the Old World than in Cuba or Southeast Asia. Although I did not see most of these activities as the devil's work, like many American liberals I worried about their impact on a world opinion that the idealism of the Peace Corps was meant to sway. The Peace Corps, not the CIA, would resist poverty and build free communities in the Third World. As for space, Gagarin and Shepard were both "making history," I wrote to my brother, and I wished we "could think solely in terms of space exploration" instead of Cold War competition.

More gloomy than I and more candid than official Washington, Dad began to predict that the Cold War might overwhelm my personal agenda. After the Bay of Pigs, he wanted the United States to stand firm and not bow to any Soviet threats. But he also feared "that Russia might use Cuba or Laos as an excuse for causing trouble in Germany, and that you might not get home in September or even to Oxford." If war should come, he wrote, "not only you and John but a million or two other young men will be called up. And of course nuclear bombs could end a lot of us civs at home." I agreed with Dad about the Soviets' using excuses, but I thought war highly unlikely.

So did my brother, perhaps because he counted on having long bull sessions with me in September. "Get home!" he ordered. John had started serious rock climbing in Yosemite Valley, and he loved the Sierra more than Berkeley. He found graduate school challenging and was pleased to have been awarded a teaching assistantship for the next academic year. Yet Berkeley was "an intellectual community in name only, a chunk of acreage on which various disciplines have set up their fluttering many-hued tents." He accused academic philosophy of ivory-towered disengagement but praised one of his professors, Joseph Tussman, for challenging students to relate philosophy to American politics. (As a teaching assistant in the spring of 1964, John would issue the same challenge to his section of an undergraduate ethics course. One of his students was Mario Savio, who went to Mississippi that summer. In the fall, when the university administration cracked down on the Free Speech Movement, John advised Savio that Berkeley was not Mississippi, that Savio's experience over the summer might not apply on campus. Savio replied, "No, it's the same, you wait and see.")

John's disenchantment prompted him to reiterate his advice that I pursue a nonacademic career after acquiring my doctorate, following in the steps of other Rhodes scholars, like Dean Rusk. "Play politics at Oxford," he counseled, and "learn how to compromise your ideals" if you intend to have an impact on public affairs.

In a long letter in April about genes and ambitions, John reflected on how Mom's absence had affected our characters. During that "period of desolation," while Dad was "hanging on by sheer guts," we brothers acquired "a vulnerability to loneliness and a craving for attention." But having been thrown on our own at that age, we also became "far more resourceful and creative than would otherwise have been the case." We must have known we were different from other kids, and that "sense of separation" had led us to believe we were destined for unique achievements. We had inherited Dad's "high intellectual standards of rationality" and Mom's "gaiety and spontaneity." This was a superb combination "if properly managed." Managing it was our major difficulty. We both had "a sense of un-explored potential, room for growth, unlimited adventure." Perhaps, for the time being, we should take Montaigne's advice to refrain from marriage "'when feverish and full of agitations, and to await another more private and less disturbed opportunity.'"

If I were to reply to John now, I would agree entirely. I would ask how we might manage our parents' combined gifts so as to maximize satisfaction with whatever we achieved. I would wonder how much our fates were determined by vulnerability and loneliness. I would compare his summary of our inheritance with the words under my photograph in the West High yearbook of my senior year, 1955: "No one takes responsibility more seriously or amusement more lightly." I would say that responsibility can wear you down, and amusement is all that's left to ward off despondency. Mom's father, Bunk, hadn't made it. Mom had, or so it seemed, and God help us if we lost the gaiety and spontaneity she had somehow regained.

At the time I received John's letter, however, my mind was not on family but on Antje, who filled me with agitations. I introduced her by mail a couple of weeks before our evening in Wiesbaden. John was impressed. "She sounds great," he wrote, "why don't you bring her to Madison in September?" Dad offered no advice: "That's your business and it's always different from what happens to every other man." Mom thought Antje sounded wonderful; "I have always trusted your good taste, so why should I doubt your taste in women?" Miss Ada was happy I had found a "Jane."

Mom avoided politics. She sent news about her reading club,

Cornell crew, and Barbos, whom she called "Chief of Staff" in the new house, but she still offered me no advice on china. She was "just bustin'" to see me in September, and indeed she mentioned September in all of her letters. Her tidbits seemed cheerful, her eagerness to see me understandable considering my plans. I did not notice that her letters became fewer and shorter in the spring.

In May I notified Rhodes House that I was applying for an early release from the army in September and asked for a document proving I had received a scholarship to study at Oxford. I knew my family counted on my homecoming, and I looked forward to seeing them. But I had set my sights on Oxford. My future lay there. Going home would be a bonus, an interlude, a holiday. It was not necessary for my story nor my family's state of mind.

I took over the A&T Platoon while its commander was on leave for three weeks. I thrived on the challenge and wondered what I would think of the army if this had happened earlier. The platoon's spirits climbed, and, as I wrote home, "we broke all unit records for speed and safety" in loading warheads during a practice alert. But by and large, I added, my battalion was like a psychologist's white rat experiment, except that no reward awaited successful performance. I was starting to count the weeks I had left in Giessen, a sure sign of considering myself a short-timer. Military service had taught me about as much as it could, and I was ready to file it away.

President Kennedy had "inspired a rebirth of political consciousness," I wrote to John, and I was "thinking seriously of a life of public service." I had "something to contribute," encouraged by Professor Ernst's compliment that I would make a superb diplomat. Although there was "an abysmal difference" between potential and actual greatness, perhaps diplomacy was my destiny after all. I seemed to have "a knack for getting along with Europeans" and was acquiring "a feel for Europe." I told John that hearing a commentator on Radio Czechoslovakia denounce, in French, the postwar ascendancy of Gens. Speidel and Heusinger "was more instructive than reading in *Time* that the propaganda war in Europe is intense. Radio Moscow, in English, is a barrel of laughs, but makes frightening sense to the uninformed."

On the last day of the month, while Kennedy and de Gaulle discussed Berlin a few days before the Vienna summit, I attended a ceremony in Heidelberg celebrating the university's 575th birthday.

Professor Ernst had me seated with honored guests in the main hall. Deane Malott, president of Cornell, was there, having come to Heidelberg to dedicate a plaque to Jacob Gould Schurman, a former president of Cornell (1892–1920) and U.S. ambassador to Germany (1925–1930). Kurt Kiesinger, the minister-president of Baden-Württemberg (and later chancellor) gave a short speech. The highlight of the program was the conferral of an honorary degree on William Somerset Maugham. When the dignitaries passed by at the end of the ceremony, I overheard him mutter to his companion, "Oh, I *would* like a *cigarette*." A few minutes later, as people milled about the foyer, Maugham emerged from the men's room, puffing and smiling. The Cold War was nowhere in sight, Oxford just a few months away.

When a smiling Parisian barber asked me early in 1996 what sort of haircut I wanted, I replied, "Oh, normal." He raised both arms in a suspenseful shrug, scissors in one hand and comb in the other. "Mais tout est normal!" (but everything is normal), he declared, and he asked me to make a decision. On the eve of the Vienna summit in 1961, peaceful coexistence was normal: between NATO and the Warsaw Pact; between the Cold War and my world's fight.

Nevertheless, something felt unusual in the spring of 1961. I lost a boyhood hero when Gary Cooper died. "Der Cowboy ist tot," mourned the *Giessener Freie Presse*. Now in unseasoned adulthood, I had begun the year with complementary aims and by the end of May had made progress toward all of them. Yet each goal was changing shape as I approached it, as if part of some protean plot to incite doubt and frustrate planning. German history had grown more difficult and my imaginary role in it more baffling. Antje looked away. Military service had become a chore that I was no longer sure I would finish in time for Oxford, whose spires looked more and more inviting. My elation of December and January had waned.

Expectant and unsettled, I was trying to reconcile these changes at the same time President Kennedy struggled with his initiation into the Cold War, Western European leaders fidgeted, and Khrushchev gloated at the sight. Thoughts of Oxford blunted my perception of Cold War tension, its effect on my family, and its responsiveness to diplomacy. I did not know how inexorably I was being drawn into the stuff of history that could wreck coexistence and normality with it.

CHAPTER 7  *War over Berlin?*

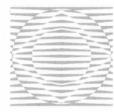

I remember the 20th of August 1961 as if I had just put on clean fatigues. The "world's fight" was abruptly here, now, sure to postpone the scholarship that was supposed to prepare me for vague battles in the future. Things had fallen apart.

After the Vienna summit, Berlin muscled in on politics and private lives like a vulgar gate-crasher. Escalation frayed the nerves of American forces in West Germany and West Berlin. My family wanted me home, while tours of active duty were extended. I proceeded as if things were normal, as if leaving the army and attending Oxford were still attainable goals along a private time line that unruly public events could not erase. But I felt a distinct change in atmosphere. I was disoriented, no longer sure that time marked progress and worked in my favor. I could not free myself from events that were becoming historical around me, hardly the story I had bargained for since winning the Rhodes scholarship. I sensed that my fate was firmly in the grip of leaders in Washington and Moscow who were losing control of the Cold War.

The Berlin crisis paralleled, and often accentuated, the everyday, the peaceful, the comical. I knew I was locked into an unusual drama, yet I could also go outside it, as if waking from a dream to find familiar surroundings. My memory preserved both everyday and unusual moments, its customary way of showing that it was on the job marking, filing, comparing.

Memory can judge Cold War realities more accurately than governments do. American troops who reinforced the Berlin Garrison in August 1961 were later awarded the Armed Forces Expeditionary Medal. The far larger numbers who stood on alert in West Germany in case the reinforcements precipitated war received no official recognition. Looking back, I think this differentiation is senseless. All of us who were in Germany in August 1961 made history and have been made by it. There is meaning in what we did and what we remember.

Shortly after I returned from the University of Heidelberg's celebration, Kennedy and Khrushchev met at Vienna on 3–4 June to discuss a wide range of issues, including Laos and nuclear arms testing as well as Berlin. Kennedy rejected Soviet proposals for even an interim settlement of the Berlin question, and Khrushchev renewed his ultimatum to sign a separate peace treaty with the East Germans no later than December, giving them control of access to a demilitarized West Berlin. "Savaged" by Khrushchev, as Kennedy privately admitted to James Reston in the U.S. embassy after the summit, the president returned home to begin preparing for the "cold winter" he promised his adversary.

Escalation soon became obvious in *Stars and Stripes*. I read it then, and it sounds authentic as I reread it now. On Sunday, 18 June, the newspaper reported Saturday's mass rally of about 100,000 West Berliners against Soviet policy, as well as Kennedy's threat that a Soviet refusal to negotiate a treaty banning nuclear tests could prompt the United States to resume the testing that both governments had suspended in 1958. Daily coverage of Berlin — usually with headlines on the first page — began on 22 June, with the regular use of the word "crisis" starting in early July.

On 21 June, twenty years after the German invasion of the Soviet Union, Khrushchev reiterated his plans for Berlin and wondered aloud whether West German leaders were foolish enough to imitate their Nazi predecessors. A week later Kennedy dismissed Khrushchev's boast that the Soviet Union would overtake the United States economically by 1970 and affirmed Western determination to protect West Berlin. The fall of West Berlin, warned the secretary general of NATO, would mean the end of the Atlantic Alliance. On 1 July we read — thanks to a news leak in Washington — that the Joint Chiefs of Staff proposed evacuating 250,000 military dependents from France and West Germany, declaring a national emergency, calling up reserves and National Guard, transferring at least one combat division from America to West Germany. On the 8th the Soviets rejected American proposals for a test ban treaty, and Khrushchev announced a turnabout in defense policy: the suspension of planned troop reductions and an increase of 25 percent in military spending for the year. President Kennedy, who expected the Soviets to provoke a long series of crises short of war, ordered a comprehensive review of America's military strength and budget. His brother Robert, the attorney general, warned Khrushchev not to repeat Hitler's mistake and underestimate the American people.

Kennedy addressed the nation on the evening of 25 July. I heard excerpts the next morning on the Armed Forces Network. He blamed the crisis on the Soviets, compared West Berlin to Bastogne and Stalingrad, said that a Communist attack upon West Berlin would be "an attack against us all," declared we would not surrender. Consistent with the doctrine of flexible response, he proposed increasing the size and diverse weaponry of the armed forces. In case of conflict that could not be limited, he recommended more spending on fallout shelters. For the army, he would double and triple draft calls, summon reserves and National Guard units, and extend terms of active service that would otherwise expire before 1 July 1962. The latter meant me. On 31 July Congress gave Kennedy the necessary authority to call up reservists and extend tours of active duty by twelve months.

By mid-June the tension over Berlin had already risen enough to persuade me that events could disrupt my plans for Oxford. In July I questioned neither the need for emergency measures nor their timing. The lessons of the Second World War came easily to mind as both sides tossed them about. I subscribed to the American version, my agnostic qualms having evaporated in the inflammatory atmosphere of threats and historical analogies. In the long run, history would justify Kennedy and American power. Khrushchev was the neighborhood bully in Europe, and the West must not give him Berlin as it had given Hitler much of Czechoslovakia at Munich. The United States must and would lead the Western Alliance clear of appeasement. (I did not know then that President de Gaulle stood firmer than Kennedy, who was more willing to negotiate on Berlin, nor, at the other extreme, that the National Security Council discussed the possibility of a preemptive nuclear attack against the Soviet Union.) If war came, it might not be as good as the war of my childhood, but it would be better than surrender.

In his speech on 25 July, Kennedy appealed to American patriotism, and soon draft boards witnessed an upsurge of volunteers. An incident in 7th Army, however, recalled Senator McCarthy's slanders and reminded me that a certain kind of American would never believe that liberals were patriotic. In June Gen. Clarke admonished Maj. Gen. Edwin Walker, who, while commanding the 24th Infantry Division, had called Truman, Acheson, and Eleanor Roosevelt "pink." Walker had also distributed materials published by the John Birch Society and alleged that the American media were controlled by Communists. The *Overseas Weekly* had blown the whistle on Walker. As if to make up for his divisive rubbish, *Stars and Stripes* lauded the ideals of Peace Corps volunteers, like the young woman from Texas who was tired of our generation's always being called silent and the marine veteran who welcomed the chance to serve God, having already served his country.

Escalation began to drown out the normal background noise of Cold War politics. Scuttlebutt and grumbling in my battalion concentrated on the fate of short-timers and dependents. Few of us expected war, but we performed our routine tasks knowing that Berlin had become an implicit contingency lurking out there beyond normality. We adjusted to our new commander, Maj. Hayes, who seemed alternately more relaxed and more nervous now that he was in charge. We responded to changes in training that resulted from Wintershield II and flexible response. Seventh Army ordered units to stop wasting time on window dressing for inspections (such as painting rocks around headquarters' areas) and concentrate on small-unit operations. USAREUR instructed 7th Army to design "combat capability tests" for missile and rocket battalions with nuclear warheads. We entertained Norwegian and Italian officers, the latter telling me that the address I remembered for the Pensione Rubens in Rome — where my family had stayed in April 1952 — could not be correct for it was that of a brothel. We prepared to leave for Grafenwöhr at the end of July for our Army Training Test.

In the summer of '61 camaraderie around the BOQs was warmer than ever before during my tour in Giessen. Perhaps the distant rumble of Berlin helped move us closer together, like backpackers who hear thunder approaching. Frank, JJ, and I belonged to a small group of officers and schoolteachers (Jo Ann, Mary, Gina, Jo) who often gathered for drinks and dinner in our rooms, at the Officers' Club, or in town. We traded memories and dreams. We looked up to all the Kennedys; Jackie had become a role model for many women who prized both glamour and public service. We speculated about why Ernest Hemingway killed himself; if there were clues in the Nick Adams stories, which I loved, I did not want to find them. JJ wished he had had the option of serving in the Peace Corps instead of the army. Jo preferred the sweetness of Johnny Mathis to the softness of Nat King Cole, missed California, and looked forward to returning to what she accurately claimed was then one of the best public school systems in the United States. I assured them all that, if I made it to Oxford, I would come back to Giessen for Christmas. At the Officers' Club we heard other bachelors enthuse over Washington's increasing interest in South Vietnam. That's where the real action will be, they said, and that's where we want to be when it hits. By some bilateral process of selection, none of these adventurers belonged to our intimate group.

USAREUR headquarters thought intimacy had gone too far in the BOQs. In March Gen. Clarke had issued a directive on morals. Disturbed by reports of drunkenness and other misbehavior, he reminded officers that, when we accepted our commissions, we were "presumed to have acquired the ethical and moral precepts of an officer and a gentleman." As the Berlin crisis escalated during the summer, Clarke apparently wanted us to save our loins for girding.

In late June word went around the bachelor officers in Giessen that the military police were going to inspect all BOQ rooms one night to stamp out unauthorized sex. Forewarned by an insider at Giessen Post Headquarters, we all slept innocently on the night of the raid. When I answered the knock on my door, there stood two MPs and a major whom I knew. I had not been sleeping with anybody, but some half-conscious jester in me turned toward the bedroom and yelled, "OK, everybody out!" The major and MPs made straight for the bedroom, their eyes glowing with triumph. They found no one: not in the room nor outside the window, where they thought they would find a knotted sheet to explain my woman's escape. I told them there was no woman, that I had been kidding at the door. They left mystified, wondering how to report their only apparent victory of the night.

I bumped into the major at the bar in the Officers' Club a few days later. "Well, Lt. Post," he said, "now that it's all over and nothing will happen to you, tell me, how did you do it?"

"Sir?"

"How did you do it?"

"Do what?"

"Aw, come on, you know, how did you hide the girl?"

I laughed and denied again that I had been hiding anyone, but my protest only widened the grins along the bar and solidified my sudden reputation as a clever night fighter.

I wished I had been hiding Antje, but she had fallen for the other guy. While falling, she had asked me what I thought of him. I should have been candid, but the cowboys on both sides of the family told me to lick salt, and Uncle John's euphemisms did not ride to the rescue. So I failed to warn her to distrust any man who reads manuals on how to smoke a pipe so he will look cool doing it. (Antje saw through him after a few months. Two years later he married another German woman, whom he persuaded to change her given name to something that sounded more American; he was a career officer.)

Recent experience informed my brother's warning to me that "no woman wants a man who is in the least unsure of himself around her." I was very unsure, I replied. I had "somewhere along the line developed a cautious, almost defensive attitude toward feelings of the heart." I did not want to "get burned," much as I wished I could "fall madly in love and get it over with, whatever the consequences." I knew these feelings went back to Mom's leaving us after the war, but I hesitated to tell John. Saying it to myself invited loneliness, and I was trying to put all that behind me. Solitude should be my choice, I thought, not imposed.

Antje and I got back together for the weekend of 8–9 July, while Khrushchev and Kennedy delivered their escalatory announcements. She meant no love, and I was too guarded to expect any. She simply wanted to fulfill her promise to introduce me to her relatives in Enkirch, a village on the Mosel where her uncle owned several small vineyards and bottled excellent wines under his Rasmussen-Bonne label. I found solace in the large cellar where he stored his marvelous 1959 vintage. Sipping and listening, I discovered differences among wines produced from the same Riesling grape growing on the same hill in what looked like the same soil; you could taste variations in drainage, minerals, and southern exposure. I bought my first case of wine from her uncle, all 1959s.

One of his helpers drew me aside later that afternoon and, apologetically, told me he had seen "terrible things" in Warsaw during the war. "Ich hab' es erlebt" (I experienced it), he repeated over and over, a litany that betrayed both shame and pride to have lived the unthinkable. My curiosity turned to disgust as he described scenes of starvation and brutality, sounding not like a perpetrator but a voyeur, going beyond what was necessary to convince someone who had not been there. Perhaps the Eichmann trial had pried open his memory, perhaps also the television documentary *Das Dritte Reich*. I pitied and loathed him for what he remembered.

West Germans continued to wrestle with their consciences and with history that summer. Feelings of guilt and persecution tangled, heightening German fears that the United States opposed Germany's reunification and might abandon West Berlin. I discussed these questions with German friends on Sunday walks. The Ernsts and I paused in the amphitheater constructed on the Heiligenberg by the Nazis for celebrating German folk themes outdoors. On the Schiffenberg, the Flörkes showed me the remains of the abbey that had been founded in the twelfth century and given over to the Deutschritterorden (Knights of the Teutonic Order) in the thirteenth. We had tea on the terrace of the small café outside the cloister wall. We looked miles to the south and covered lots of ground — Eichmann, guilt, Berlin, Kennedy, NATO. Gen. Flörke felt responsibility for the Second World War but not guilt, and he did not lament Germany's losing. He found mistakes in Western policy during the course of the Cold War, and he thought Kennedy and NATO should have taken a stronger stand on Berlin right after the Vienna summit. But he accepted historical reality. Unlike many German veterans and conservatives, he knew the United States could not have joined Hitler against Stalin, and he reconciled himself to the probable finality of the new German-Polish borders. He had faith in Kennedy's word and America's will to defend West Berlin.

On 25 July President Kennedy acknowledged that "studies or careers will be interrupted." The next day I wrote to E. T. Williams at Rhodes House in Oxford: "As a result of President Kennedy's new defense proposals, my tour of active duty will probably be extended for one year." I saw little hope that the army would approve my request for an early release in September, and I asked whether I could hold onto the scholarship until fall 1962: "Perhaps such a rain check is wishful thinking, but I cannot convince myself that I must forgo Oxford altogether."

I wished I could trade the army's rules for Oxford's. Williams had written to me earlier in the month about Oxford's prohibition against undergraduates having cars there. He advised me to ask New College's permission to bring mine. "Not as of right but as of grace," he added, for "in the past some Rhodes Scholars have implied it was part of the American Constitution whereas our statutes are older and different, if you see what I mean." My pessimistic letter of the 26th was forwarded to him on holiday in Devonshire. His encouraging reply reached me at Grafenwöhr. The Rhodes trustees would certainly give me a rain check. "I can but hope," he continued, "that you'll be free to appear in Oxford next term, but we'll all understand — and sympathize — if you can't."

Miss Ada saw me where I was, not where I wanted to be. On the first night of the Vienna summit, she wrote that it was "pouring down rain" in Haskell, good for the ranch. She was thrilled by television coverage of the Kennedys and Khrushchevs meeting in Vienna but asked me, "Is all this visiting and cablegrams, etc., going to get us anywhere?" She had "seen ole soldiers buried who fought in the Civil War & World War — their families were very proud of them and I am proud of you." My "brand" — my officer's rank — would stay with me all my life, she declared.

Reading Miss Ada's letter now, along with her other letters of 1961, I find something between the lines that I did not see then. She had seen other generations of men go to war. She recognized, more intuitively than I, the possibility that I might fulfill my childhood ideal of heroism in battle. She knew better than I that, once you have tied your destiny to such an ideal, history does not readily let you loose because you would rather be a civilian at Oxford. That was a hard lesson for me to learn. I saw Berlin as an untimely threat to Oxford, not my inexorable rendezvous with history.

Even before Kennedy's emergency measures, I warned my family that I might not obtain either leave or early release in September. Dad knew the crisis was serious, and the anxiety in his letters rose along with the international tension. In early June, before the import of the Vienna summit was clear, he had regained hope that they would see me in September, "one-and-a-half years since that miserable Sunday when we took you to Fort Dix — Mom and I were more miserable than you!" He had two fine red wines "to go with fatted calf" to celebrate my homecoming. Three weeks later he suspected I would have to defend Berlin and regretted he was "partly responsible for your being born into this lousy 20th century." The day after Khrushchev's announcement of 8 July, Dad wondered whether we ought not to compromise over Berlin since "the Russians and E. Germans are so much more powerful than we are," and he feared something "over there will upset your fine plans." Surely the United States could spare "a man who has such an opportunity as yours."

John, in Madison for the summer, could not believe that Mom was now fifty and Dad fifty-nine. Dad's bad back had improved but would remain intermittently painful. Mom seemed to have "accepted the fact that from now on she will have to devote her life to taking care of him." John urged me to "get home for Mom's sake." Silent about Berlin and porcelain, Mom consoled me over my disappointment "in the Ladies Department." She missed me "more than ever" because John was home. On 20 July she closed, "Sois sage" (be wise). It was her last letter that summer.

I barely noticed changes in the tempo and tone of family correspondence. I seldom wrote after the Vienna summit. I was trying to get over Antje, starting to say good-bye to Giessen, and could offer no assurances about how things would end in Germany or begin in Oxford. John implored me to give them information. Dad ascribed my silence to nonexistent emergency maneuvers that he thought must have prevented their letters from reaching me. I figured John and Dad were exaggerating the danger of war; after all, they were far from Germany and had been counting on my homecoming. For the same reasons I was not worried about Mom, just impatient she would give me no guidance on china. The dwindling of her letters after Vienna did not alarm me, nor did their lack of humor; no more wordplay in them like returning from Europe on an Honest John instead of a shield.

I badly underestimated the anxiety on the home front. Dad's sudden willingness to compromise with the Soviet Union should have tipped me off, as well as Mom's quiet and John's ordering me to come home for her sake. To them Europe was no longer a peaceful grand tour for the family's prodigal. It was a dangerous place for their son and brother who had already done his patriotic duty, and homecoming meant his survival. Mom needed me. That much became clear after the crisis.

Less clear, even now, were the historical parallels at work back home. I would guess that my family were fighting the Second World War more than I was. Dad and Mom may have remembered 1939, when Hitler upset their fine plans to spend a year in Europe. Was Khrushchev now hitting close to home? Perhaps John's memory of the Second World War warned him that the Berlin crisis had begun to depress Mom in a similar way, worse than the occasional freezing and brooding she had told him about the previous summer. Could her silence have echoed mine? In her mind, maybe postwar Europe was betraying both of us, no longer the liberating climate that had helped her recover in 1949–1951 and that I sought after college.

I don't know how else to explain the forebodings that I failed to perceive in the summer of 1961. To me, Berlin was not as perilous as my family thought, Europe not a combat zone, and coming home not imperative. Berlin was a nuisance, causing a dissonant crescendo of military escalation and private plans. I wanted out of the Cold War and on to New College. Something had to be resolved; when and how were unknown.

In July 30,000 East Germans fled to the West, the highest monthly total since 1953, followed by another 20,000 during the first twelve days of August. The numbers reached intolerable proportions for the East German regime and brought East-West relations to the kindling point. When East Germany blocked the exodus, President Kennedy decided on military retaliation only if the East Germans or Soviets entered West Berlin or denied Western rights of access to that half of the divided city.

My battalion spent the month at Grafenwöhr. We left at the end of July, a few days after friends of Miss Ada's had asked me to keep their daughter from straying into danger while she traveled in Germany, a few days before Gen. Clarke tightened USAREUR restrictions on leaves and passes as a "readiness measure." Our minds were on training, not on fighting, but we knew that governments were flirting with war. I remember a unique convoy, crates of nuclear warheads, an exhausting training test, Pvt. Karp's sanity, a strange odor of suspense. Most vividly of all, I remember the alert called on Sunday the 20th, when I finally grasped Miss Ada's lesson about history.

When the battalion departed for Graf, Maj. Hayes left Lt. Newman and me behind in Giessen to safeguard our warheads until further notice. He did not explain this change in procedure, but we inferred that the battalion might have to return quickly to Giessen, perhaps in order to take up our general alert position in the Fulda Gap. Late that afternoon plans changed again. Newman and I were to transport the warheads to the halfway point east of Würzburg, where the battalion would wait for us. The two other artillery battalions in Giessen would furnish vehicles, drivers, and guards.

Next morning, after loading and briefing, our little convoy moved out from Giessen. The men seemed glad to escape their units for an unconventional trip and take orders from two unfamiliar lieutenants. It was an ideal summer day — mild, dry, brilliant blue sky dotted with benign cumulus. Newman and I took turns leading the column while the other patrolled up and down to insure the proper interval between vehicles. The drivers held excellent convoy discipline, the best I had ever seen, and we made good time. More than the usual number of American military police and German highway police directed traffic in our favor at critical junctions, and a v Corps helicopter hovered overhead near Frankfurt. The pilot radioed, "You're lookin' good. Good luck," when he turned back toward his base. I was intoxicated by the mixture of responsibility and freedom. We were transporting warheads expeditiously and safely, observed by experts who admired our work, unfettered by senior battalion officers. We carried an apocalypse, but my mind was on looking good. Our luck held, and soon we passed the medieval walls of the Marienberg fortress at Würzburg. When we pulled into the battalion's bivouac area, majors and captains took over, fussing like hens. Newman and I backed away, exchanged smiles, and shook hands, knowing we had accomplished something special.

On 6 August I wrote home from the field, which was "dusty one day, muddy the next." "Still no word on my early out," I reported, but at least I had not yet been extended, "bless J.F.K." I asked Mom again what sort of china she wanted, still stymied by what I presumed was a simple case of her procrastination.

During the next six days, Khrushchev gave two belligerent speeches, citing American hysteria and German revanchism, warning that, if war should break out over Berlin, it would quickly become a thermonuclear holocaust in which the Soviet Union could destroy American bases around the world. Kennedy issued an executive order calling up reservists and extending for one year the active duty of anyone who was eligible for release before 1 July 1962. West Point cadets who had been attached to units in Germany for a month of summer training and looked forward to German girls and beer were restricted to base. NATO intensified joint planning for war. The East German government announced that it was prepared to take necessary steps to end West Germany's "head-hunting and slave-trading" of East Germans.

Paranoia came out of the woodwork. In Washington Senator Strom Thurmond stepped up his attacks against Senator William Fulbright for criticizing partisan speechmaking by generals and charged that there were "Marxist Socialists" in government and the press. At the front, battalion headquarters sent me on a secret mission: keep track of a three-star general who was visiting Grafenwöhr and who intended to make surprise visits to units in the field. Pvt. Karp may have been deficient in botany, but he knew comedy. Like someone who gets a running inside joke, he nodded and grinned as we shadowed the general around Grafenwöhr post for most of a day, radioing his whereabouts to battalion every hour.

My headquarters did not ask for reports on events that were overtaking us. On Sunday the 13th the East Germans closed the border between East and West Berlin, shutting it to their own people, not to West Berliners nor to the Western allies. On the 15th, when the East Germans put up barricades, my battalion loaded up vehicles for the ATT that would decide whether we were combat effective. While we were in the field, from morning of the 16th to evening of the 19th, the crisis escalated sharply. Disappointed by inertia in Washington, West Berliners at a mass rally shouted, "What are the Americans doing?" Mayor Brandt compared East Germany's move to Hitler's remilitarization of the Rhineland in 1936 and urged President Kennedy to take strong action. The East German government threatened to blockade Berlin if West Germany imposed economic sanctions. NATO governments sent protests to Moscow, calling the barricades illegal and accusing the Soviets of violating four-power agreements on Berlin. President de Gaulle ordered a number of French units to be shifted from Algeria to France. The Pentagon announced that extensions of active duty and other measures were not merely a response to the Berlin crisis but part of a general buildup in military strength "to meet the world-wide threat." The Soviets and East Germans moved reinforcements into districts bordering West Germany, as well as the countryside around West Berlin. Kennedy decided to send an American battle group from West Germany to West Berlin in order to reinforce the Berlin garrison and reaffirm Western rights of access. An American political mission arrived in West Berlin on Saturday the 19th, headed by Vice President Lyndon Johnson and including Lucius Clay, a hero to Berliners for defying the Soviet blockade of 1948–1949. The East Germans closed all but a handful of crossing points between East and West Berlin; their barricades grew into a wall.

We passed our Army Training Test. During the test, Pvt. Karp, my weathervane, warned me of normal snafus such as contradictory orders, changes of plan, vague messages. I catnapped a couple of hours each night, sitting in the jeep, mixing dreams and radio traffic, wearing my "steel pot" and waking up whenever it banged the dashboard as I slumped over. Karp surpassed himself in provisioning our small corner of the free world: coffee, cookies, rolls with jam, peanut butter sandwiches, cans of the choicest field rations (he knew I liked beans and wieners), pancakes wrapped around squares of butter, pieces of cherry pie stuffed into plastic coffee cups. During a lull one sunny afternoon, Karp spread out the makings of a snack on the hood of our jeep under the camouflage net. "Hey looteen," he said, admiring his work, "if we had hot doowogs we could have a real picnic."

Although too busy to follow events on the Armed Forces Network, many of us felt generally uneasy about the outside world. It was the first time we expected bad news to greet us after an ATT. When we returned to the barracks on Grafenwöhr post late on Saturday the 19th, we washed the dirt off vehicles, refuelled them, sorted gear and were told that Sunday would not be a day of rest. Too tired to discuss rumors about Berlin, most of the battalion showered and hit the sack shortly after midnight, the officers together in one large room, our air mattresses and sleeping bags on the concrete floor.

Capt. Haggerty, duty officer that night, woke us up around six o'clock Sunday morning shouting, "Alert! Alert! Alert!"

"Aw bullshit, Haggerty . . . You gotta be kidding . . . Get outta here . . ." voices mumbled from inert sleeping bags.

"No, I'm not kidding," Haggerty yelled, "it's an alert, goddammit, a real alert. I'm serious!"

We got serious in a hurry, shaved, dressed in clean fatigues, and gathered for a briefing. We learned that an American battle group was on the East German autobahn heading for Berlin, badly outnumbered by Soviet and East German forces. The 1st Battle Group, 18th Infantry Division, had left its quarters in Mannheim early Saturday morning and bivouacked that night near Helmstedt, a few miles from the inter-German border, under orders to cross the border Sunday morning and proceed to West Berlin. USAREUR had called the unprecedented stand-by alert in case the Soviets and East Germans blocked the battle group and shooting started.

The Cold War never earned its paradoxical name more fittingly than on the morning of 20 August 1961. The 1st Battle Group was ready for a fight but did not look for one. When the Americans moved out from their bivouac around 6 A.M., a West German spectator eyed the convoy skeptically and asked, "Where are the tanks?" Extraordinary shows of force observed ordinary bilateral procedures. The Soviets insisted on transit protocol, and the Americans obliged. Upon reaching the Soviet checkpoint between Helmstedt and Marienborn, the battle group's commander, Col. Glover S. Johns Jr., ordered his troops to dismount so the Soviets could count heads and compare this figure with the manifest that American officials had given them the day before according to rules in place since 1945. In 1959 the Americans had started the practice of dismounting (and of giving the Soviets advance warning of long columns of vehicles) so as to expedite the processing of convoys, which East

German and Soviet guards had been delaying with bureaucratic harassment.

In Grafenwöhr we were unaware of transit protocol and did not know whether shooting would start. We were exhausted from the ATT, but there was little griping. We stayed near our vehicles, certain that, if the East Germans or Soviets fired on the battle group, "the balloon would go up" and the battalion commander would open the white envelope containing top secret orders for our deployment far from Giessen and the Fulda Gap. Military service had more to teach me after all. Several officers looked terrified, their faces pale and immobile. I began to visualize panic in combat, wondering how it might spread from individuals to missiles. The atmosphere was much more tense — and we were closer to war — than many histories suggest. One of several rumors flying around the battalion mentioned Dresden, but I did not know whether that meant an objective for a NATO advance or, more likely, one of the enemy's points of concentration for an offensive and thus a likely target for our nuclear weapons.

The mention of Dresden caused a chain reaction of memories and reckonings. I associated that city not only with Allied saturation bombing but with Grandmother Post's Meissen tea service, long a symbol to me of delicacy and refinement in the parched landscape of West Texas. In a secluded storage area at Grafenwöhr two weeks before our ATT, I had sat atop crates containing our nuclear warheads, peeling an orange and swinging my legs during a sunny break for lunch. Sitting in my jeep on the 20th, I wondered whether my platoon would be sent back to the storage area to load the warheads that Newman and I had skillfully transported halfway to Graf. I estimated that the number of kilotons on which I had perched in the sunshine far exceeded the combined power of the atom bombs dropped on Japan and the conventional ones that devastated Dresden in 1945. I thought about the annihilation of German civilian life and the loss of my own, in Germany but not against Hitler. I was ready to obey orders.

Pvt. Karp could tell I was hurting. He kept looking at me out of the corner of his eye, like someone who hesitates to offer an arm to a blind person. "Lootenen," he consoled, "you gotta be da unhappiest guy in da ahmy." I may have been.

My family, too, was hurting. Dad's letters had increased in number and chagrin during August. He feared war but hoped "negotiation will go on." He was proud of my military service but resented "American complacency and Eisenhower stupidity" for causing "this trouble in which you are caught." Too many students were exempted from military service, and too many intellectuals were "convinced that because war is bad, it is not necessary and therefore armed forces are not necessary." He wished I would write, "for no news here is so important as the news from you," but he assumed I was too busy, "maybe on the very frontier." He clung to the hope that I would be released in time to come home before going to Oxford. So did John, who would postpone his return to Berkeley if I gave the word. We could drive north together in September for a weekend of camping on the Big Two-Hearted River. "What the hell's the scoop over there?" he asked. "WRITE!" Mom did not write.

I did not blame Ike or any other American for my predicament. Nor did I think the army needed intellectuals at this time. Not an ounce of my agnosticism questioned the wisdom of sending the battle group to Berlin. I believed in defending West Berlin, in its symbolic importance for freedom's larger struggle against Communism. If it came to war, I was willing to die for a cause more important than my own destiny. That conviction belonged to the better person I had been inventing for myself since the Second World War, and it belonged also to Camus's rebel. But I did not summon Camus on 20 August 1961. Oxford, not war, was my next test; thither, not to avoid combat but to get on with my life. I did not see myself as a coward nor as a rebel against government autocracy. If I was resisting what Camus called the autocratic power that history can wield over individuals, I did not feel a moral responsibility to do so.

I was hurting not for family but from self-centered confusion. The Berlin crisis had demolished my sense of history as a purposeful sequence in which I had some freedom of choice about timing. For the past eight months I had projected into the future my ambition to make history. I would carry to Oxford all the tales, memories, mentors, knowledge, and experience that, combined with an Oxford degree, would equip me for the "world's fight." Suddenly, events were saying not so fast, your fate lies in this fight.

Oxford looked far away, outside time. So did I in the photo taken by another lieutenant while we drank coffee in the mess hall. After years of using my historical imagination to picture what I might do in a crisis, here it was. I knew I was part of history but not how my small story would play itself out inside this large one that had taken me by surprise. I wanted to be worthy of grandmothers, cowboys, men with pipes, Mom, and John. But what would happen to this idealized heritage when it came down to one heir in a real mess? As the two stories collided on 20 August, my riddle shrank to two questions. First, if hell broke loose, would I fight well; would I row well? I used to wonder on the way to the starting line of crew races, and now, for the first time in my service with the 3/79, I felt serious prerace jitters. Second, if peace prevailed, how and when would I get to Oxford? If asked which outcome I would eventually prefer to tell my children about, I would at that moment have unhesitatingly said going to Oxford, leaving this Cold War history behind me and with it my chance to become the military hero of my childhood.

The American battle group drove toward Berlin, preceded by an East German jeep that held the convoy to 25 m.p.h. A reporter for the *V Corps Guardian* saw "bushes filled with East German People's Police" and feared the consequences of "any jittery false move" by either side. But the Americans reached West Berlin without incident early in the afternoon. As I heard several years later from Professor Hans Herzfeld of the Free University of Berlin, who watched the column arrive, West Berliners cheered the troops as if they were liberators. The soldiers, who had not fired a shot, flashed V for victory signs and adorned their helmets with the red and yellow flowers strewn their way. On Monday Secretary of the Army Elvis Stahr told the press that war was now unlikely over Berlin. "If there were to be war," he said, "it would have started yesterday. If there were to be war, that battle group would not have arrived [in West Berlin]."

Late Sunday afternoon our alert ended, and we began to act as if it had never been called. When the battalion returned to Giessen on the 23rd, I was surprised not to find orders extending my active duty. USAREUR and 7th Army had recommended approval of my request for early release, but the Department of the Army had not decided. On the 28th I drove to USAREUR headquarters in Heidelberg, where a sympathetic officer in personnel told me he would ask about my case when he called the Pentagon in a few hours. I returned to his office after a restless walk around the base, during which I discovered the concealed swastikas at the front gate. He gave me news I had nearly convinced myself I would not hear. As an "exception to policy," I would be released from the army in early September — at Fort Dix, New Jersey.

I so wrote Oxford and wired my family. My mind turned to buying china, flying home, and sailing to Britain with other Rhodes scholars. I would let others worry about Berlin, Honest Johns, Moscow's announcement that it would resume nuclear testing, Indian prime minister Pandit Nehru's warning at a conference of nonaligned nations that the world was "at the very brink of war," Richard Nixon's criticizing Kennedy's decision to send the battle group as an "empty gesture."

At Mettenheimer Porzelan in downtown Giessen, I bought a dinner set of Rosenthal, defying my mother's silence and my government's lectures on spending abroad. It wasn't Meissen; saturation bombing and the Cold War had seen to that. But it was the best I could do. Before the army shipped it to her, I would be able to describe its design to her in person: a long-stemmed rose, elegant and understated like her, in an autumnal brown that I knew she liked. I said good-bye to the Flörkes, promising to stay in touch. Did I see regret on Antje's face or just want to believe she knew she had made the wrong choice? I packed my bags at the BOQ, made arrangements to leave my Bug and case of Mosel wine with JJ until I could come over from Oxford at Christmas to retrieve them. I had no time for bull sessions at the Officers' Club bar, where dreams of glory were shifting back to Southeast Asia as the Berlin crisis subsided.

But Berlin would not let go easily. Telephone calls to Rhein-Main Air Base failed to secure me a seat on a military transport plane to the States. I had orders to report to Fort Dix on 5 September, and my battalion expected me to leave for good. Its farewell gesture was to provide the jeep that took me to Frankfurt on the 1st. I dumped my bags in a room at Rhein-Main's transient BOQ and went to the office that handled army transport. I sat there in limbo for two days, hoping the major in charge would assign me to a flight home. He gave me every reason for pessimism, but I held off wiring home. The major had bloodshot eyes and an unquenchable thirst for black coffee. On the afternoon of the second day, he blew up.

"Listen, Post," he thundered, "I've got thousands of dependents flying to the States and thousands of reinforcements flying back here. This is an emergency for Chrissake, and I don't have room for anyone who's going to Oxford!"

Later, as I started to leave for another lonely night at the BOQ, the amiable specialist 4th class who ran the outer office motioned me over. Experience had taught me that unruffled "spec 4s" ran the army, and he proved it again.

"Lieutenant," he whispered, "I know I'm not supposed to do this, and for God's sake don't let the major find out, but I've never had a chance to help someone go to Oxford, so just show up here tomorrow morning before 0600 and I'll put you on a plane."

He did. I called home when I arrived at McGuire Air Force Base and said I'd be in Madison as soon as paperwork allowed. I was released from active duty at Fort Dix on the 5th, a few hours after surviving a sergeant's announcement to a large roomful of surly reserve officers newly recalled to active service that "Lt. Post is the one who's getting out!" I didn't feel guilty. On the 6th I flew to Madison on a civilian airline, changing planes in Chicago, proud to wear my uniform and eager to shed it. John met me at Truax Field, where we had been enthralled by wartime aircraft as kids, and during the drive home I began telling war stories. He said Mom and Dad couldn't wait to see me, that it was a "damned good thing you made it."

We pulled into the driveway of the new house on Cable Avenue at about 11 P.M. My parents and Barbos came out the front door. I motioned for Mom and Dad to stay put while Barbos tried to figure out who was this stranger in uniform. He approached slowly, then stopped, nose up, tail low and tentative.

"Hello, Barbos," I said softly. He knew my ancient smell.

I hugged my parents, threw duffle bags into my new bedroom, and took off for the last time my dog tags and my jacket with the 7th Army patch on the shoulder. When I walked into the living room, I began to explain to Mom how I had gained fifteen pounds in Germany. She came over without a word and held me in a long embrace. "Oh kid," she said, "oh kid."

Soon I opened the bottle of Mosel wine I had brought back for the occasion, a '59 Rasmussen-Bonne Spätlese.

"Son, this is the finest German wine I've ever tasted," Dad said.

My Cold War was over.

# Epilogue

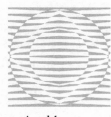In the weeks before I left for Oxford, my mother pampered me as if I were a schoolboy recovering from the flu. I could tell that she was recovering from something more than a normal case of motherly anxiety over the Berlin crisis. She had become despondent, and my homecoming revived her.

I felt I should have come to her aid during the Second World War, and I had been bracing myself ever since then never to let her down again. Lately, I had borrowed moral grounds for unselfish action from the writings of Camus and the lessons of German history. But going to Mom's defense in September 1961 was inadvertent and unconscious, not in the least heroic, and I have never congratulated myself for it.

Would she have suffered a relapse if I had not come home? Maybe not. Still, I saw at last that my time of service abroad in the Cold War had reached the limit for my family. I came back for only a month, but that was long enough to refuel my search for self with a strong reminder of origins and debts.

In 1967 Mom did have a relapse, in Princeton, where Dad had joined the history department three years earlier. Late in August he called me at Stanford to report that she was very depressed. "I don't know why she's so down," he said, "but thank God it's not as bad as in the forties. She'll have to spend a few weeks in the hospital, and you don't have to come home unless it gets worse." It didn't. She soon pulled out with complete rest and new medications. She would use these remedies several times thereafter to curb depression and avoid hospitalization.

Dad retired in 1970, four years after winning the Haskins Medal of the Medieval Academy of America for his book, *Studies in Medieval Legal Thought*. He was terribly disillusioned by the radical politicizing of college campuses during the 1960s. John and I had tried in vain to persuade him that the Free Speech Movement at Berkeley made valid criticisms of educational bureaucracy and that the war in Vietnam had become senseless. "Just remember one thing about youth movements throughout history," Dad rebuked us as if we were card-carrying naifs bent on revolution, "they grow old." It was a lousy time for him to grow old, and I was sad to see him embittered at the end of his distinguished career.

Dad and Mom moved to Haskell in 1971, living in Miss Ada's bungalow that had been rented since her death while I was at Oxford. They were happy in Haskell until Dad's health deteriorated and they both realized how much they missed college towns. Only a few of the regulars who gathered for morning coffee at the drugstore on the courthouse square caught on when Dad claimed to have discovered that "Home on the Range" derived from a bucolic Roman song, "Domus in Prato," written at the time of Virgil. Dad died shortly before Christmas 1986. His pallbearers were two farmers, the druggist, a hardware storekeeper, and a grocer. We gave him the epitaph he had requested shortly after returning to Haskell: "Always devoted to family and to the study of history as two necessities of civilization." For many months after his death I thought daily of having been named after him, and I had to be ready to leave the room if I pictured him during a class or committee meeting.

After a year of living alone, Mom asked John and me to find her a nice retirement home before she grew so old she would resent us for putting her in one. We found a remarkably benevolent home in nearby Abilene, run by the Methodist Church. John moved her there on a gray, sleety February day. "Only a Yankee would take his mamma to an old folks' home on a day like this," she said with characteristic humor to break the emotional tension that John was trying to hide with silence.

During her last few years, she filled a few of the many gaps still remaining in what I knew about her relationship with Dad. She had begun to fall for him at a Sunday picnic held on the lawn of the local water company, when he leaned over to the group she was sitting with and handed her a small bouquet of tiny daisies he had picked from the grass. "I crown you Queen of the May," he had said.

I hesitated to quiz her about the war years or the time between her breakdown and Paris, and she volunteered little. But she gave me much of what I needed when I took her one morning to a small historical museum in a restored brick hotel across from Abilene's old railroad station. As we stood near the reception desk in the former lobby, a woman entered with her two towheaded sons about four and five years of age. Mom went straight over to the boys and put her hands softly on their heads, her touch and the love in her eyes calming the startled threesome. I took her out to dinner that evening, and she thought I was Dad. "How are the boys?" she asked. "When can I come home? I'll try to do my part." She died in April 1995, a few months before I left for my sabbatical year in Paris. At the graveside service in Willow Cemetery on the western edge of Haskell, a stiff wind from the southwest flapped the awning over the site. "There goes Katie ridin' by," an oldtimer sitting behind me said.

John left Berkeley in 1965 for a position in the philosophy department of Vanderbilt University, where he still teaches. He married Patricia Trueblood in December 1966. They have two sons, John Gavin and David Gaines. Although my brother has published learned books and articles on metaphysics, presuppositions, and symbolic logic, he has never quite adjusted to the many-hued tents and academic politics of the American university. Both of us were misled about our profession by growing up in Madison when the University of Wisconsin came as close to the ideal of an intellectual community as any American university ever has.

I sailed for Oxford on 28 September 1961 aboard the SS *United States*, ten years after my first voyage to Europe on the *Liberté*, six days after my twenty-fourth birthday, delighted to be back on course toward my indefinite "world's fight." I "read" modern history at New

College, as the College of St. Mary of Winchester has been called since founded in 1379 by William of Wykeham, Bishop of Winchester and Chancellor of England. Modern history at Oxford began with Roman England and ended in 1914; anything since then was "politics." I joined the Fisher Society, the college's history club. When we visited Winchester Cathedral, the verger showed us six reliquaries containing the bones of five Anglo-Saxon kings and one queen. He apologized that no one could say with certainty whose bones were in which reliquary, for Oliver Cromwell's Roundheads had "mixed them all up" when they used them as missiles to shatter the cathedral's stained glass windows during the English Civil War.

Oxford's antiquarianism muted Cold War clatter. So did the lifelong friendships I made there. Our long discussions dwelt less on world politics than on courage, love, death, Lawrence Durrell's *Alexandria Quartet*, and vacations on the Continent. The Americans among us viewed the Cuban missile crisis of October 1962 with less alarm than did our families. Khrushchev's withdrawal of Soviet missiles, I thought, would strengthen Kennedy's international clout and return American attention to Europe, where it belonged.

A year later I had barely begun graduate study in history at Stanford University when President Kennedy was murdered. Kennedy's assassination marked the beginning of my sixties. Much of my enthusiasm about public service was buried with him. Yet, as I wrote to my parents, his death also convinced me that my fight was in education; "they should not be put in jail," Adlai Stevenson had said about Dallas citizens who struck and spat upon him, "but in school."

I knew I wanted to become a college teacher. I prepared for this career during a virtual civil war that shook my Cold War agnosticism and shattered the peaceful order by which my generation had presumed it would succeed Kennedy's. Protest welled up where obedience or acquiescence had been the rule in the 1950s, from civil rights to education to war, leaving me in a quandary over the ideals of resistance I had inherited from Europe's struggle against Nazism. I moved to the left of my politics of the fifties but retained enough faith in institutions and elders to stop short of the Left of the sixties.

I watched Martin Luther King Jr.'s electrifying Washington speech of 28 August 1963 with my parents on their small black-and-white television set a few weeks after returning from Oxford. "I have a dream," he intoned, and for the first time in my life I began to grasp the injustice of racism in the United States. I did not enlist in the fight for civil rights, as did my girlfriend, Anne, who, after graduating from Stanford in June 1964, headed for Mississippi to live with a black family and help register voters. But I became a staunch supporter of affirmative action, partly from a sense of guilt, but largely because of the agile minds of black students at Stanford to whom I taught Western Civilization while working on my dissertation, 1966–1969. One of them was Mike, a lanky fellow from Long Beach who liked to tinker with automobile engines. One day in January 1967 my class discussed Henry Adams's *Mont-Saint-Michel and Chartres.* The conversation moved from medieval culture and Gothic architecture to spiritual values in American society, the sort of classroom migration that had become common during the Vietnam War. Mike asked, "What are our flying buttresses today?" He wondered whether they were collapsing, or would they one day stand firmly enough to support the entire edifice? Moments like that, I wrote to my parents, "make teaching worth more than Solomon's treasure."

The next day Clark Kerr, president of the University of California, was sacked by the university's regents at the behest of Governor Ronald Reagan. Kerr's vision of the modern university as part of the post-Sputnik "military-industrial complex" fueled by public funds had been rejected by the Free Speech Movement, founded at Berkeley in the autumn of 1964 when Mario Savio and others recently returned from Mississippi insisted that the civil rights movement belonged on campus. While Stanford remained relatively calm for a few years, many of its undergraduate and graduate students agreed with Savio and with the Free Speech Movement's charge that universities overemphasized research and slighted teaching. Although not a radical by a long shot, I accepted the movement's premises that civil disobedience formed a bridge between the academy and social reality, that Camus's rebel would always be "relevant," that universities must not become industrial corporations, that Reagan and his sort endangered academic freedom. I have often wondered what academic good might have resulted from the Free Speech Movement had the Vietnam War not captured most of the baby-boom generation's rebellious energy and brought violence onto campus.

From the congressional Tonkin Gulf Resolution of August 1964 until the summer of 1966, I supported U.S. intervention in Vietnam. The fight seemed consistent with the policy of containing

Communism around the world and protecting our strategic interests in the southwestern Pacific. Although I had never been ordered to report to a reserve unit while at Stanford, I did not resign my commission in the army reserve after my six-year military service obligation expired in June 1965. Nor did I try to earn the "retirement point credits" during the next twelve months that would have enabled me to stay in the reserves. I received my honorable discharge on 9 June 1966, a few weeks before returning from a year of dissertation research in Germany and Britain: "This certificate is awarded as a testimonial of Honest and Faithful Service."

I came home with strong doubts that we belonged in Vietnam and great relief that I had already served. While I was abroad, the European press poked holes in America's preoccupation with containment in Asia, which weakened NATO's posture in Europe. My research concerned secret military planning in the Weimar Republic, which had undermined the moral and legal foundations of Germany's new democracy. Interviews with former generals of the Wehrmacht showed me where obedience and reason of state could lead. Official pronouncements from Washington jeopardized American democracy with inaccurate versions of the truth.

My feelings of suspicion and resentment grew during my first year of teaching at Stanford, as I watched my own students confront the escalation in Vietnam. They found nuggets in the readings that I had overlooked, turning "Western Civ" into a timeless morality play. Ideas mattered to them, my mind was still open, and we found common ground in the Beatles and Sophocles' *Antigone*. Heady times for learning, the most exciting intellectual atmosphere of my career, the sixties stretching consciousness and generating idealism out of both anguish and hope.

Unlike me, my students could not build a justification for military service out of memory of the Second World War, willingness to safeguard democracy in Europe, and trust in the judgment of older men who issued orders. Our differences surfaced one evening in May 1967, when a number of male students asked me over to the dorm to talk with them about the draft. Since "don't trust anyone over thirty" had become one of their generation's slogans, I figured I still had four months to go.

They were fine young men who would not have hesitated to volunteer in December 1941. They had perceived ironies in the World

War I poems of Wilfred Owen, which we had read a few weeks before; "My subject is War, and the pity of War," Owen had written from the trenches on the western front. "The poetry is in the pity." These students were not radicals or dropouts; they planned to enter careers in law, business, medicine, and engineering. They opposed the war, distrusted President Johnson, and questioned their duty to serve their country in what they viewed as an unjust and indefensible war. Several said they would rather go to jail than submit to induction. All of them were about to return home for the summer, and they wondered what they should tell their parents.

To their underlying question, "what can we do?," I suggested that they follow their conscience. Your parents might as well learn now that how you grow and what you grow into may not coincide with their dreams for you. Once they learn that, you and they can develop new familial bonds that will allow you more independence. At the same time, I hope you won't denigrate patriotism just because of this war. "I will write letters to draft boards in support of those of you who object to the war on moral grounds," I assured them. "In return, I want you to leave ROTC alone."

That plea must have been a vestige of my belief at Cornell that Camus and military service were compatible. I was turning dovish. Perhaps subconsciously I blamed the war for Mom's relapse in August; in my first letter to her after she went to the hospital in Princeton, I excised draft portions about the war and campus unrest and adopted a completely cheerful tone.

The bloody Tet offensive of January–February 1968 ended any remaining agnostic qualms I had about opposing the war. In mid-March I drafted a letter to President Johnson. I introduced myself — Madison, Texas, Cornell, military service, Oxford, Stanford. "With utmost respect for your achievements as President and your qualities as a leader," I continued, "I urge you to de-escalate in Vietnam." My reasons were military, political, and social. I was "convinced that America's domestic progress and harmony [were] closely related to its foreign policy — we cannot continue this war at the present or higher level without deepening the political fissures and social animosities (including race) that have already become abnormally deep." I considered these reasons "more compelling in the long run than our loss of face at backing down." Unless you de-escalate, I concluded, "I will not vote for you in November."

I never mailed the letter, but LBJ got it. I set it aside to grade papers and recover from the flu. A few days later, encouraged by Senator Eugene McCarthy's strong showing against Johnson in the New Hampshire primary, Robert Kennedy announced his intention to run for the Democratic presidential nomination. On 31 March Johnson withdrew from the race.

No sooner did I begin to regain hope for the country than Martin Luther King Jr. was assassinated in early April. Then Robert Kennedy in June. "We lose our best men to violence," I noted sadly in my journal. "Violence has become a habit with such oppressive regularity that I feel myself abandoning healthy skepticism and a sense of social mission for cynicism and self-interest."

I struggled with my dissertation that summer, emotionally drained by what felt like an endless series of deaths in the family. Stanford had begun to catch up with Berkeley; arsonists demolished President Wallace Sterling's office in July. John and Pat spent the summer in Berkeley. Telegraph Avenue smelled of tear gas, so we found restaurants elsewhere. We escaped to the Sierra in August for two weeks of backpacking in the John Muir Wilderness, our circuit marked by Bishop Pass, Dusy Basin, LeConte Canyon, Muir Pass, Evolution Valley, Humphreys Basin, and Piute Pass. On Friday the 23rd, when we turned on the car radio as we drove from roadhead down to Bishop, post-trip jubilation turned to dejection. The Red Army had invaded Czechoslovakia to suppress the democratic yearnings of the "Prague Spring," and Chicago police were mobilizing for combat against the antiwar movement at the Democratic convention scheduled to open on Monday. A few days later the Chicago police began clubbing demonstrators, looking far more brutish than the Paris gendarmes who had come after me in October 1951.

America had succumbed to its "frightening dichotomy of freedom and violence," as I wrote to an English friend. "We have so much in us that is greatness," I went on, "yet so little that is tranquility and forbearance. Political assassination is not confined to the crazed loner or the hired gun; it rears its venomous head in the words of conservative Max Rafferty (California Republican candidate for the Senate), who labels the Supreme Court as 'a bunch of social reformers, political hacks and child-marrying mountain climbers,' and in the no less politically absurd allegation from the visionary Left that Johnson and Rusk are 'Fascists.'"

Estranged by the politics and language of hatred, I joined no group. "Commitment" was a charmed word among those who combined against racism, war, and university bureaucracy. But I held back, resisting the urge to rebel because, though I felt it, I feared losing my independence to the organization and momentum of a vehement cause. I was committed to family, friends, and a career in teaching, which would provide me an honorable way to resist my old enemies no matter what the times. Ignorance, chauvinism, deceit, and autocracy would always undermine democratic societies.

As the tragic year drew to a close, I met a graduate student in English named Jean Wetherbee Bowers. Since leaving the army in 1961, I had slept with several women, including Antje — at last uninhibited, during my year of research in Germany. I did not want to spend the rest of my life with any of them. I did with Jeanie. She grew up in Boston, attended Wellesley College, and taught for a year in a German high school near Cologne before starting graduate study at Stanford. She was pretty and slim with terrific legs, like Mom. She had dark hair, blue eyes, graceful hands, gentle voice, and warm heart. She did not know mountains but had spent summers on Cape Cod and loved the sea. I proposed to her in February on a rock above the secluded tidal pool I had found at Point Lobos, overlooking the Pacific, during my first year at Stanford. A few weekends later I showed her Yosemite Valley, a more symbolic engagement gift than any diamond. I had camped there alone several times just to clear my head, once during an overnight snowstorm that almost covered my small tent and in the early morning hours gave me the valley to myself, like John Muir.

We married in Brookline in July 1969 and settled in Austin, where I taught at the University of Texas. We soon bought a small limestone house surrounded by oaks and junipers. Mom sent Jeanie the Rosenthal china that had arrived in Madison without a scratch shortly after I left for Oxford in 1961. While living in Austin, Jeanie and I adopted our two children, Katherine Doris and Daniel Lawrence, and we took them as often as possible to see their grandparents in Haskell, sometimes on the way to the mountains of New Mexico and Colorado. In 1983 we moved to Claremont, California. I have been on the faculty of Claremont McKenna College since then.

In my research, I specialized in German and European history after the First World War because I wanted to comprehend the origins of the second. My two major books dealt with the Weimar Republic and British appeasement in the 1930s. Both cases included resistance against antidemocratic forces. In both I objected to authorized versions of the story but could not keep Europe from falling apart. In my teaching I have advised students to read Camus, novels, and memoirs. And to be skeptical about the misuse of history for ideological ends by the Right and the Left, about jingoistic claims of winning the Cold War, about glib talk of the end of history, and about pronouncements on American culture — that nothing good came from the sixties, for example — from critics who have never dug a latrine. I take such presumptuousness personally. I urge my students to imagine what it might have been like to be someone else. I tell them that a former general in Hitler's Waffen-ss thought he was complimenting me when he said in 1966 that I was tall enough to have been in Sepp Dietrich's elite ss division, the "Leibstandarte Adolf Hitler."

I came to Claremont to be dean of faculty and thought I might go on to a college presidency. A year or two earlier the former president of one of the country's best liberal arts colleges had told me a college president needed both high principle and low cunning. "You have plenty of principle," he observed, "but you are rather short on cunning." I remembered his warning during my first year as dean when one of the faculty's chief bullies, his voice dripping with contempt, accused me of trying to be fair. When I wrote an op-ed piece for the *Los Angeles Times* three years later on the need for solitude in higher education, I suspected I wasn't cut out for administration after all. How can anyone manage faculty politics and raise money when he believes he is still fighting the Second World War?

# Singular Lives